AN ALTERNATIVE PLAYLIST

Forty Songs That
Should Have Topped
The Charts

AN ALTERNATIVE PLAYLIST

Forty Songs That Should Have Topped The Charts

© **Steve Roach 2023**
All rights reserved. No part of this book may be reproduced or used in any manner without the prior written permission of the copyright owner, except for the use of brief quotations in a book review.

This book is a work of critical commentary and review.
Song lyrics are quoted with this view of 'fair usage' for critical review purposes only and are all credited accordingly.

All images used in the book are used under the 'fair usage' right for critical review purposes only. If you are the Copyright holder and object to an image being used please contact the author to request it be removed from future editions:

steveroachwriter@gmail.com
facebook.com/writerroach

Additional contributions from James Griffiths and Hollingworth are © these authors respectively.

For my brother Andy.

Special thanks to Lloyd Hollingworth for proofreading, suggestions, additions and corrections. This is undoubtedly a better book with your input.

As always, thanks to Steph for the love, support and additional proofreading.

CONTENTS

Introduction

Big Black Delta — *Capsize*
Band of Skulls — *Himalayan*
1000 Homo DJ's — *Supernaut*
Afghan Whigs — *Matamoros*
Ween — *Take Me Away*
Pop Will Eat Itself — *Karmadrome*
Primus — *Wynona's Big Brown Beaver*
Violent Femmes — *Country Death Song*

Interlude 1

New Model Army — *White Lights*
Pixies — *Gouge Away*
Clutch — *A Quick Death in Texas*
Revolting Cocks — *Beers, Steers & Queers*
Fields of the Nephilim — *Endemoniada*
Curve — *Chinese Burn*
Primal Scream — *Kill All Hippies*
PJ Harvey — *Long Snake Moon*
The Fall — *Guest Informant*
Jane's Addiction — *Been Caught Stealing*

Interlude 2

The Cure — *A Japanese Dream*
Mudhoney — *Here Comes Sickness*
Nine Inch Nails — *Only*
Buzzcocks — *Lipstick*
Jean Michel Jarre — *Ethnicolor*

Interlude 3

Prodigy — *The Day is My Enemy*
Mike Oldfield — *Ommadawn*
The Sisters of Mercy — *This Corrosion*
Cardiacs — *Is This The Life*

Best Videos

Instrumentals

Album Spotlight – Zoolook

EMF	*Light That Burns Twice as Bright*	
Siouxsie & the Banshees	*Peek-a-Boo*	
Sleaford Mods	*Jobseeker*	
Rage Against the Machine	*Bullet in the Head*	
Orbital	*The Box*	
Nick Cave and the Bad Seeds	*Stagger Lee*	
Talking Heads	*The Listening Wind*	
Madness	*Grey Day*	
Richard Hawley	*Don't Stare at the Sun*	
Ultravox	*Mr X*	

Guest Contributions

Magazine	*Goldfinger*	(James Griffiths)
Julian Cope	*Strasbourg*	(James Griffiths)
Helmet	*In The Meantime*	(Lloyd Hollingworth)

Bonus Content   One Offs

The Bolshoi	*Away*
David Byrne & Brian Eno	*The Jezebel Spirit*
Killing Joke	*Love Like Blood*
Freeland	*We Want Your Soul*
Grimes	*Player of Games / We Appreciate Power*
My Bloody Valentine	*Soon*
Eat Static	*Survivors*
Ozric Tentacles	*Half Light in Thillai*
Amyl and the Sniffers	*Guided By Angels*
The Temper Trap	*Sweet Disposition*
James Ray & The Performance	*Texas*
Fishbone	*Bonin' in the Boneyard*
Morphine	*Honey White*

About the Author
Other Books by Steve Roach

INTRODUCTION

When I started this book I had no idea that it would take so long. I expected the project to last 6 months from conception to publication, but I ran into a bit of a problem. I'm writing about bands that I love but there are so many of them and it's been impossible to keep up with everything every band here has ever released. So, when researching, I'd go through bands' back catalogues and would sometimes discover great music that I should have known already but was discovering for the first time – and I'd play it to death.

Generally, when doing a piece on a certain band I'd listen to nothing else except for music by that band. And some of the music stuck with me and I couldn't move on until I'd finished playing – I got stuck on New Model Army's back catalogue for months, and then Cardiacs had the same effect. So it's taken almost 2 years to complete this book, probably the longest project I've ever worked on continuously.

Another problem I found is that it was really hard to impose a limit on my choices. There are so many bands and great tunes that have been left out – at some point in the future there will be another volume and that will be addressed. The second volume will also heavily feature other contributors – the people I spoke to when writing this book all had suggestions of their own and my advice was for them to follow the format template I lay out here and write a piece of their own to contribute. Hopefully we'll see that come out in 2024.

Now, if you had written this book there's a very strong probability that your preferred tracks wouldn't include any of the ones I have chosen. These days, music is so diverse and so easily accessible that it's very easy to gather a personal collection of favourite songs that nobody else knows (or you might have a digital playlist anonymously compiled for you by an algorhythm). It's natural that you'd want to spread the word and share the love. I mean, if you like the tracks so much, there's a good chance that other people might if only you could tell them why they should listen.

So, here's my selection of tracks that I'd like to share with everyone I can get to listen. I'm not getting paid to do this by the record companies and some of the bands no longer even exist. Some of the people involved in making this music are dead and won't care either way. But I think it's important to bring these songs back into the light, however briefly. Any song included here is, in my opinion, subject to a sprinkling of genius, brilliance or some magic that's hard to define, and hopefully by the end of the book you'll agree with me, even if it's only for a couple of tunes.

In a slightly alternative universe, some of the tracks would have topped the pop charts. Some occasionally did break into our particular universe's Top 40, albeit briefly, but on the whole the songs here didn't make much of a dent on mainstream consciousness.

That is a terrible injustice and this book is my small part in helping to correct that cosmic blunder.

Deliberately mainstream pop songs are catchy, generally shorter pieces of music that are easy to whistle and get everybody's feet tapping. They are mostly lightweight, insubstantial bits of colourful fluff that gently massage your eardrums for a pleasant three minutes or so before settling, like snowflakes, on the historic drifts of popular culture.

Although pop music can be great, with occasional spikes towards the sublime, on the whole it can be repetitive, unoriginal and often bland. The same glossy pop ideas are regurgitated for the masses over and over. Once you see pop music for what it is, there's no turning back. 99% of pop songs are about a) someone falling in love with someone else or b) someone moaning about how they've been dumped by someone else or c) overexcited idiots singing about sex (dressed up in all manner of euphemisms but always about sex).

Everybody gets laid, big deal. Evolve. Sing about something else for a change. When pop stars mature a little bit (or, God forbid, they get old) the reality of them still singing about this banal pap is frankly embarrassing. I get why it happens – the market for pop music is mostly teenagers, who love that stuff, but once you understand the mechanics of what's being sold it all becomes a bit too 'meh!'

Often people who like this sort of mainstream music won't delve any deeper into what music can be or do. They write off huge swathes of creative genius because they think it's too dark or somehow just not for them. That's such a shame. Or maybe they just don't know what else is out there – and here's where I can help.

If you're one such person then the following pages offer you a mind-expanding world of awesomeness and discovery. If you're open to listening to some new music – music that veers a little bit from the path you're used to but goes through some interesting and colourful territory of its own – then this could be the best book you ever read in your life. By the end of it, you may have a dozen new favourite bands and a playlist that will keep you going for years.

Some of you reading this book may be doing so because you know many of the bands featured and are looking for something in the same ballpark to listen to. That works too, and the chances are that if you already like some of this stuff then you're going to end up liking most of it.

I'd suggest that the songs featured here are pop songs, in a slightly twisted way. They are catchy, full of musical hooks and choruses – the only difference is they're made by people whose appearance may be unconventional and musical approach atypical, and there's often a lot more depth to both music and lyrics. If a regular pop song is a sweet little 12 year old girl in pig-tails and a yellow dress, these songs are her older brothers, still part of the same family but wearing leather jackets and carrying a well-thumbed cult paperback book. They're a bit more grown up and worldly-wise, sometimes even a bit moody.

They might be songs you've never heard because the bands are on an indie label and they've never made it to a mainstream channel broadcast. They could be by bands that are 'before your time' – you might be 25 years old and many of the bands here had broken up before you were even born. Or, they might be by bands that are better known but, for one reason or another, the featured song was largely ignored by the masses upon release. Whatever the reason, keep reading – you're in for a treat.

For every track I'll give a little introduction to the band to provide you with some background information regarding the people who put it together. I'll also offer my opinion on which of their albums to date is deserving of your further attention – it might not be their most popular or commercially successful but rather what I'd consider to be the best introduction for new listeners to the band.

It's never been easier to sample music you've never heard before but I'd like you to step outside your world of curated playlists, and recommendations that follow a suggested path, and take an interesting detour with me.. In a way I'm jealous that you get to hear all of this stuff for the first time! Enjoy!

BIG BLACK DELTA

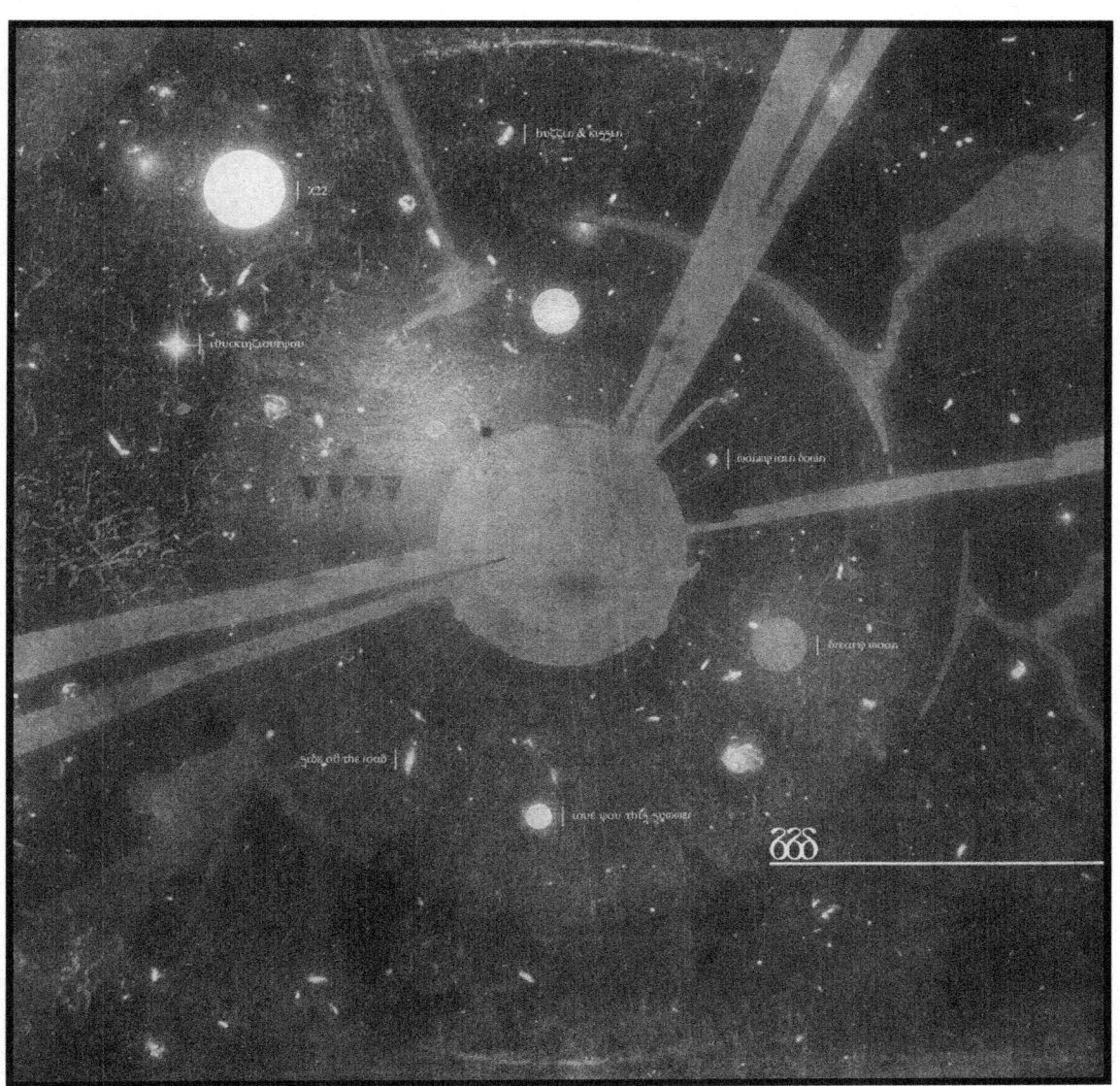

CAPSIZE

BIG BLACK DELTA – CAPSIZE

About the Band
If you've heard of this band at all – actually a solo endeavour by LA musician and singer Jonathan Bates – it's most likely that you heard the track **Huggin and Kissin** from Netflix series *The Sinner*. The song was a powerful presence in the show and is a good gateway track for getting into the rest of their catalogue.

Bates sang and played bass with Mellowdrone for ten years, achieving a certain level of success with tracks appearing in TV shows, movies and video games. He eventually grew tired of being in a full band and all the hassle that comes with it, deciding that it was time to try something different, with more freedom, as a solo artist. Armed with some instruments and a laptop, and initially helped by long-time Nine Inch Nails (more on them later in the book) collaborator Allesandro Cortini, he has released four albums to date and despite having some high-profile fans such as Jay-Z, the band has remained off the radar of most people. Quite how that's happened is impossible to say, as the man writes some outstanding material.

BBD's most recent activity at the time of writing includes what appears to be a flight simulator clip uploaded from his channel onto YouTube. No new music, no explanation, just three and a half minutes of this, whatever it is. The previous chronological clip has him saying there'll be loads of new material coming this year (2023) but somewhat seems like an exercise in making a video with some UFO nonsense in the background. Perhaps this is how his particular genius creates, I don't know.

About This Song
Capsize opens on a metronomic beat that sounds like a wrench tapping on a metal pipe, before a gentle keyboard riff joins in the lead up to the vocal. Drums and a distorted bass come aboard. A wall of noise hits for the chorus, dropping out for the emergence of additional drums and backing vocals for the second verse.

This song builds and builds before a longish fading outro. Not a typical pop song but there's enough there to love if you succumb to its charms. Sometimes the virtues of a song are hard to explain, and trying to make an audio experience sound interesting from dry words is a bit futile. This said, I'll quote verbatim from an online reviewer called 'channel Five': *this song makes me feel like I'm breaking through the atmosphere of an alien planet on the outskirts of some distant cosmos.* Do reviews get any better?

This music can sound cold, alien, robotic, distant but there's more to it than that - it's essentially retro-futurism in the sense that it's simultaneously modern and yet also retro/nostalgic. This genre is constantly referencing 1980's sources like soundtracks to sci-fi/horror films from that era. It's no coincidence that 80's nostalgia-fest Stranger

Things uses similar music. The retro animated videos – seemingly always with lots of neon pink - that you see in every YouTube video further reinforce this retro aspect.

Essential Album

The eponymous album **Big Black Delta** is an ever-so-slightly flawed masterpiece. I personally think there are a couple of weaker tracks on it right at the end (some people may like these as a sort of come-down from the rest of the album) but for me the first ten tracks are enough to justify future-masterpiece status.

Opener **Put the Gun on the Floor** sets out Bates' intent from the get-go, laying the groundwork for what follows. A modern take on Eighties synth-based pop, tracks feature distorted and layered vocals on top of dirty, throbbing basslines and dense layers of music with more than a touch of an influence from the Industrial genre.

Despite the noisiness of some of the instrumental sections, all of the songs retain strong pop sensibilities and work wonderfully together to produce a cohesive album. Your choice of standout tracks can change every time you listen to it, and there always seems to be something new to pick out that you've never noticed before.

Money Rain Down is perhaps the most obvious choice for comparisons to more mainstream pop and once heard it should be hard for anyone to deny that such a song easily competes with the output of bone fide pop stars like Pharrell Williams and The Weeknd.

Mania-infused **IFUCKINGLOVEYOU** is a belter, as is follow-on track **x22**. I could pick out more individual songs for high praise but they're all worth a listen. This might just be the best album you don't yet own.

Second Choice Song

Although it's not my favourite track of theirs by a long way, it has to be the aforementioned **Huggin and Kissin**. It's such an immediately in-your-face slab of thick pop that it demands your attention and despite the association with *The Sinner* is a strong enough track to stand on its own. As of writing, the YouTube video for this stands at five million views, a country mile ahead of all his other stuff which comes in at low six figures.

If you've any doubts about my first track choice, this will settle the matter for you. It's just a fantastic pop song, hardened by the choices of production and instrumentation, with a gloss of weirdness in the vocal delivery for a particular section I'll let you discover on your own.

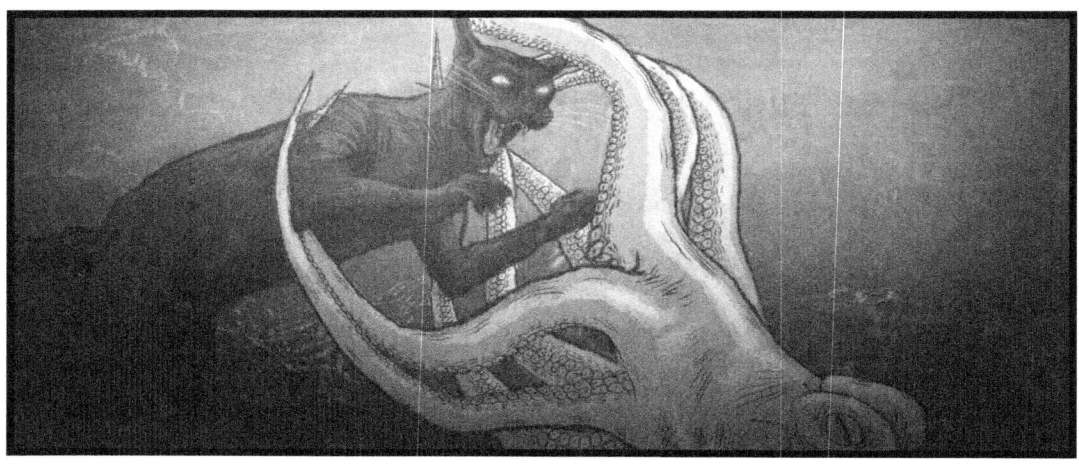

The accompanying video – and I'll often mention videos for songs in this book if I think they have merit and are worth viewing, and YouTube is an endless and free resource that hasn't let me down yet – is an animated film with a unique look detailing the adventures of an astronaut that lands on a red planet (returning home, possibly) and starts following a cat.

He finds his home and wife and there's a montage of children. And Christmas. There are occasional interruptions from an octopus. At some point the cat starts fighting the octopus, and it feels as though our friend the astronaut might be a little insane. A glimpse of another 3 dead astronauts means that we may be witnessing the dying thoughts of a man far from home. Whatever the hell is going on, it bears little resemblance to the lyrics but it a pretty cool background to watch whilst you're soaking up the tune itself.

For now, if you like the two tracks I've highlighted above, you have four albums to explore and enjoy.

BAND OF SKULLS

HIMALAYAN

BAND OF SKULLS - HIMALAYAN

About the Band

Band of Skulls were a three piece from Southampton, featuring Russell Marsden on guitar and vocals, Emma Richardson on bass and Matt Hayward on drums. In the main, Marsden sings on most of their tracks, with backing from Richardson, who occasionally becomes the primary vocalist.

Founding drummer Hayward left the band in 2016 and Richardson recently left (November 2022) to pursue a full-time painting career. There's something about being in a band that attracts people who have other artistic capabilities, and many musicians seem to paint during the downtime and transition to artists when they've had enough of working on music full time (see also Sarah Jones, Cardiacs, in this book).

Although the band survived the loss of Hayward, the effect of also losing Richardson remains to be seen. Certainly, what made Band of Skulls what it is will possibly lack a certain chemistry or magic from now on but it's also entirely possible that such a devastating personnel change will bring about a level of success that has currently eluded them.

To date, the band have released five studio albums (with a further three live albums), and their musical style has encompassed indie rock, blues rock and pop. They have also been described as *'ferociously heavy'* (they can be, but often aren't) and garage rock. In short, they're basically a rock group with blues and pop elements, but that description barely does them justice either.

Some of their poppier tunes are perfect 10's. When you hear songs like **Himalayan** and **Brothers and Sisters** you have to wonder why they didn't break through and get to the very top of the charts. The only answer I have is that their name possibly puts people off. They sound like a heavy metal band, maybe even death metal, and when those audiences check them out they find the songs aren't what they were expecting. Conversely, casual music fans are probably too put off by the name to even give them a try.

Consequently, of 17 single releases made between 2009 and 2019, not one appeared in the UK Top 40. One lonely track broke the US Alt Rock charts (the epic **Sweet Sour**, peaking at no 28). 2013's **Asleep at the Wheel** cracked the US Main Chart (peaked at no 33) and that is probably their biggest success.

Despite most people not knowing they even exist, success has come in other forms, with an early Channel 4 documentary and a few tracks appearing on TV show soundtrack Friday Night Lights Vol 2, a Guitar Hero software release and a track appearing in one of the Twilight movies. Overall, their lack of mainstream success is genuinely baffling.

About This Song
Himalayan is up there with the best of them. From the opening guitar riff, this catchy rock-pop hybrid makes you want to, as the lyrics themselves say: *Throw your hands up, kick back your heels and dance to the beat*. The whole song is dripping with euphoria, and even the middle lull is interesting enough to barely halt the momentum.

I can't imagine anyone who heard this song saying anything bad about it, which can only mean that the only reason it didn't take over the world must be because not enough people heard it. And, more importantly, because some idiot at the record company didn't see this for what it was and put it out as a single.

Maybe the band stymied any such release but whoever made the decision (if there ever was such a conversation) made a serious, serious error. It's bouncy, has fun lyrics, a great guitar solo, singalong choruses – I mean, there's seriously not one thing about it that's hard to love. This would have dented the charts in a big way on both sides of the Atlantic. Listen to it and see if you don't agree. Actual single release **Nightmares** sounds a little flat and underwhelming in comparison.

Essential Album
This isn't necessarily a dig at the band, saying more about me than them, but I do find it hard to pin down a particular album in general to recommend. It's rare for a band – any band – to put out an album that doesn't contain some filler material, stuff that doesn't quite hit the mark and you only give a listen to because it's a band you normally like. Back in the days of vinyl (I appreciate that those days are sort of here again) then you often listened to the filler tracks because skipping a song involved getting up and physically moving the stylus. These days, on MP3 players and Spotify etc, filler tracks get bounced after five seconds.

There are a lot of bands I consider myself a fan of but don't like everything they've recorded. I think that's pretty normal. **Bands of Skulls** are definitely one of them. This said, there are tracks that I really like on every album they've put out. Sweet Sour is a phenomenal album purely on account that it has three stellar singles, it doesn't really matter what else is on there.

If I really had to pick one, I'm going to go for 2013's **Himalayan**. It kicks off in style with **Asleep at the Wheel**, arguably their best selling single, followed by **Himalayan** itself, and then **Hoochie Coochie**, a blast of jittery rock with more than a touch of Glam about it. Track four is a slower ballad with an exceptional vocal performance from Richardson. Then you get the aforementioned **Nightmares**, followed by insanely catchy **Brothers and Sisters** (another massive blunder on the record company's part for not forcing this through as a single release, this would have surely breached the Top 10 in the UK and properly launched the band).

I've only covered half the album and there's more than enough to recommend it. For me personally, the album dips a little after such a breath-taking start but maintaining such excellence was always going to be a difficult proposition.

Second Choice Song
This is a really difficult choice because it should be, hands down, **Sweet Sour**. What a song! The video is superb as well, a hilarious black and white inner-city snapshot of feral kids with nothing to do but break stuff and dance. It's a no-brainer that this should be on anyone's list of music to try. In fact, give it a try now, I'll wait... Brilliant, eh?

Close runners up include **Bruises**, and **The Devil Takes Care of His Own** but, pipping them at the post and larging it up as my second choice must be the opener from their 2019 album **Love is All You Love**, a dazzling bit of rock infused with electronica called **Carnivorous**.

Much like my first choice song, Carnivorous is really easy to dance to, more than leaning towards disco territory. An introduction sets the stage before the song kicks in properly around the 18 second mark and within 10 more seconds you know you've got a monster on your hands, and I mean that in the best way possible. This song is HUGE, thundering along like a juggernaut with steroids in the diesel.

Once again, the band opt for a lull to bring a temporary halt to the song. This quickly builds up to the latter half, and strips back the power a little bit before launching you once again into the fray. It's a song that sounds loud even when you're playing it quietly, and when you do get the chance to put this on at a volume that would distress your neighbours, man it's fucking awesome.

Between the two songs profiled for Band of Skulls, there should be enough of a hook there for you to check out some more of their stuff. If you don't, the musical gods will one day judge you, shaking their heads in disbelief that you passed up such an easy opportunity for hearing some great new music.

1000 HOMO DJ'S

SUPERNAUT

1000 HOMO DJ'S - SUPERNAUT

About the Band
1,000 Homo DJ's discography amounts to a couple of 12-inch singles between 1988 - 1990. The fact that one of those singles is so goddamned good is the reason why they're in this book.

The band was, according to Wikipedia (and accurate information is rather hard to come by elsewhere), a side project to release some outtakes from Ministry's 1988 album **The Land of Rape and Honey**.

Aside from Ministry frontman Al Jourgensen, the band included fellow Industrial alumni Paul Barker (Ministry), Martin Atkins (PiL, Ministry, Killing Joke), Will Reiflin (Pigface, REM and King Crimson), Mike Scaccia (Revolting Cocks, Ministry, Lard) and Trent Reznor – briefly! (Nine Inch Nails). Also involved, working under the pseudonym of Count Ringworm was Jello Biafra of Dead Kennedys / Lard fame. So this was quite the supergroup, a bunch of talented folk coming together to produce pure gold.

The band's name – undoubtedly one that would struggle to gain traction in the modern world and would probably get everyone involved de-platformed – is attributable to Wax Trax! co-owner Jim Nash, although there are conflicting anecdotes behind the related quote.

In notes for the 1994 triple-disc retrospective compilation release **Black Box**, one story says that Jourgensen and Nash were listening to a(n unathorised) remix of a Revolting Cocks song (one of Jourgensen's many other side projects) and Nash declared: *"No one's gonna buy this. It'll take one thousand homo DJs to play this for one person to buy it."*

The other version of the moniker's origin comes from a 2004 Jourgensen interview, where Nash said more or less the exact same thing but this time about demos of the as-yet-unnamed project itself. Either way, Nash came up with the name and Jourgensen liked it enough to christen the project.

The band split in 1990 due to potential legal pressures faced from Reznor's involvement and the usage of various samples (see below for more info about those). Whilst destined to be only a short-lived project, the band made an indelible mark on the Industrial scene and burned very brightly for that briefest of moments.

About This Song
Supernaut is a cover of a 1972 album track by Birmingham's finest, Black Sabbath. The original version was often hailed as a classic by musicians such as John Bonham (legendary Led Zeppelin drummer), Frank Zappa and **Beck**, who named the **Supernaut**

guitar riff as his favourite of all time (tying with a Neil Young riff for **Cinnamon Girl**).

For this cover version, original vocals were recorded by Trent Reznor (Nine Inch Nails main man) but due to a dispute with his own record company this version was never released at the time, only turning up four years later as part of a retrospective box set for label Wax Trax! Records.

Myth tells of Al Jourgensen simply distorting Reznor's vocals and releasing the track anyway, whilst other variations of the story have Jourgensen re-recording the track himself. The fact that the vocals are so similar to each other doesn't help matters. I could have sworn the version I've been listening to for years was the Reznor version, though I'm possibly wrong.

Due to his own vocal style, you could easily throw Revolting Cocks and frequent Jourgensen collaborator Chris Connolly into the mix as well, as the vocal track sounds a lot like him too.

Regardless of who gets the final credit, and whether or not that actually matters, what you have here is a towering beast of a song, taking the original Sabbath metal number – itself a stone cold classic, so they were already standing on the shoulders of giants – and turning it into a raucous 'death disco' stomper, maxing out the feelgood factor to 11.

Everything about the song is loud and a little bit over the top, although not too dissimilar to the original. Everything Sabbath did is present and correct with a few little extra changes and flourishes from Jourgensen's crew to improve upon perfection. The urgency to the vocals, the repeated shouts of *'Supernaut'* (missing from the original), the stellar guitar solo work, the perfectly chosen samples, they all serve to give this version an authority over the song, a mastery of it. Industrialisation removes something of the looseness of the original but with a jump from 1972 to 1990 and a complete transformation of recording styles that's only to be expected and it works really well.

The opening sample monologue is attributable – but extremely hard to track down – to Art Linkletter in a speech to President Nixon, and is included in full here:

Practially every one of the top 40 records being played on every radio station in the United States is a communication to the children to take a trip, to cop out, to groove. The psychedelic jackets on the record albums have their own hidden symbols and messages as well as the lyrics to all the top rock songs and they all sing the same refrain: it's fun to take a trip, put acid in your veins.

Honestly, these people are a gift to musicians like Jourgensen – the very things they are speaking out against in an attempt to shut down are like a beacon of light to the curious young, the best advertisement for the 'bad stuff' ever. Ironically, given the epic virtue signalling Linkletter is guilty of, many Americans knew who he was for his appearances on Bill Cosby's *'Kids Say The Darndest Things'*. You couldn't make this shit up.

(Further research on this reveals that Linkletter's 20 year old daughter, in a state of depression after LSD usage and possible bad trips, leapt to her death. Now I feel bad.)

The countdown sequence vocals appearing just before the four minute mark of the track are from official coverage of the Apollo 11 launch, the voice of which is NASA's Public Affairs Officer Jack King.

Falling down a rabbit hole, and remembering that the song was released by the Ministry side project from Al Jourgensen, he then went on to cover this song with his own band Ministry in 2008 as part of an album made up of cover versions. To satiate your curiosity and save you a mouse click, the album also featured songs by T Rex, Deep Purple, ZZ Top, The Beatles, Bob Dylan and Louis Armstrong.

Essential Album
A difficult question to answer as they never released one. If you like what's going on with this song, I'd probably suggest going back to the original and checking out some Black Sabbath, or maybe taking a sideways leap and listening to Revolting Cocks' Beers, Steers & Queers album (covered elsewhere in this book).

Second Choice Song
I'm going to cheat here. As **1,000 Homo DJ's** was pretty much a one hit wonder, I'm going to pick another of Jourgensen's side projects that also released very limited material. The track is **No Name, No Slogan** and the band is **Acid Horse**. It's a repetitive dance track with a Spaghetti Western twist, sung by frequent collaborator **Chris Connelly**, and is a really interesting and fun tune that in all likelihood you've never heard of and never would unless someone points it out. You're welcome.

I also cant resist mentioning another very short lived project from Jourgensen featuring Paul Barker and Connelly on vocals again – **PTP** released the single **Rubber Glove Seduction** in 1989 and reissued it in 1993. It became a minor club hit and was included in the Black Box compilation. Again, this is something that you're unlikely to come across unless someone recommends it and I thoroughly recommend all three tracks covered above. Hopefully you will too, one day.

AFGHAN WHIGS

MATAMOROS

THE AFGHAN WHIGS - MATAMOROS

About the Band

The Afghan Whigs is one of those band names that seems to put people off listening to them (see Band of Skulls). It obviously brings to mind the country of Afghanistan, not noted for its lasting contribution to Western Rock, and also the status of any US citizen who *'supported independence from Great Britain during the American Revolution'* (thanks Wikipedia). It's not even deliberately pre-empting the 2001 US invasion of Afghanistan in retaliation for the 9/11 atrocity, after all, who could have predicted that?

The band appropriated the name of a *'little known biker gang of White Muslims, who were objectors to the Vietnam War'* (thanks again, Wikipedia). Wherever it comes from, it's not an appealing combination of words you'd expect for an American rock band and may have played a part in their absence from the mainstream.

The band has had two main eras, operating from 1986-2001 the first time around and then, after a long hiatus, reforming in 2011 to the present day.

They started out in Cincinnati and signed to the Seattle based Sub Pop label in 1989. Sub Pop would really break big with Nirvana's globe-busting **Nevermind** album and are credited with nurturing the 'Seattle-sound'. Early Afghan Whigs fitted into that mould, touring with the likes of Mudhoney, but the Whigs didn't really flower creatively until they changed musical direction and brought in influences from R&B and Motown.

Their music is a blend of rock, blues, soul, grunge with a bit of funk and a seasoning of jazz. This heady mix of styles blends perfectly and resulted in a trilogy of sublime albums between 1993-8 in **Gentlemen**, **Black Love** and **1965**. Disappointing sales coupled with a change of labels portended doom for the band, ultimately splitting in 2001 due to – *and this is a reason you won't get a lot of younger bands falling out over* – geographical differences and family commitments.

They were well regarded for their choice of cover songs, some recorded and some captured live at concerts and now available on YouTube. Standouts include a cover of TLC's **Creep**, James Carr's **The Dark End of the Street**, and an awesome version of The Beatles' **I Want You (She's So Heavy)** filmed at a rehearsal in 2001.

There's a stronger Beatles connection with singer Greg Dulli, having performed on the soundtrack of *Backbeat*, a 1994 Indie film recreating the early days of the Beatles as they played in Hamburg. The featured songs weren't original Beatles material, instead highlighting the covers they chose to perform of other artists, and Dulli was the voice of John Lennon on that album. Other contributing musicians included Dave Pirner (Soul Asylum) as McCartney, Thurston Moore (Sonic Youth), Mike Mills (REM), Dave Grohl (Nirvana) and Henry Rollins (Black Flag). Illustrious company indeed.

A brief Afghan Whigs reunification during 2006 resulted in a couple of new tracks and then another five year hiatus. Late in 2011, they reformed and played live dates through the following year and came to realise that it was working out (minus the original drummer) and new material was coalescing. This came out in 2014 as the album **Do to the Beast**, a solid album with a couple of bangers, but the recording produced a casualty as the original guitarist also left the band.

Their most recent album, after 2017's **In Spades** (which heralded another long gap of five years) was **How Do You Burn?,** gaining decent chart positions in Belgium and Scotland of all places, but otherwise under the radar of most people. That's a tragedy – listen to opening track **I'll Make You See God** and see a band still motoring along better than 99% of modern bands and still producing great music after 30 years.

About This Song
Matamoros is from the second era Whigs, released on 2014's long-player **Do To The Beast**. To me, it sounds harder and more polished than anything they've done before. Songwriter / vocalist / guitarist Greg Dulli said he built the song around the drumbeat, which cracks like gunshots and drives things forward at a heady pace. There are obvious hip-hop influences, as well as R&B stylings in the chorus and Middle-Eastern inspired orchestral strings. Honestly, this song has everything you need and clocks in at under three minutes.

The accompanying video is well worth a look, featuring dance crew W.A.F.F.L.E. decked out in suits and skull face paint, performing moves and acrobatics on a New York subway car.

Essential Album
Probably, as an all-round intro to the band and containing three great tunes in **Blame, Etc**, **Going to Town** and **Honky's Ladder**, the 1996 album **Black Love** is a good choice. Archived website Drowned in Sound describe the album as *'orchestral film noir sprawl'* and if that isn't a great description then I don't know what is.

This said, my favourite album is **1965** (released in 1998) as it's less intense and brings in a lot of soul and R&B influences, which generally hold no interest for me but I love what it does to this record. Lead track **Somethin' Hot** really opens up the band's sound, moving away from the darkness of previous albums but still retaining elements of singer Greg Dulli's obsessions. Even the weaker, filler tracks like **66** and **Citi Soleil** are decent. Apart from a 24 second long wet fart at track four, there's not a duff song on the album.

The album was mostly recorded in Louisiana and once you know that it seems impossible to think of it being recorded anywhere else, the record would sound right at home performed in a bar in New Orleans. 1965 received mixed reviews and comes across and overshadowed by previous albums **Black Love** and **Gentlemen**, but it's easily their most accessible record and contains some of their career-best work. It deserves more airings and a wider recognition. It's very hard to think of a reason not to love this record, and it should fit into most people's music collections with ease.

Second Choice Song
By all rights it should be **John the Baptist**, a phenomenal track from **1965** but just pipping it are the two tracks that sign off the album and actually play out as an epic, conjoined track. Building slowly, **Omerta** begins with a tappy little hi-hat groove, some back ground keyboards and a little falsetto vocalisation from Dulli. The verses are sung in a low key manner, ticking along and establishing the main grooves, building and exploding into a singalong chorus that leads back to a quieter second verse. The momentum builds again, exquisite in it's release, and foreshadows the follow on track with the element of loose abandon and instruments coming to the boil. In the background, Dulli sings "yeah yeah yeah" and you can't help but join in.

There's a brief gap, no more than a stutter, a wall of rising instruments building quickly into **The Vampire Lanois**, an instrumental extended outro to both the album and Omerta, and the band are firing on all cylinders and just play their hearts out. It brings the total time of both tracks together to 9 minutes, all of them glorious. As a final sign-off to an album, things don't get any better than this.

WEEN

TAKE ME AWAY

WEEN _ TAKE ME AWAY

About the Band
Ween started life as a two-piece in Pennsylvania, US, in 1984. Aaron Freeman and Mickey Melchiondo renamed themselves Gene and Dean Ween respectively and embarked upon a career that has so far lasted almost 40 years and nine studio albums (preceded by a half dozen home-made cassette only albums).

Apart from the alt rock or experimental rock labels (neither of which is an entirely accurate description) Ween are pretty much unclassifiable, switching genres and musical styles as fancy takes them. Over the years, they've dabbled in funk, country, prog-rock, punk, soul and a dozen other genres it would be too pedantic to list.

With the release of the album *Chocolate and Cheese* in 1994, the line-up expanded to include a bassist, keyboardist and drummer, creating a more conventional touring band than two guys and a backing tape.

"Each of us had different things in our record collections that the other one didn't have. Aaron's dad had a lot of psychedelic records, I was really into punk rock, and we would just turn each other on to music."
Ween 2015 interview on YouTube, posted by tonwich.

Although Ween have never achieved mainstream success with the general public, they have many admirers. Global hit cartoon *SpongeBob SquarePants* was, according to its creator, heavily influenced by 1997 album **The Mollusk** and many episodes contained references to the band. They also appeared in an episode of *South Park* and have worked a few times with SP creators Trey Parker and Matt Stone. Although still active as a band, they haven't released a new studio album since 2007's **La Cucaracha**.

About This Song
Take Me Away evokes an image of a washed-up Elvis, having survived the infamous toilet trip and subsequent heart attack, still plying his trade some years later to a handful of mostly disinterested pensioners in a smoky dive somewhere in Vegas. I'm hardly selling the song based on that description but that's what I see every time I hear it and this song gets regular airings on my playlists.

It's impossible to say why I think this song is so great, I just do – from the very first time I heard it (2005 on a US road trip) to the present day, it has never gotten old and I break into a broad grin and sing along every time. For a Ween song, it's a pretty straightforward composition with few frills, though it is a song with a swagger in its step whilst throwing a wink at the listener. It's also one of the easiest ways to get into the band – a lot of their tunes are so out there that you need to get acclimatised first!

Essential Album

Ween change their sound and style a lot (even on the same album) so you could go with any album and you might like it or hate it, there's no telling. They do whatever they want and for the most part they get away with it (if you don't believe me just play the first few songs from the aforementioned **The Mollusk**, a concept album with a nautical theme that the band themselves feel is their favourite release, blending elements of prog rock, psychedelia and sea shanties).

For me, though, it's **Chocolate and Cheese** simply because it's been a treasured cd in my collection for many, many years and stands up to oft-repeated playings. Songs come close to sounding like parodies but pull back from the brink before everything collapses into complete lunacy.

Production values on this, Ween's fourth album, are higher than on previous work as this was the first to be financed by a major label and recorded in a professional studio. Quite what the engineers made of songs like **I Can't Put My Finger On It** and **Buenos Tardes Amigo**, (both excellent tunes but decidedly offbeat) I can't say but everyone did a fantastic job.

Baby Bitch is beautiful and savage at the same time and **The HIV Song** is just full-on bonkers. It's hard to think of another band that would release a song like **Spinal Meningitis (Got Me Down),** and even harder to describe the feelings you get whilst listening to it. I'll understand if this particular track doesn't get added to your favourites playlist, it's a tough sell in anyone's book.

Overall, it's a quirky, deadpan, humour-laden set of often misery-drenched songs, where somehow even the slow ones become an uplifting listen. Chock-full of classics, if you click with the album you're sure to give it many listens. The world is undoubtedly a better place with *Chocolate and Cheese* in it, that's for sure.

Second Choice Song
Anyone who knows the SpongeBob movie will have a soft spot for **Ocean Man**, but my choice is **Voodoo Lady**, a song I first heard on the Mark and Lard radio show in the 1990's, the presenters having some affection for the tune. Chart-wise, it peaked at number 97 in the UK, 58 in Australia and 32 in the US Alt Airplay chart. Not a massive success but enough to get noticed by one or two influential radio DJ's.

It's the aural equivalent of something primal crawling from a slime-filled Louisiana swamp. The narrator tells us about some red and hazy eyed, spicy-lipped woman that's been driving him crazy with some voodoo and some *'boogie oogie oogie oogie oogie oogie oogie oogie'* before she goes about howlin' and stompin' and making love to some swamp 'gators. So, not your typical pop love song.

Again, Ween walk a tightrope balancing act between parody/novelty and a serious entry into the historical rock canon. In common with a few other tracks in this book, if people hear you listening to this they're more than likely to ask, with bafflement writ large across their faces, "What in the actual fuck are you listening to?" How you answer that question, either with a dismissive shrug or with an urge to convert the uninitiated, is up to you.

POP WILL EAT ITSELF

KARMADROME

POP WILL EAT ITSELF - KARMADROME

About the Band
Somewhere in L.A., in a mansion up in the hills complete with a home music studio and framed posters of movies that he has soundtracked, a short haired man imagines a warm splash on his leg and shivers at the half-buried memory, still haunting him almost four decades on...

Pop Will Eat Itself (PWEI) are a Midlands band and leaders/pioneers of the Grebo movement. They were notable for their live performances as they eschewed a traditional band line-up and performed to backing tapes. I remember seeing them live in Birmingham once when the backing tape broke down and it wasn't pretty, but they eventually got the tape fixed and carried on. Such episodes were widely mocked in the music press at the time.

They were one of the first all-white UK bands to actively perform with a rap aesthetic, which drew much ridicule (*and much anger from audiences when on a tour supporting Public Enemy*). They were also one of the first traditional rock bands to thoroughly immerse themselves in the sampling scene, their work 'borrowing' sound clips from other artists predating the first full length sample-only album released in 1996 by DJ Shadow by nine years.

Because of their Black Country accents, and because of the songs they wrote, many serious music fans wrote them off as a joke, when in fact they were way ahead of the curve and before long many more bands were taking the same approach to making music.

They didn't help themselves when it came to being taken a little more seriously, releasing songs like **Beaver Patrol** (a cover version of a Wilde Knights 1965 release) – which is a great song but could easily be dumped in the novelty record category and time hasn't been kind to it. A quick play of that tune in the wrong place, such as a woke university campus or an office party, is liable to get you expelled or sacked these days. It would be pretty much impossible for such a song to be released in today's political climate. For an early release, it gained a boost by appearing on the soundtrack to 1988 film *The Great Outdoors*, foreshadowing the band's connection – or rather vocalist Clint Mansell's connection – to future film scoring.

Behind the perceived convention that the band were a bit of a joke, they actually had some fantastic tunes and broke new ground in the way they performed and recorded. Although regular musicians and perfectly capable of performing as a live band (their initial incarnation formed in 1981 and called themselves From Eden, and featured two members who would go on to form The Wonder Stuff), their heavy use of samples in the creative and recording processes left them at the mercy of a backing tape when playing live.

They recruited drummer Fuzz Townsend to beef up their overall sound (and add to the live aesthetic) and embraced Industrial influences (by bands such as Nine Inch Nails, who later signed PWEI to their *Nothing* label), evidenced on 1994 single **Ich Bin Ein Auslander**, which also showcased their anti far-right wing political stance. But it was too little too late – their move into making more serious records, and playing more as a band, didn't deter their decision to split in 1996.

Clint Mansell's friendship with movie director Darren Aronofsky proved fruitful as Mansell scored a number of his films, which led to subsequent gigs on movies like *Moon*, *Muta* and Ben Wheatley's version of *Rebecca*. If you'd have asked any PWEI fan back in 1986-96 if they thought Mansell would become an award winning, Golden Globe and Grammy nominated film composer living in Los Angeles, they would have laughed so hard they'd have ruptured their spleen, but he had the last laugh. No more number nine bus for Mr Mansell, that's for sure.

Way back in the late 1980's, sometime around 1988-89 as far as I remember, my brother was pissing in a urinal in the Barrel Organ, a goth/rock haunt close to the bus station in Digbeth, and Clint Mansell walked in and stood next to him for a slash of his own. My brother, being a little inebriated and a little surprised to see Grebo royalty polishing the porcelain in our favourite pub, turned to Mr Mansell and asked if it was really him. Being inebriated, as he turned, he forgot he had hold of his still spraying winkle and pissed all over Mansell's leather trousers!

And back in L.A., in the present day, Clint Mansell shivers and reburies the memory. He won't be putting up with that sort of thing these days, that's for sure.

About This Song
Karmadrome comes from PWEI's fourth studio album **The Looks or the Lifestyle?**, sometimes unfairly panned as a lacklustre effort when in fact it contains a handful of great tunes including **Eat Me Drink Me Love Me Kill Me**, **Harry Dead Stanton** and the bands highest charting single, **Get The Girl + Kill The Baddies** (reaching number nine in the UK charts).

By now, Fuzz Townsend was a full-time member and helped to produce a more layered sound. Like singer Mansell, Townsend is an interesting character with more than one string to his bow. As well as becoming a college lecturer, his CV includes time as a solo artist, a touring musician, a journalist and then editor in the car magazine industry and time as presenter of tv show *Car SOS* on the National Geographic Channel. A busy, talented man. And one showing off excellent drumming skills on my chosen track.

It's hard to categorise **Karmadrome**, drawing as it does on dance, rave, rock, pop and industrial influences – it's an unholy mash of styles and it all works beautifully. Equally at home played in a field, a pub or even a stadium, this is how great pop music can be and it should have stayed at the top of the charts for at least a year. As it happened, the track peaked at number 17 in the UK chart before disappearing. Sometimes, life just isn't fair.

Essential Album
Too tough a choice to make. PWEI evolved so much during their initial decade long existence (*1986-1996*) that every one of their first 5 studio albums has at least half a dozen fantastic tracks. For a band often written off as a bit of a joke, they made dozens of superb tunes. With six different compilation albums to choose from, it's hard to even recommend a greatest hits package. **Wise Up Suckers** is great, but includes nothing from debut **Box Frenzy** or final album **Dos Dedos Mes Amigos**, both of which contain diamonds in audio format. The only thing to do is listen to them all, but if I had to pick a single album that makes a great introduction to the band it would be the aforementioned **The Looks or the Lifestyle?** which perfectly bridges the gap between their earlier, more radio friendly leanings and their eventual move towards a harder sound that began to crystalise on their follow up (see below).

Second Choice Song
Ich Bin Ein Auslander, (German for '*I Am A Foreigner*'), standout track from 1994 album **Dos Dedos Mis Amigos**, (Spanish for '*Two Fingers My Friends*'). The band obviously had a penchant for naming their songs in other European languages at this point. One of the heavier songs in their repertoire but still catchy enough to dance to, it barged its way into the UK charts and reached number 28. The lyrics examine attitudes towards immigration and are an effective statement against intolerance and discrimination, detailing what it would be like to be an outsider in a foreign country and dealing with the associated prejudices that sometimes come with that. Great lyrics (see below and remember these are the same people that decided to cover **Beaver Patrol**), trippy video, a superb swan-song for a band that never got the wider recognition they deserved.

If they come to ethnically cleanse me
Will you speak out? Will you defend me?
Freedom of expression doesn't make it alright
Trampled underfoot by the rise of the right
Ich Bin Ein Auslander © Clint Mansell / Universal Music Publishing Group

As a final note, I have to mention an absolute corker of a tune called **Not Now James, We're Busy**, which completely rips the piss out of James Brown and his worst excesses. Great track, heavy beats, hilarious lyrics. Bless you PWEI, I can't think of another band that would have put out this slice of perfection.

PRIMUS

WYNONA'S BIG BROWN BEAVER

PRIMUS – WYNONA'S BIG BROWN BEAVER

About the Band

If you have been taking this book seriously and giving every suggestion a go, you might think you've already peaked with the lunacy after hearing some Ween tunes. Primus take things up a notch. What saves them from parody is the fact that the songs are really great and the musicianship is on another level.

I'm always amazed at how good some of the musicians are in these bands that never storm the charts. You must have noticed something wrong with the *Matrix* whenever you see some megastar boy band on the TV and realise, with a creeping horror in the back of your brain (that never fully breaks you free of the bullshit and makes you escape your docile slavery to the idiot lantern by smashing it to pieces) that most of these fuckers can't play an instrument (and can barely even sing in tune). Usually, there's one member of the band (take a bow Gary Barlow, or Tony Mortimer) that comes up with the goods and the rest just do backing vocals, dance and try to make themselves attractive for their core audience of teenage girls (there's that feeling again, you know it's wrong).

But with some of the bands here, bands that you may never have heard of before reading this book – I can guarantee that most of these people are exceptionally talented musicians. Trent Reznor from Nine Inch Nails, for example – classically trained pianist, plays guitar, keyboards and I believe has a bash at the drums now and then. Members of Tool are so technically proficient at playing their instruments that they get bored of traditional song structures and write music based on the Fibonacci Sequence.

Back with Primus you have chief songwriter Les Claypool, surely one of the top 10 bass players on the planet. Then there's guitarist Larry LaLonde who somehow elicits six-stringed magic to perfectly compliment Claypool's madcap visions, and top notch drummer Tim Alexander, who can not only dazzle you with polyrhythmic percussion but is also a competent guitarist and singer in his own right.

In the course of writing this book, I would play through each band's songs a few times to orient myself. With Primus, I ended up playing a lot more of their back catalogue than I expected. It's not an exaggeration to say that listening to Primus stalled the writing for months because I just couldn't stop listening to them. (I had the same thing with New Model Army, which is partly why this book has taken so long to write).

Primus are awesome and I misjudged them for decades. Quite why Claypool uses his almost supernatural abilities to make the kind of records that Primus make is a mystery, one that I didn't understand when I saw them support Jane's Addiction on their UK 1991 **Ritual do lo Habitual** tour. I had no idea what to make of them then and until very recently I still didn't. I'd give **Tommy the Cat** another go every few years and each time walk away mystified.

Researching the band with the intention of recommending Tommy The Cat and little else, I fell down a Primus YouTube wormhole for about an hour, which may have led to irreparable damage, but something clicked for me. Some of their videos are amazing, and this paved the way for an acceptance of a few more of their songs. Then a lot more. Which is why they are now more than a mere footnote somewhere and get an entry all of their own.

I have to say that as one gets older, finding new music to like becomes increasingly more difficult. Everything just sounds like watered down derivatives of the stuff you liked when you were 20. One of the great joys has been looking at some of these bands, of which I might have liked a song or two, and finding that I really like the rest of their stuff as well. I've listened to so much new music over the last 18 months of writing, and a lot of it isn't even new at all, it's just been there waiting, all this time. So, even if you don't like a lot of the stuff I'm recommending here, I would suggest going back to the things that you liked a few years ago but never fully got into the band or artist, and checking out some back catalogues.

Back to Primus again… the potentially off-putting thing about a lot of their tracks is the fact that the lyrics are sung in a sort of comedic voice. Claypool would probably admit that he's not the world's best singer, and I think using his voice in a different way initially helped him to overcome feelings of inadequacy (I'm sure I read that in their oral biography **Over The Electric Grapevine** but really don't want to read the entire thing again just to track down the exact quote.) If you can you clear this hurdle, you'll realise that the music beneath is often sublime and once you get a feel for a song you'll even start thinking that it wouldn't have been quite the same if Claypool had sung in a normal 'rock' voice anyway. Bizarrely, the perceived weakness of the singer's vocal delivery turns out to be a strength for the songs. Behind the strange voices, the humorous and often childlike content of their videos, there can sometimes be lyrics probing some serious issues that appear buried until careful listening brings them out. In 2022's **Conspiranoid** they're more surface level and are openly critical about issues Claypool feels strongly about. And, of course, there are songs about big brown beavers.

About this Song
Wynona's Big Brown Beaver could have been, a straightforward satire about Winona Ryder's nether regions, which is what most people will interpret from the title. However, this is actually a song about a beaver with no sexual innuendoes included and nothing at all to do with Ms Ryder. I think. In the oral biography mentioned earlier, there's a whole explanation of the trouble the band had getting the track played on MTV because the studio execs thought it was about somebody's private parts. Their

hesitancy to believe Claypool's explanation that it wasn't – and it clearly isn't, from the lyrics, unless the subtlety is beyond me – may have stemmed from the title of a 1989 live album called **Suck on This**. And later, once the single did get airplay, the decision to release a single in 1997 called **Shake Hands With Beef** may have left them sitting in a quiet room with their head in their hands thinking they were right after all. (They weren't.)

Being the most accessible of their tunes, this is your gateway into Primus' world. And, if you can get your head around any of it, you might find you like it there. Like many Primus videos, this one is amazing and if you haven't done so yet I thoroughly recommend you dropping everything immediately and going to watch that video. I'll wait.

Essential Album
Each of their albums seems equally baffling to the casual listener, so I would suggest their greatest hits album, **They Can't All Be Zingers**. Brilliant tracks include the following (many of which have equally brilliant videos):
Wynona's Big Brown Beaver *(see above);*
Tommy the Cat *(see Second Choice Song);*

John the Fisherman
Shake Hands With Beef
Jerry Was a Race Car Driver
American Life
Mary the Ice Cube
Southbound Pachyderm
I could go on like this for ages.
Pudding Time. Candyman. My Friend Fats.

If you like this handful of tunes you're sufficiently equipped to take a deeper dive into their back catalogue. Basically, 30 years after first hearing their music and writing it off, I eventually fell in love with Primus. And when I realised that their best years were probably behind them, they go and release that brand new 11 minute single **Conspiranoia**, which is up there with their best.

Second Choice Song
Tommy The Cat is a prime example of the musical madness Primus generate. It's a sort of funk-metal workout that sounds a lot like early Red Hot Chili Peppers hijacked by some sort of bluegrass mentalist. Imagine if Waylon Thibodeaux dropped a shit-ton of speed followed by half a pint of liquid LSD then you're halfway there. I have seen an online comment that sums them up quite well: *"Primus are Tool for hillbillies."*

They are pretty much the coolest band you've probably never heard of and there's a good chance that if you listen to a few of their songs you'll have a new favourite band and a stack of really interesting videos to watch. Enjoy!

VIOLENT FEMMES

COUNTRY DEATH SONG

VIOLENT FEMMES – COUNTRY DEATH SONG

About the Band

Milwaukee's Violent Femmes started their recorded life as a 3-piece, achieved initial early success and never quite reached the same dizzy heights again, though patches of success are scattered throughout the rest of their long on-off career.

Their early sound is distinctly off kilter, with guitarist/vocalist Gordon Gano sometimes coming across like an escaped lunatic accompanied by a skiffle band. Tracks have a hillbilly vibe, mixed with folk and even punk sensibilities. Often stripped back and featuring instruments like violins, xylophones and banjos, their songs sound completely unique.

Founder members Brian Ritchie (bass), Victor DeLorenzo (drums) and Gano played together for 13 years before DeLorenzo left, replaced by Guy Hoffman for about a decade before rejoining and then leaving for good in 2013.

Gano and Ritchie have a relationship that has sometimes been difficult, particularly between 2007-9, when the bass player sued the vocalist for selling the rights for one of their most popular songs – Blister in the Sun – for a Wendy's commercial. Ritchie addressed the band's fans by saying: *"I see my life's work trivialized at the hands of my business partner (Gano) over and over again, although I have raised my objections numerous times. As disgusted as you are I am more so."* As much as the use of the music disgusted him (there was nothing he could do as Gano is the sole credited creator of the song and owns the publishing rights), what seems equally annoying to Ritchie was the fact that Gano is a vegetarian and therefore selling the rights to a chain that sells burgers and chicken nuggets (amongst other things) seemed hypocritical.

For Gano, head of a band that he'd dedicated his life to but which has never really brought in the money they perhaps deserved, it was a quick cash grab and one has to wonder whether there's anything overtly wrong with that. It's a question that only creators of underappreciated music can fully answer, and some of the vitriol spewing fans that abhorred the decision have never faced the same dilemma: If selling a piece of your soul to corporate America pays for you to keep making music for the next few years, rather than calling it a day and punching a clock somewhere in a dead end job, wouldn't you do it?

The argument caused a complete cessation of band output and activity until 2013, where newly made up Ritchie and Gano were joined by a compliment of Brian Viglione (drums, percussion), John Saparrow (also drums, percussion) and Blaise Garza (sax, percussion, keyboard). This version of the band have released a couple of albums, the last of which appeared in 2019. They are still an active entity, having toured as recently as 2023.

About This Song

Country Death Song features a man who slowly goes mad and kills one of his daughters by throwing her down a well before hanging himself in his barn in shame. Happy fare indeed. It starts with a simple, repeating baseline that underpins the entire track, quickly joined by drums and guitar. The usual stripped-down sound deliberately draws on traditional Appalachian musical influences. The track shifts up a gear when the banjo kicks in and the narrative gets fully underway.

Bob Biggs, president of Slash Records (the label who put the record out), really wasn't impressed when first hearing it, dismissing the song with the comment: "It's OK until that piano comes in and ruins it." When the president of a record label mistakes a banjo for a piano it doesn't bode well for anyone, but thankfully nobody else thought like this and the song was released successfully and endures to this day, becoming a fan favourite and a concert staple.

Special mention needs to be made for a particular Country Death Song video, one that really stands out from the assortment of live versions and other clips used for this song on YouTube. Simply animated with a predominantly black and white palette, cutout paper figures act out the scenes and completely draw you into the dark world of the lyrics (inspired by a newspaper article Gano had read). It's the work of fan Cory Latoki and perfectly captures the energy and mania of the song, and beautifully illustrates the dark narrative at its core. It started life as a finals piece for his animation class and now lives on YouTube so we can all appreciate it.

Essential Album
The debut album, also called 'Violent Femmes', contains a number of the band's best known tracks including Blister in the Sun, Add It Up and Gone Daddy Gone. Most of the songs (and those of follow-up album 'Hallowed Ground', with its change of direction towards gospel and more experimental songs with overt Christian leanings) were written when Gano was just 18 years old and still at school. The record gained a cult following and steady sales, receiving gold status 4 years after release and platinum status another 4 years after that, finally cracking the Billboard Top 200 (peaking at #171) some 18 years after debuting.

The album received a 40th Anniversary Record Store Day vinyl picture disc release, issued in April 2023. It features the same 10 songs and that iconic cover, a photo of 3 year old Billie Jo Campbell peering through the window of a dilapidated old house somewhere in LA.

Second Choice Song
Taken from the debut album, Add It Up is one of the band's best known tracks and is a stone-cold classic. Chosen to headline the compilation album **Add It Up (1981-1993),** the live version included here is spectacular, eclipsing the original and showcasing a band firing on all cylinders.

Astoundingly, **Add It Up** wasn't a single release for the band and never officially charted as a standalone song. **Country Death Song** was also never released as a single, which means that both of my choices for this band are album tracks. Whether this has any relevance to the band's failure to achieve mainstream popularity is open to question but deliberately choosing to keep two of their best songs out of the singles charts surely didn't help their cause.

INTERLUDE 1

BEST VIDEOS

BEST VIDEOS

I already realise that this section is a doomed endeavour. All of my recommendations in this book are personal favourites and I can only hope that you will agree and embrace some of my choices so they become your favourites too. But choosing my favourite videos on top of the music seems to be taking things a little too far. Maybe. I don't know.

Promo videos for songs really came of age with Queen's **Bohemian Rhapsody**. It's impossible to hear the song without picturing the video (or the film clip from *Wayne's World* and those bobbing heads in the car). Some videos do this, they're so fantastic that they lock themselves onto the music forever, impossible to separate. Think Peter Gabriel's **Sledgehammer** - horrifically (charmingly) dated now but stunning at the time - or the late Sinead O' Connor's weepy face on **Nothing Compares To You**.

Of course, pop videos existed way before 1974. Al Jolson even has a video for his 1927 song **The Jazz Singer**. French perv Serge Gainsbourg appears in one from 1959, **Le Poinconneur Des Lilas**. You can find promo clips (and even entire movies) for bands like The Beatles, The Kinks etc from the 1960's. Bob Dylan came out with a much-imitated promo for **Subterranean Homesick Blues** in 1966. But the one that changed everything was arguably Bohemian Rhapsody. Seven years later came the launch of MTV and suddenly every single band on the planet no longer had a choice about music videos – they were a necessity if you wanted some serious airtime.

As you've been working your way through the book, you've no doubt been heading across to *Spotify* or *YouTube* to check out my choices for yourself. If you picked *YouTube*, you'll have probably seen lots of new videos already, especially if I highlight the appropriate promo clips within my main selections.

What follows is a short selection of great videos. I've tried to choose ones that don't just feature the band standing around playing their instruments and nothing else, but rather have taken us on an unexpected and delightful journey into a strange new world. Some of the choices feature bands that didn't make it into the rest of the book for lack of space, and will probably feature in a second volume, but more on that later.

For now, enjoy these videos and hopefully they'll add an extra layer of appreciation for the bands and their music.

THE HIVES – BOGUS OPERANDI

We'll start with a new one from 2023. **The Hives** are a Swedish rock band formed in 1993 (or possibly 1989, like Trigger's broom with a different name and a different sound – is that the same band?) and steadily worked their way towards breaking Europe. Creation Record's Alan McGee signed them to a new label (Poptones) in 2001 and released a compilation album of their early material which then broke them in the UK.

Shortly afterwards the band signed a Deal with Universal worth a reputed 50 million dollars. I shall repeat that number because I can hardly believe it myself – 50 million dollars. I think they're good but *that* good? Is anybody worth that much?! I'll court a little controversy and say that my limited sampling of their wares leaves me feeling that their material sounds a bit samey, songs firmly embedded in the garage rock genre with little exploration outside that (although there are some experimental tacks like **A Stroll Through Hive Manor Corridors** that are pretty decent). And they've definitely had their share of bangers – **Hate To Say I Told You So** and **Tick Tick Boom** are both awesome, for example.

But **Bogus Operandi** takes the biscuit for me. Great song (I've basically been playing it to death since first hearing it), and a spectacular video. Put together they may just be the best thing in this whole book. It's basically a retelling of *The Evil Dead* with the band being terrorised and murdered by implements like a shovel, a broken bottle and a spoon. It's incredibly gory in places, but clearly made with a reverence and a love for the source material and a great deal of humour.

Being murdered/undead doesn't deprive them of their usual stylish snappy dressing, bringing out uniform black suits with white flashing for the latter half of the song. I often say that I can't recommend things highly enough – I do have a trait where I get very excited about things with a level of intensity bordering on autism – but in this case I really can't. This tune and this video are superb.

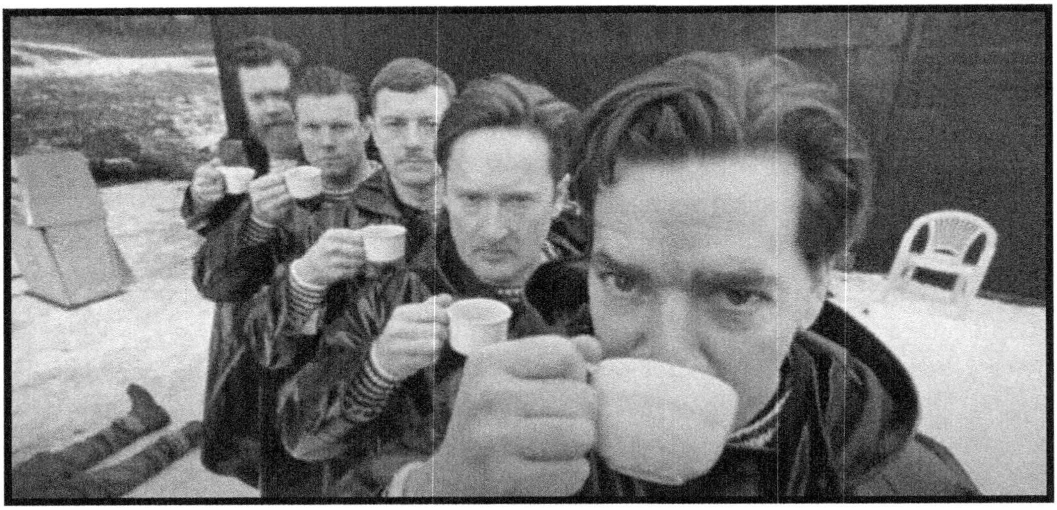

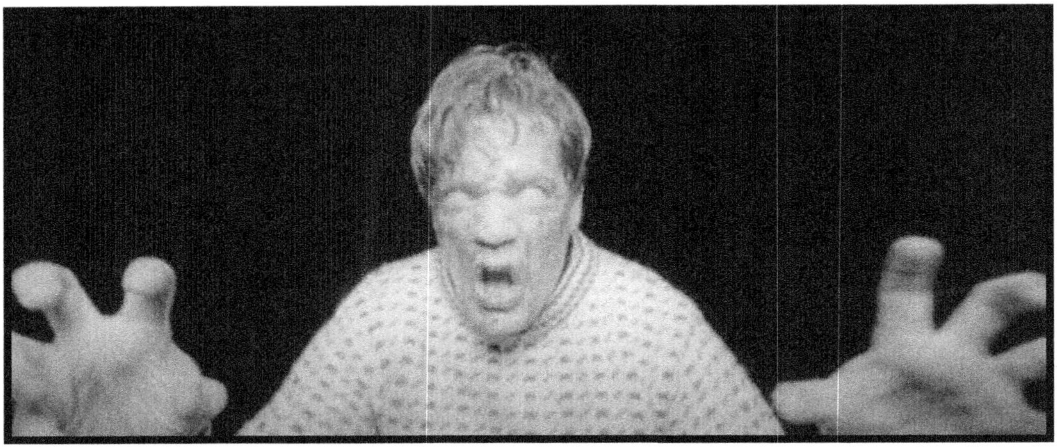

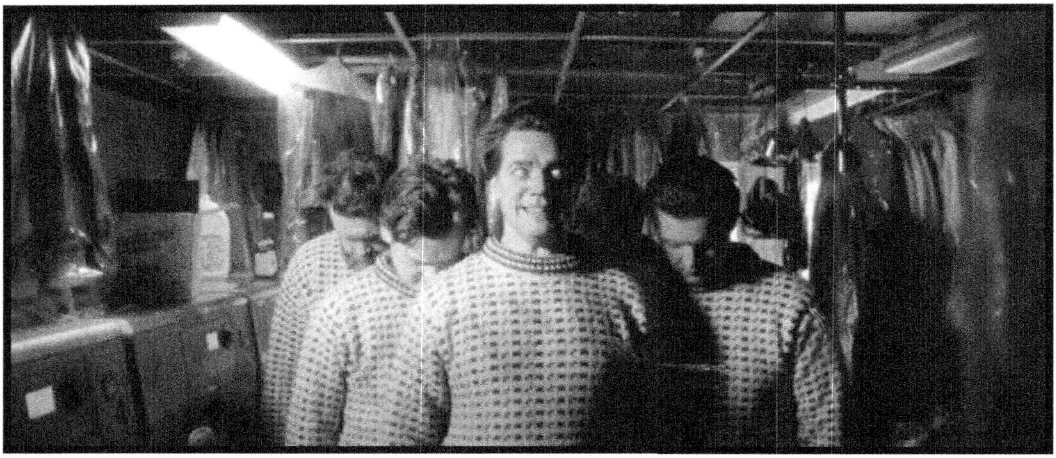

BASEMENT JAXX – WHERE'S YOUR HEAD AT?

We're going back over 20 years for the next one and it's another blinder. You could probably make this one with today's computer technology for a few thousand pounds but back then it was pushing at the technical limits (and most definitely budgetary limits) of special effects.

This fantastic tune, one of their many hits and taken from their 2nd studio album **Rooty**, charted well in Europe, the US and Australia, and one can only imagine the faces of unwitting folk who stumbled across the video expecting some light-hearted dance promo with more traditional visuals.

The band really went for it on this one, and they created one of the most disturbing and hilarious pop videos ever made. In the guise of a short horror film, a music journalist arrives at a large hospital building to report on "the latest thing in pop music". A bunch of scientists in white coats and monkey fixations greet him and try and sell him on the idea of monkeys playing instruments. But all is not as it seems, as will soon be revealed. Disinterested, the journalist seems ready to leave and then one of the head scientists makes the decision to let him see the next phase of the program.

He's taken into an isolation room and some monkeys come in to give a live performance. But these monkeys have human faces! (Two of the monkey faces are band members Felix Buxton and Simon Ratcliffe). The monkeys become increasingly agitated (and top marks to the band for their acting skills, the performances are terrific) and revert back to more animalistic behaviour, destroying the equipment and threatening the journalist, who tries to escape via a small chute (after seeing the laboratory where the transformations take place, and their dastardly plans for him).

This is a fabulous, superbly inventive video that won a couple of awards and a spot on my playlist forever.

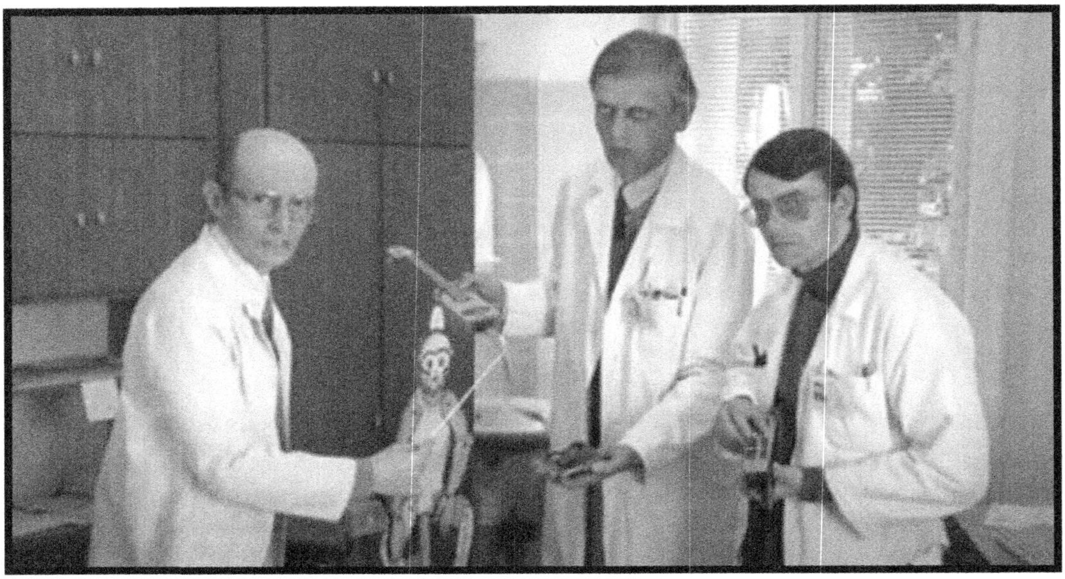

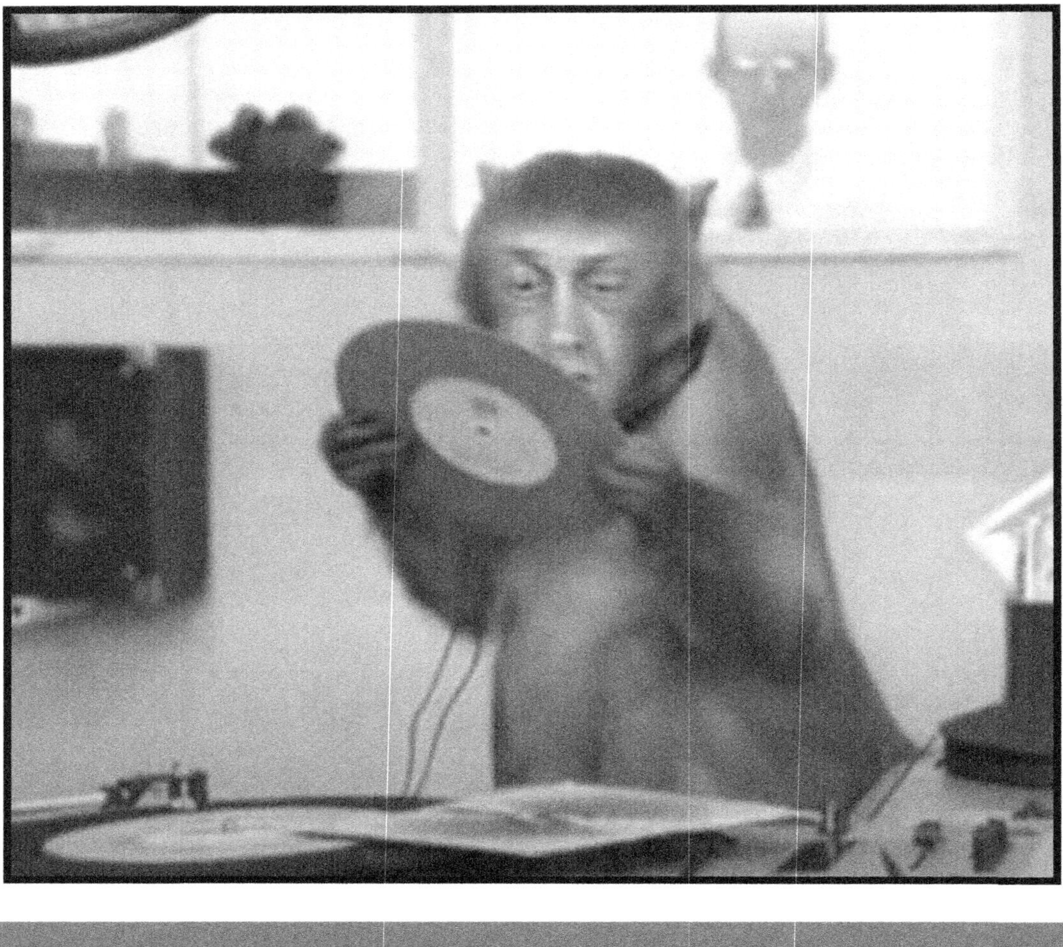

BAND OF SKULLS – SWEET SOUR

Back to more rock-oriented fare now. You may have already watched this video due to my praising it in the section on **Band of Skulls**. If you haven't, you are in for a treat. Like all of these videos, it goes without saying that the songs behind them are top notch – great videos won't make a shit song better, after all. **Sweet Sour** is one of the band's early singles from an album of the same name. It's a measured number, showcasing the band's talents without any showboating, one the New Zealand Herald aptly summarises as "slow-burning but blistering".

The video, filmed in black and white (and probably the cause of many heart attacks from the Daily Mail readership), shows a small group of energy-filled children with nothing better to do than terrorise their wasteland of a home environment with petty acts of vandalism and casual violence. And dance. The group come across a young boy in the middle of a junction and after some intimidation there's a dance and an acceptance of this new little fellow into their gang. More casual vandalism ensues before they head into an old warehouse with a boombox on the floor and finish off the song with a dance worthy of an *X-Factor* audition. (Wierdly, the young girl in the video really did turn up on a *Britain's Got Talent* audition!)

It's effortlessly cool song, enriched by a surprisingly touching video and your life is incomplete without experiencing both at least once.

APHEX TWIN – COME TO DADDY

I've just noticed that quite a few of my video choices contain horror elements. That's not necessarily a bad thing, just an observation. This next choice is definitely one of the most disturbing things most people will ever see. It's also very funny, extremely well done and a highlight of both contributors' CV's. This said, it is the most challenging video – and piece of music – in the book. I don't expect many people to like this one. I'm not even sure if I do myself, but I certainly admire the work that's gone into it and I definitely recognise the creative genius of both artists.

Aphex Twin will be covered in Volume 2 – he's a very interesting bloke from Cornwall called Richard James and he's basically like Alcatel (now Alcatel-Lucent), the French company that pretty much no-one has ever heard of but is absolutely integral to the infrastructure of the Internet and the modern world. Richard James is like that with electronic music. A niche artist, his tunes have influenced more of his contemporaries that we'll ever know. A prodigious talent with a reported backlog of unreleased material lasting hundreds of hours, he generally avoids the spotlight and lets the music – whatever limited releases he puts out – do the talking.

Chris Cunningham, the film-maker and collaborator on this project (and also Aphex Twin releases **Windowlicker** and the seriously warped **Rubber Johnny** short film, soundtracked by Aphex Twin), has a very unique vision and brings that to all of his work. Other bands he has worked with include Autechre and Squarepusher. According to *Wikipedia*, he's been approached to direct the film of the William Gibson novel *Neuromancer*, but it's been stuck in early pre-production for two decades. More successful movie endeavours including working with Stanley Kubrick, Richard Stanley (who did some videos for Fields of the Nephilim) and David Fincher.

Once viewed, **Come to Daddy** is something you will never unsee. It will be in your head forever. I'm almost afraid to recommend it to you but I feel that I must, and that is for one simple reason – it may be one of the most bonkers and disturbing pop videos ever made but it is an absolute work of genius.

An old lady walks her dog across the wasteland of a mostly abandoned inner city estate, all litter and broken shopping trolleys, stained concrete and high-rise flats. (Filmed at the now-demolished brutalist Thamesmead Estate, which Stanley Kubrick used for a lot of the location shots for A Clockwork Orange). She encounters a very scary discarded TV set and a group of very odd children. They run riot as she tries to avoid having a heart attack (and I suspect the creators of Band of Skulls **Sweet Sour** promo have seen this video and it's had a lasting influence on them). From the television emerges a demon figure – and this imagery precedes cult Japanese horror film *Ringu* by a year, where the big scare was Sadako engaged in a similar tv-birthing scene – and in one of the most amazing sequences ever produced for a music video, the demon stands in front of the old lady and SCREAMS, subjecting her to a wind of filth so strong it ripples her cheeks and blows back her hair as if she's in a High-G testing machine.

How you return to normality after watching this video I don't know – maybe bridge the gap with another offering of Aphex Twin called **Windowlicker**, a tune equally as inventive but far mellower. This said, the video for that is just as disturbing and may just tip you over the edge.

Regardless of your final judgement on these tracks, I find it really exciting that people like Aphex Twin and Chris Cunningham are out there, making such unhinged pieces of art, countering the bland *X-Factor* bullshit that the masses are being spoon fed. I don't expect even a fraction of the same audience to like it but it's so nice to have a choice.

THE CURE – CLOSE TO ME

The Cure have always had interesting videos, at least between **The Hanging Garden** (1982) and **Friday I'm In Love** (1992), whereby all of the singles videos except two were directed by long-time Cure collaborator Tim Pope.

Pope brought imagery that exactly complimented Robert Smith's off kilter songs, and the band's pairing with the director was a perfect match, bearing rich fruit such as the classic videos like **The Caterpillar**, **Inbetween Days** (almost my choice here), **Just Like Heaven**, **Lullaby** and **Fascination Street**. All are vibrant examples of how to present a band like The Cure in their best light, accentuating the offbeat humour that the band aren't often noted for, but which is obvious when you look a little more closely.

Take, for instance, the video for **Close to Me**. The band are packed tightly into a wardrobe perched precariously at the top of a cliff. Pope captures the claustrophobia of the environment (and, indeed, the lyrics) perfectly.

There are 2 versions of the song, and the various horn additions are absent from the more compact album version. Thankfully, the single release was extended slightly and horn sections were added, which if you know both versions you will appreciate just how much those additions round out and really make the song what it is. This is the version used for the video.

Halfway through, the wardrobe falls off the cliff and we see the band tumbling around inside. When you think about the logistics of what Pope accomplished with this video, it really is a remarkable achievement. The wardrobe ends up in the sea, and inside the band have to make the best of the constricted space now filling up with water. I remember reading an interview with Smith where he says the water came from some fire engines and it was freezing and it stank – and there we all were, thinking how glamourous the life of a pop star must be!

Clearly the video looks a lot of fun, and the band can't contain their joy in making it, so let's just forget that the actual premise involves them all drowning! For a little lighthearted refreshment you really can't go wrong with any of the Tim Pope videos, and all of the band's music from this period marks their golden era as well.

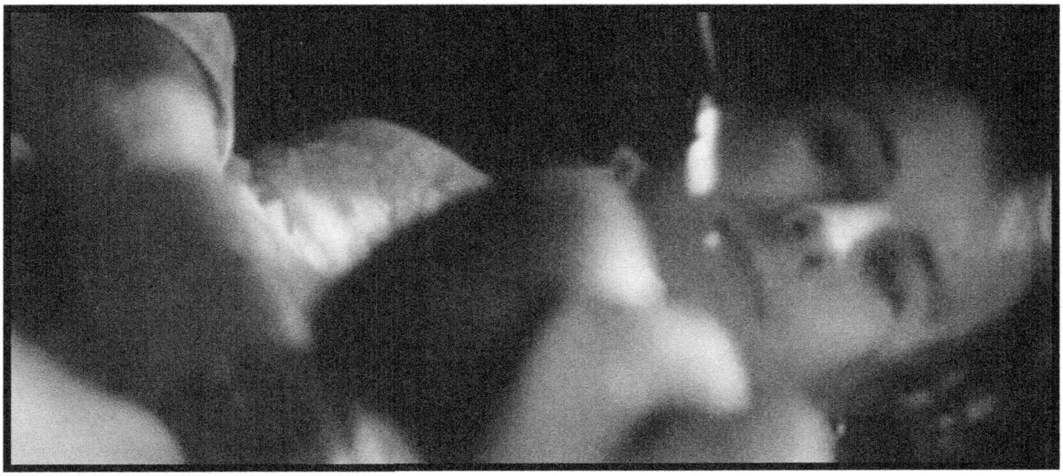

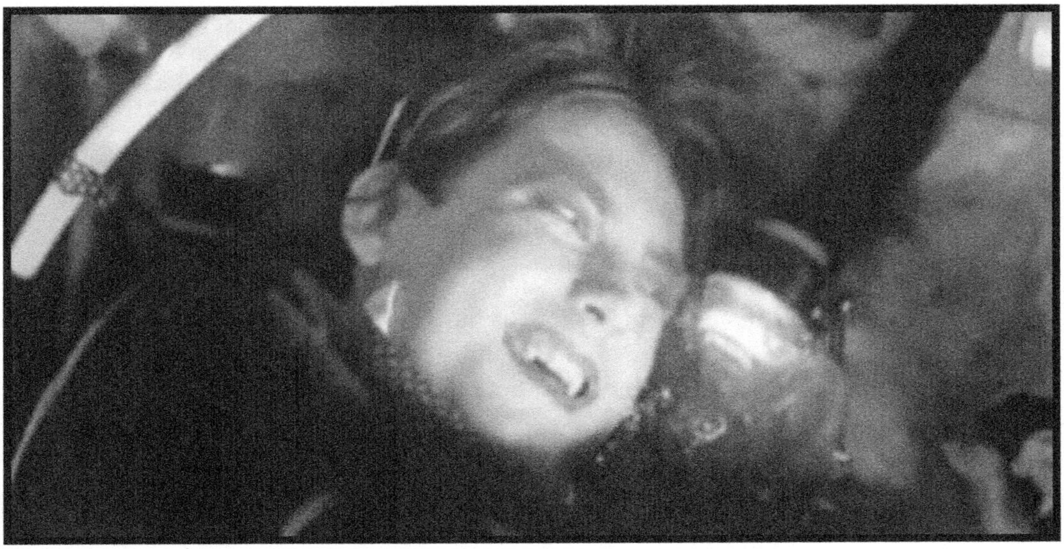

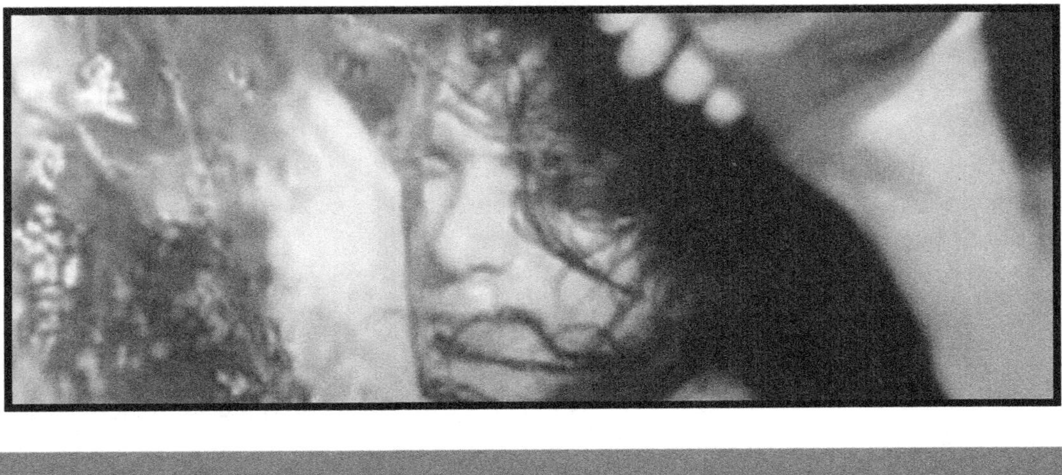

MASSIVE ATTACK - ANGEL

It all starts with the song. None of these videos would work with anywhere near the same level of awesomeness if the underlying songs themselves weren't any good. Each is pretty much a classic before any associated imagery gets tacked onto it.

Angel is the opener to Massive Attack's mega-successful 1998 **Mezzanine** album. It's a relatively slow-paced affair with a crawling keyboard bassline and a throbbing bass guitar on top, and beautiful vocals from collaborator Horace Andy (who appears in the video, and also on a couple more tracks on the album including the fantastic **Man Next Door**, which samples heavily from The Cure's **10:15 Saturday Night**).

The track slowly builds momentum, adding additional layers and bristling with an underlying menace. Heavier drums join the lighter drum machine thread, guitars bring more volume and intensity and there's a long fade as the instruments peel away one by one. It's a sublime piece of work, one of the strongest songs from that era of British music history.

The start of the promo video is band member 'Daddy G' (Grant Marshall), who parks his car at night in a seemingly empty multi-storey car park, gets out and starts walking, soon realising he's being followed. Initially only by Horace Andy, but other shadowy figures emerge, including Massive Attack band members Robert del Naja and Andrew Vowles. All three commit to their performances and the video seethes with tension.

Before too long, dozens of people are following him and, understandably nervous, he picks up the pace. He's a frightened animal and the pack have sensed the fear and are closing in. He breaks into a run, and the chase is on. There's no reason given for any of this, there's no sense to it – it's just a primal, animalistic hunt and the fear from the victim is palpable. They chase him out of the car park, now hundreds strong, across open ground where he comes to a wall. Trapped, he turns to face the mob.

And here is where the true genius of this video lies. The subtleties and nuances of a facial expression, the slow blink signalling the acceptance of his fate. The smile of the hunter but edged with something else. The sudden, unexpected realisation that the balance of power is shifting. The eyes of the hunters widen slightly with their own fear. The tables turn and the victim takes a single step forward, and the effect it has on the mob is genuinely shocking. None of them can seem to believe it. He tests them again, and a movement ripples through the mob. Panic sets in. He starts walking forwards and they back away. He runs. They flee in terror.

Here is an example of a promo video that has been boiled down to its essence – just a single, simple idea stripped back of any frills and executed to perfection. Like all of the best videos, I never tire of repeat viewings. This one gets an airing every few months and each time it fills me with the giddy wonder of watching something amazing.

The video has 52 millions views at the time of writing so the secret on this one is already out and there's a chance you've already seen it. If you haven't, and this goes double if you've never even heard the song before, drop everything right now and get it on!

NINE INCH NAILS - ONLY

Here we have another band that makes innovative and interesting videos, usually based around performance rather than flights of fancy. Early videos flirted with bondage imagery, which I sort of ignored as I loved the music, and the band eventually grew out of that and moved onto other themes, but not before leaving behind the highly upsetting and pretty much banned everywhere video accompaniment for the **Broken** EP. I wouldn't recommend watching it out of anything other than a morbid curiosity if you really like the band, but it's really not necessary.

The video for **Only**, though, is. Despite the dark lyrics, the tune itself is one of NIN's poppier numbers and feels really upbeat. Directed by David Fincher (director of *Zodiac* and *Fight Club*, and multiple time collaborator with Trent Reznor, who soundtracked Fincher movies *The Social Network*, *Gone Girl*, *Mank* and *The Girl With The Dragon Tattoo*), the video features various bits of office paraphernalia rocking in time to the music.

A sterile desk environment comes alive, with various bits of equipment like a laptop speaker, a Newton's Cradle and the surface of a cup of coffee shown in macro detail vibrating along with the beat. The star of the show is one of these Pin Art toys, which is shown in extreme close up before appearing to contain NIN main man Reznor performing the song. It's a clever idea and really well done. Although the office itself looks real, pretty much every single thing in the video is CGI, with the exception of the director's hand initiating the song sequence at the start and some blurry cars in some background shots.

Even if you don't end up liking the song (an unimaginable proposition, surely!) the video is worth watching for the sake of seeing an unusual and creatively artistic approach to making a promo video for a song. And it's essential viewing for fans of Fincher's films, bringing in elements of his work from some of those films (particularly the close-up CGI work featured at various points in *Fight Club*).

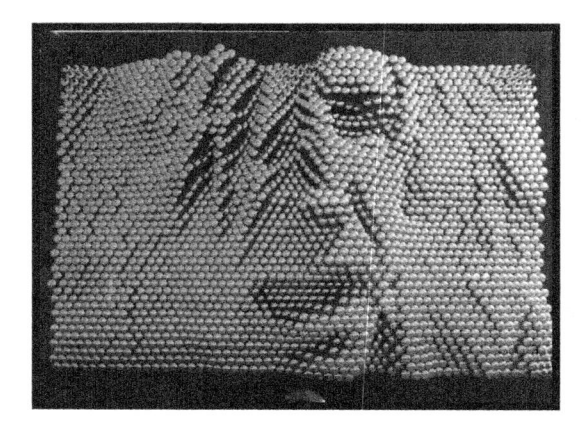

PRIMUS – SOUTHBOUND PACHYDERM

I was spoiled for choice with **Primus** videos, they have so many classics. Three that come to mind immediately are **Candyman**, **Winona's Big Brown Beaver** and **Lee Van Cleef**. I could easily sit there and watch those three on a loop all day.

However, for my choice here I've gone with **Southbound Pachyderm**. The song itself – although I love it – is not as obviously catchy as the others just mentioned. You go on more of a journey with it. The intro alone, led by the bass and reminiscent of the **Dead Kennedys'** **Holiday in Cambodia**, lasts over 2 minutes on the unabridged version, but here is cut to about half that. Knowing how expensive video is to make, that minute probably saved them many thousands of dollars.

Although the band do appear in the video – on monitor screens observed by the antagonist – the majority of the action is stop-motion animation featuring clay figurines. Story-wise, the titular pachyderms (thick skinned non-ruminant animals such as hippos, rhinos and elephants) are being hunted by a group of gun-wielding poacher-types orchestrated by a Big Bad Villain. A couple of scientists are bringing pachyderms to a safe place away from the hunters but realise they've been discovered and send the large creatures away with harnessed propeller-powered wings. They're heading south, presumably, for the time being out of reach of those guns.

The video is great fun to watch but contains a serious message, one that Primus main man Les Claypool feels strongly about – the conservation status of these large pachyderms and the extinction threat. It's something we should all feel strongly about, for the generations coming up behind us will no doubt live in a world where such creatures are only known about through books and old videos.

The shoot for the video lasted six weeks, and the animators produced ten seconds or less of useable footage per day. An alternative video accompaniment to the song was featured in an enhanced DC version of the parent album **Tales From the Punchbowl**, but after viewing it for research purposes I can safely say that I won't be revisiting that version and you should maybe not bother at all. (Sorry Mr Claypool, the 'proper' video is so much better.)

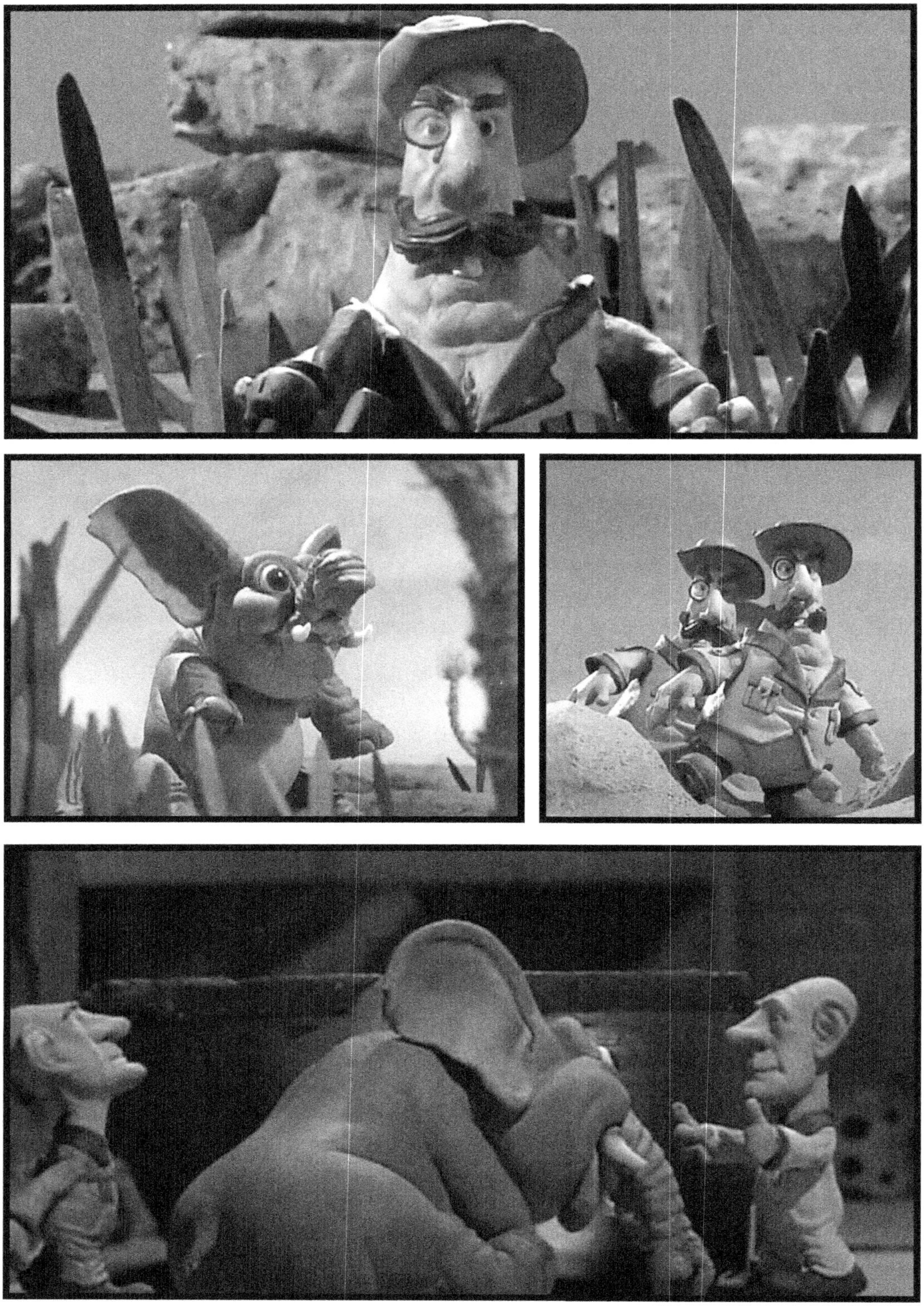

NEW MODEL ARMY

WHITE LIGHT

NEW MODEL ARMY – WHITE LIGHT

About the Band

Like any band that's been around for decades, New Model Army has been through numerous incarnations, with the only constant member being songwriter / vocalist / guitarist Justin Sullivan. Sullivan went by the name of '*Slade the Leveller*' in the early years, an act that sets out his stall with regards to political beliefs, character and a foreshadowing of many lyrical themes the group would follow during their career. Additionally, myth has it that he used the name so that he could pursue his musical ambitions with paid gigs and still claim benefits.

During the course of their career they've released 15 albums (with additional live and compilation collections) and have DNA laced with punk, folk, rock, metal, goth and most importantly, Northern sensibilities. Despite Sullivan being born in Buckinghamshire, his spiritual birthplace is surely Bradford and the wild moors of the North.

They are a unique band and hard to pin down to any particular category, and the one thing that can be said with any degree of certainty is that they're criminally underrated and have, with the odd minor interlude, been ignored by the mainstream for most of their existence.

Their music, especially the earlier recordings, sounds quite menacing. Bass and drums lock together in a thunderous wall and Sullivan – who, with the best will in the world, can be a genuinely scary looking fellow – sings about savage things over the top of it all. His songs often tell stories and, beneath the heavy backing of the music, can be angry, dismissive, rebellious but also poignant, righteous and moving at the same time. Sullivan was singing about themes that mattered long before it became worthy to do so.

They are a band that has aged well. Many bands get comfortable and mellow too much as they grow older, producing songs that lack any sense of urgency or fiery spirit. New Model Army, Sullivan in particular, continues to see injustice in the world and it fuels a deep anger that continues to offer a wellspring of inspiration.

2016's **Winter** album is as good as anything that came before it, and is bookmarked either side with strong releases in **Between Dog and Wolf** (2013) and **From Here** (2019), which features my second choice song. To pick two songs from the same band almost 30 years apart from each other shows that NMA have been quietly producing quality material, without much fanfare, for decades. They are a great British institution and long may they continue.

About This Song
White Light is a pretty straightforward rock song by NMA standards and is an album track from 1993's **The Love of Hopeless Causes**. Apart from being an opener to gigs around that time, the track has no particularly notable reason to stand out but it's one that I've happily played to death without ever getting tired of it, and still play on a regular basis.

They have better songs, and I originally chose **Vagabonds** (read more about that song shortly), but I'm taking a chance that you'll listen to Vagabonds anyway and it would be impossible to dislike it so let's try something a little different here. **White Light** is simple in structure, not overly flowery in terms of musicianship and is just a solid, dependable rock song, one that elevates itself to a higher level with repeated listens.

There's a brilliant live version on YouTube from a 1997 concert at Sziget, where Sullivan appears in lesser-spotted shorn hair mode. Well worth a watch.

Essential Album
Thunder and Consolation is not only one of the best albums by New Model Army, it's also one of the best albums by any band in this book. The trio of Sullivan, Rob Heaton (drums) and Jason Harris (bass) were at the top of their game and the album gained an extra dimension by featuring the violin work of Ed Alleyne-Johnson.

Opener **I Love The World** is the heaviest track in the collection and encapsulates everything that the band does in a single song – intelligent lyrics, immaculate playing from everyone involved, a great arrangement and structure. Sullivan is one of those singers that can make dense, complex lyrics sound effortless.

"Well I never said I was a clever man,
but I know enough to understand
That the endless leaps and forward plans
will someday have to cease.
You blind yourselves with comfort lies,
like lightning never strikes you twice,
and we laugh at your amazed surprise
as the Ark begins to sink."
I Love The World © Sullivan/Heaton

The music is superb, as always, and the lyrics equally so. Sullivan's themes of the distrust of religion, technology and science, are present. Prescient, even. And then you have lyrics of **Green and Grey**, telling the story of a young man who resists the urge to fly from his small town, to not follow the young men whose previous exodus left those that remained in an even more desperate plight as their hometown withered before their eyes. It's a heartbreaking, oft-repeated story, captured perfectly here.

Green and Grey was a single release, along with **Stupid Questions** and the phenomenal **Vagabonds**, a highpoint of the long-established folk-rock genre and occasionally played live with a compliment of between 2-6 drummers. It's an anthem, a definite jewel in a crown already overloaded with riches. When I say that the rest of the songs on the album are just as good, we're left with a record that is a benchmark for how this kind of thing should be done, an album that should be inducted into the Rock Hall of Fame for Albums when they finally invent it.

Second Choice Song
Never Arriving (2019) features an older, greying Sullivan walking across his beloved moors in the sopping rain. Again, this is a song of lyrical complexity and one that evokes vivid imagery. The fact that I'm going to quote even more of Sullivan's lyrics should show how great they really are:

I drove you South through the landscape that you love,
all those medieval towns with the cobbled stones
washed by the blood of the martyrs,
in the last great stand of the true believers.
The hilltop villages baking in the afternoon sun,
the walls pocked with old bullet holes
and the stone and iron that broke the people's backs
all laid out for the tourists.
Never Arriving © New Model Army / Sullivan

That's not even the best verse! Fantastic stuff. And we haven't even gotten to the music yet. Powered by a throbbing bassline and solid, pounding drums, the song throws in some jangly guitar and brief backing vocals for the louder choruses. There's a deliberate lull in the middle, a brief pause before the chorus powers back in for a lead out finale. For my money, the quieter verses are the driving force and the more interesting parts of the composition.

It's not as obviously likeable as White Light or Vagabonds, but a couple of listens will definitely be rewarding. And, of course, there's that video, mixing in band footage and some scenes shot from a drone and a moving vehicle, but it's the bits focusing on the endlessly watchable Sullivan just walking and singing that fascinate the most. In places he's no more than a dot in the open wilderness, and listening to his music you pick up lots of clues that this is where he is the happiest.

On a final note here, I really struggled to find just a couple of songs to showcase, and in various drafts of this piece I changed my mind about half a dozen times before finally settling on these. Before this book, I knew the band and **Thunder and Consolation** would have made my top 10 albums anyway, but a much deeper dive into their music (which stalled the book for months as I just couldn't stop playing them!) unearthed a boatload of classic tunes that are really too good to just ignore. So, if you like what you've heard so far, whether it's for the music, or the poetic lyrics, or even the videos, you must also try these and see if that opens up the door for further exploration on your own:

The Hunt (1986)
Lights Go Out (1986)
Here Comes The War (1993)
Winter (2016)
Born Feral (2016)

PIXIES

NO. 13 BABY

PIXIES – NO. 13 BABY

About the Band

Formed in Boston in 1986, Pixies would have a monumental effect in guiding the sound of music over the next two decades, influencing the likes of Nirvana, Radiohead, PJ Harvey, Smashing Pumpkins and dozens more. Any band that embraced the *quiet-LOUD-quiet* aesthetic of making music owes a real debt to them.

At the beginning, Charles 'Black' Francis and Joey Santiago had *some* idea of what they were doing, and supercool Kim Deal joined the band as their bass player without knowing how to play. Drummer David Lovering had once met Kim at her own wedding reception and got a spot in the newly forming band from that introduction alone. Hardly an auspicious beginning, more like a jape, but once rehearsals got underway the four disparate elements that combined to make the Pixies symbiotically produced pure gold.

They released an EP mini album called **Come on Pilgrim**, followed by their first 'proper' album proper, **Surfer Rosa**. In the UK, Surfa Rosa incorporated the EP, but in the US the releases were kept separate. Undoubtedly the sound of the band on the second record was sculpted by producer Steve Albini (Big Black, Shellac), a man to whom, post Surfer Rosa, numerous bands came looking for him to produce their own music, including The Jesus Lizard, Murder Inc. and Pigface (a supergroup featuring various musicians in the book, one of whom – Chris Connelly – readily admits that they never lived up to their potential and sadly produced only disappointing material).

4AD label boss Ivo Watts-Russell almost passed on the band until his girlfriend convinced him otherwise. Without her, we might never have heard of them. **Smells Like Teen Spirit** – you know the one – was written by Kurt Cobain as a conscious effort to rip off the Pixies song writing style, so we would never have had that, or the whole grunge movement, which influenced the overall rock sound of the 1990's onwards. Indeed, without Watts-Russell's girlfriend, music today would sound very different.

The follow up album **Doolittle** dialed back on the ferociousness a little, being filled with cleaner and more melodic tunes with tightly controlled bursts of nuclear strength fury. With a higher production budget and overseen by Gil Norton, their music was corralled into a collection of songs slightly more sympathetic to the ear and the album really launched them, in Europe at least. Old touring partners Throwing Muses, The Wolfgang Press and the like were replaced with stadium filling acts like The Cure and U2 and headline slots at Reading. (Looking back at their 1990 Reading poster, where they headlined on the Sunday above bands like The Fall and Jesus Jones, I can't help but wonder at the line up on the Friday where Jane's Addiction sit low on the bill just above An Emotional Fish (I actually had one of their singles, it wasn't too bad) and beneath Gary Clail). In retrospect, pretty shocking.

Pixies success didn't initially translate to their home country. Although well-known in Boston and their home state of Massachusetts, the rest of the US was slower to catch on (**Surfer Rosa** took 17 years to achieve gold status there).

Touring for the **Doolittle** album created division amongst the band members, with Francis and Deal eventually refusing to communicate with each other. More friction came in the form of Deal's resentment of Francis' control over the band, wanting to have more of an input and being batted down once too often. She would eventually leave the band and form the instantly mega-successful The Breeders, along with Tanya Donnelly (guitarist and backing vocals for the aforementioned Throwing Muses) and bassist Jo Wiggs. Their hit **Cannonball** was a mainstay on MTV for quite a while and gave them lots of exposure.

Pixies' third album **Bossa Nova** brought in more of a surf-rock sound to the band but in the fickle world of rock n' roll, the fact that they were changing their sound and not producing more of the same began to see general interest in the band start to wane. Follow up **Tromp Le Monde** continued the downward sales trajectory and the band would split shorty thereafter and not release any more material until 2014's **Indie City**, a gap of 23 years.

As the juggernaut of Nirvana, and all the bands they dragged in their wake, began to edge Pixies to the side-lines, it must have been a frustrating time for main songwriter Black Francis, watching as this upstart band from some rainy corner of the US, who openly admitted to being influenced by Pixies, eclipsed them and basically took over the world. When Francis ended the band in 1993, the first people he told were the interviewers at BBC Radio 5 in the UK. Relations with Deal and Lovering were so low at this point that he informed them the band was no longer an ongoing concern by fax. At least guitarist Joey Santiago got an actual phone call.

Black Francis changed his name to Frank Black (his real name is Charles Michael Kittridge Thompson IV, so you can see why he used a much cooler pseudonym) and released a few albums, some of which Santiago played lead guitar on. Kim Deal found success with The Breeders. David Lovering turned down an offer of a spot with Foo Fighters (a decision he would probably come to regret) and instead turned himself into a performer of physics-based magic called The Scientific Phenomenalist. By the time Pixies reformed in 2004 he was in a bit of a state, portrayed in the (Pixies) documentary *loudQUIETloud* as a bit of an alcoholic sad sack reduced to playing childrens' parties like some prototype Mr Jelly from *Psychoville*.

The band continued to tour to sold out crowds for a number of years. In 2013 Deal left the band again, this time for good. After a brief turn by Kim Shattuck, the bassist role was permanently filled by former A Perfect Circle bass guitarist Paz Lenchantin. New recorded material emerged as a set of EP's, which were grouped together in 2013 to form the album **Indie City**.

Since then, Pixies have released 3 more albums with solid sales, none of which match their commercial peak but enough to show that the world still wants Pixies in it and is willing to buy their records and concert tickets and thus continue their existence. A lot of bands would settle for that kind of deal, especially ones that have already been around the block a bit and seen the madness that comes from silly levels of success.

About This Song
No 13 Baby is the longest track on **Doolittle** and buried at number 11 in the running order. It's one of the less showy tunes from the album and has its work cut out competing for the listener's attention by being surrounded by a ton of classic tunes.

It's a typical Pixies song, with lots of noisy guitars and with Francis squawking high-pitched lyrics over the top and if it wasn't for the sudden change in dynamic around the two-minute mark, it might not have made quite the same impact. That change makes something very good into something great. The song relaxes, it breathes, it offers each of the musicians a chance to shine in a lengthy (for Pixies) outro, one that's impossible not to tap your foot along to.

Key to the song's power is once again the bass sound and performance of Kim Deal. Now, Deal is no Les Claypool (**Primus**, see elsewhere in this book). She's most comparable to that other bassist that rarely goes for flowery, showy stuff but provides the backbone to many a great tune and that is Tina Weymouth from **Talking Heads**. Deal's basslines are like rocks in a river that the water must flow around. They provide structural support and although they don't do anything overly fancy they do seem to be the one thing that truly defines each song. So many tunes in the Pixies catalogue (up to 2013) are anchored and lifted by Deal's playing. Without her, those early records would not be the same.

And yet you could easily say the same thing about Joey Santiago's guitar work, or Black Francis' lyrics and vocal delivery. Although Lovering isn't often credited for his drumming, and rarely (if ever) makes lists of the greatest rock drummers of all time, he is a superb musician and an excellent fit for the Pixies sound.

All of these elements combine perfectly in **No 13 Baby**. It competes for attention amongst tunes that are instantly more accessible but it has a little something extra, something undefinable – some magic ingredient that keeps me coming back again and again for repeat playings.

Essential Album
Seeing as both song choices come from the same Pixies album, I'm going to have to choose that album. I played **Doolittle** to death when it came out, over and over and

over until all of the songs were burned into my brain forever. Each day, my favourite songs would change and I must have cycled through every single track being a favourite at some point.

It's a flawless album, not only brimming with top quality tunes full of sass and attitude, full of simple yet melodic instrumentation and some quirky time signatures here and there, but it built on the sound developed through their **Surfa Rosa** album and refined it. If you want to have a comparison, I'll use the oft-mentioned Nirvana again and say that Surfa Rosa was Pixies **Bleach**, and Doolittle was their **Nevermind**. Beefier production, a realisation that songs don't have to scream, act a bit slutty or fight for attention. On Doolittle, Pixies relaxed into their songwriting and performing skills, and their burgeoning confidence allowed their music to breathe and loosen up a little, resulting in classics like **Hey** or **Silver**, both truly magical songs in their own way, both completely different from each other but undeniably Pixies and impossible to imagine any other band ever writing them.

Of course, there were still plenty of faster, raucous offerings to balance out the calm, and tracks like **Tame**, **Mr Grieves** and **Crackity Jones** continued the trajectory of earlier ferocious classics like **Something Against You**, **Broken Face** and **Oh My Golly!**

Amidst all the madness of Pixies earlier works, you get the classic singles (and album tracks that should have been singles) like **Gigantic**, **Where is my Mind?** and **Cactus**. On Doolittle, they knocked up a couple of classics in **Monkey Gone To Heaven** and **Here Comes Your Man**. Arguably, opening track **Debaser** could easily have been a single as well.

Rounding out the album are fan favourites like **Wave of Mutilation**, melodic pop tunes like **There Goes My Gun** and the gentle **La La Love You**, where drummer Lovering did his Ringo bit and took on lead vocals.

Seriously, there isn't a bad track on the entire record, and clocking in at a short and sweet 38 and a half minutes you get 15 songs and a beautiful album of delights. As a quick anecdote regarding that short length, producer Gil Norton came to test Francis' patience by continually suggesting tracks be lengthened, sometimes with additional verses. A frustrated Francis proved his point in a devastatingly simple fashion by taking Norton to a record store and showing him a Buddy Holly album. Nobody would ever argue that Holly wasn't a talented songwriter. What might surprise a lot of people is just how short some of his classic songs actually are. It surprised Norton, anyway, who backed down and let Francis get on with things his way.

Doolittle is such a great record that even after the band had initially split for ten years it was still selling between 500-1000 copies a week. A few of you reading this will already know the album and will almost certainly treasure it – it's time for the rest of you to be let in on the secret.

Second Choice Song
Gouge Away is also from **Doolittle**, the closing track and one of the most straightforward. This said, it's also one of the most influential, and pretty much a blueprint for 1000 bands that followed. The big sound, the bass at the fore, the sudden dynamic changes between the quieter verses and the very noises choruses – people have been copying this style since the moment they first heard Gouge Away in 1989.

If there was a Hall Of Fame for the most important (not necessarily commercially successful) songs in music, this album track from Boston's finest would be somewhere near the top.

It ends the Doolittle record with a bang, cycling through three verse-chorus loops with a couple of instrumental bridges, getting slowly more intense and building the layers as Francis' vocals get louder and a little more unhinged.

And the sound of that bass! So clean and crisp, so huge it could fill a cathedral. The odd time signature feels a little weird, being normal 4/4 but with what feels like 5 bars crammed in to make 5/4 or possibly 4/5 – whatever is going on in there, it adds a little extra dynamic to an already brilliant song.

The lyrics bring together some of Francis' favourite themes in death, religion and eyeball damage, and the song is a fan favourite live with audiences singing (and then shouting) every single word. The power of the song hasn't diminished over time and still blows audiences away to this day.

CLUTCH

A QUICK DEATH IN TEXAS

CLUTCH – A QUICK DEATH IN TEXAS

About the Band

Clutch are a US rock band formed in Maryland in 1991. Apart from a more-or-less immediate switch-out of the original vocalist to Neil Fallon, and a brief interlude in the mid noughties where keyboard player Mick Schauer joined and left after 2 albums, the line-up has remained constant for three decades.

Fallon likes to mix things up a little, appearing on many other band's tracks as a guest vocalist, including Volbeat, Dozer and Mastodon. A dedicated rocker, he needed surgery in 2013 to repair herniated discs (partially as a result of years of headbanging, partially a childhood neck injury returning to haunt him).

Although a moderately successful band due to their early output and solid work ethic for touring, more widespread recognition came late for the band, with releases of **Earth Rocker** (2013) and **Psychic Warfare** (2015) giving them the best commercial success of their career. This path is the opposite to most bands, who heartily decline after years of output, and Clutch seem to be aging like fine wine, still belting out bangers after more than thirty years.

Psychic Warfare was influenced by the writings of Philip K Dick, with whom Fallon shares a similar philosophical outlook on the world. Although that influence has underscored selected Fallon lyrics down the years, it's perhaps never been more prevalent that in 2022 single **Red Alert (Boss Metal Zone)**, with PK Dick themes, a *Bladerunner* influenced video and lyrics incorporating overt references and quotes from the film.

Going another level deeper, the song was Fallon's way of actually writing about a particularly disturbing yet hilarious episode from the COVID pandemic through a lens that he understood. In Italy, conspiracy theorists shared a diagram through social media that purported to be a schematic for an injectable COVID 19 5G Chip. Many theorists believe that 5G is a way for the governments of the world to somehow control our brains with a broadcast frequency that will somehow turn us into compliant zombies (as if we're not that already!). The schematic, however, turned out to be nothing more than the diagram for a guitar distortion pedal called the Boss Metal Zone. You couldn't make it up. Except somebody did, and people actually believed it. (They'll be telling us the Earth is round next, right?).

Briefly heading back to **Pyschic Warfare**, the band set up a hotline for their fans to engage with the record, calling it 'Clutch Roadside Assistance'. Fans could call up and leave messages and ask questions. That's not the only quirky promo idea they've run with though. Back on their 'Pure Rock Fury' tour in 2001, the band travelled with an ice cream truck, fitted with a full local broadcast sound system, which would park up outside venues before and after shows and play their tunes loud to attract the fans.

At the time of writing, they are 13 albums deep into their career. Their musical forte is predominantly heavy metal / hard rock, though they tackle various styles and sometimes their songs are laced with a pop sensibility (and often with an undercurrent of dark humour). Although the evolution of the band has never deviated much from a projected trajectory, they do bring more to the table with each new album.

The band runs their own annual *Earth Rocker Festival* in West Virginia, though it has been on hiatus during the COVID pandemic and current research attempts looking up the website resulted in a DNS lookup failure. One presumed it was successful enough for a return one day.

About This Song
A Quick Death in Texas is taken from **Psychic Warfare** and mixes some funky guitar riffing with hilarious lyrics. The video, set in a wild west town, sees Fallon dragged behind a horse after upsetting some of the locals, and towards the end the band are all lined up against a wall and shot. That all sounds a bit gloomy but the whole thing is done with a liberal sprinkling of humour and more than a nod to the spaghetti westerns of yore.

With all of the entries in this book, I listen to the band I'm profiling as I write, and playing this tune makes me want to push aside the laptop and grab a guitar. Once you know the song, it's impossible not to feel the urge to sing along, to join in. AQDIT is a powerful song made by musicians at the top of their game.

Essential Album
I'm going to confess that I haven't yet learned much of their back catalogue. My introduction to the band was through **X-Ray Visions** and **Firebirds!**, both from the blazing glory that is the Psychic Warfare album. Without even having a deep knowledge of their older work, in my mind their legacy would be cemented with this album alone.

After a short spoken word intro over ambient background sounds, the album launches with the full on attack of **X-Ray Visions**, a startling number that has a great accompanying video. As proven by this track, Clutch can kick some serious ass when they feel like it. At the end, when you think you've already seen level 10 of the mad-o-meter, they crank things up to 11 with the next offering, **Firebirds!**

Things go down a notch or two with the aforementioned **A Quick Death in Texas**, and they turn up the heat again with **Sucker For The Witch**. After my second-choice song (below) the band rock out for a few more tracks before closing with the epic **Son of Virginia**. Total album length is just under 40mins but it packs enough punches to knock out Mike Tyson.

Second Choice Song
Our Lady of Electric Light is a slower offering on the album but no less catchy. Immediately preceded by the short prologue track **Doom Saloon** (which is basically an extended intro), the song quietly soars, fully showing the confidence and maturity Clutch bring to the song-writing table.

I'm not entirely sure what it's about, but I could say that about a million other songs too. It feels at home in a Wild West setting, sharing some DNA with A Quick Death in Texas (and has a great unofficial video on YouTube by fan *The Sonic Void* chock full of Wild West imagery*)*, but lyrical clues perhaps point towards an American Civil War setting (it feels at home there, too, and there's mention that a war is raging on). Ultimately, both these theories are done in by the mention of a Rock-Ola jukebox, which only began production in 1927.

So what is the song about? Fuck knows. Doesn't matter. It has a relaxed feel and yet rocks at the same time. Classic American alt-rock by a classic American band. Fabulous stuff.

REVOLTING COCKS

BEERS, STEERS + QVEERS

THE ALBVM

BEERS, STEERS & QUEERS

REVOLTING COCKS – BEERS, STEERS & QUEERS

About the Band
Revolting Cocks was initially a side project for Ministry frontman Al Jourgensen, Front 242's Richard23 and fellow Belgian Luc van Acker, a trans-Atlantic project of industrial experimentation. Richard23 left the band before they found commercial success after an argument with Jourgensen, known to be an occasionally unstable individual.

The group was boosted by the presence of additional member Chris Connelly, a Scottish collaborative powerhouse and founder of Finitribe with links to dozens of side project bands like Pigface, Murder Inc and one-off, gold producing Acid Horse. Connelly deserves additional mentions for the sheer number of projects he's been involved with and the surging creativity he manages to corral and keep going with more than 20 solo albums released in the last three decades.

Completing the line-up in time for the seminal album **Beers, Steers and Queers** were Paul Barker and Bill Reiflin, both in Ministry at that time. It was essentially a supergroup made up of different band members from pioneers of the burgeoning industrial music scene.

The music was a mix of industrial, hard rock and electronic dance, all thrown together with bunches of samples and an overt sense of humour that bordered on blatant piss-taking. They were bought out from label *WaxTrax* by *Sire*, who were interested in Al Jourgensen's various side projects.

Arguably their heyday was the second incarnation of the band that lasted until 1994. The band had 2 further revivals between 2004-11 and 2016-present with no new albums since 2010's **Got Cock?**

About This Song *Remix Version*
The song starts with a sample from the 1972 movie *Deliverance*, where poor Ned Beatty's character Ed is raped by a pair of hillbillies ordering him to "Drop them pants!" and "Come on, squeal!", followed by their impressions of a squealing pig. (The original album version starts with a phone-in radio show clip discussing an upcoming appearance by the band, which from the name is believed to be a "male strip show".) It's followed by some DJ scratching, a heavy repetitive drum loop, numerous samples (including a barking dog) and some lyrics that essentially paint the state of Texas in a very disparaging light.

If ever there was a record that was made just for the fuck of it, this is it. Clearly, all involved are having a blast and don't give a flying fig about, well, *anything*. From the band name to the song (and album title), to the *Deliverance* sample and the lyrics, the song is a snowflake's soundtrack from Hell but regardless of all that the song is a powerhouse, a dance club floor filler if only you'd surrender to its charms.

"Texas is full of women and willies,
Eyes too close, filthy hillbillies
Who are these people, raised in barns?
Ghouls and fools, sex on farms.
Texas hoedown, this is the lowdown
You're full of shit, destined to go down."
Beers, Steers + Queers © Revolting Cocks

Admittedly it doesn't look so charming from the above lyrics, but everything about the song screams how much fun it was putting it together - you can imagine the band sitting around laughing their heads off when they heard the final version. When the house sample kicks in towards the end, it elevates an already genius record to sublime levels. I love this tune, it gets a few airings every couple of years and even now, thirty years after its release, it never sounds old.

Essential Album
Beers, Steers and Queers the album is my personal favourite and one that I would recommend above the others. They just nail a sound and style of music that's both industrial, heavily dance influenced and outright hilarious, something a lot of po-faced industrial bands avoid like the plague.

Although the record tapers off towards the end, the first five tracks make it an essential offering. It took all the things that made debut album **Big Sexy Land** good and just injected proceedings with a swagger and a sense of humour that elevated it. Before or after, nothing in the band's stop-start career matches the perfection of this album. Later albums seem a lot heavier in places and lose the easy charm that makes BS&Q so loveable.

Second Choice Song
For me, it has to be **In The Neck**, Chris Connelly's vocals are just amazing on it but at first listen you probably won't think that. If you aren't used to this kind of music, you might think the vocals and delivery come across as somebody having a laugh, or maybe it's the sound of an animal in pain. And the odd percussion with minimal musical

accompaniment from keyboards and bass might feel a little underwhelming or sparse.

But keep listening. The magic will come. Suddenly, everything will make complete sense and this will be your new favourite record. Because if you give yourself to this song, let it smash into you like a tsunami and envelop you completely in its world, you'll find that it's insanely catchy and everything about it has been tooled with extreme precision. Nothing is wasted, everything present is necessary. The verses tug you along for the ride and then the choruses put you in a zorba ball and roll you down a gentle hill with a pleasing momentum. Once you learn the words, you'll find yourself singing along, trying to match the falsetto high notes delivered by Connelly.

If you 've listened and still don't believe a word I'm saying, try again. This is a record made by serious musicians, prolific musicians. Singer Connelly himself is currently a vocal instructor at Oak Park School of Rock in the US, a position they don't hand out to just anyone. Listen to the song again. Still don't like it? Listen again, you're wrong. Listen until you see I'm right, until your ears bleed if it takes that much. You'll thank me, one day.

FIELDS OF THE NEPHILIM

ENDEMONIADA

FIELDS OF THE NEPHILIM - ENDEMONIADA

About the Band

Fields of the Nephilim formed in Stevenage in 1984 and became one of the more successful bands ploughing the gothic rock furrow in the late 80's. The name refers to a biblical race of giants and their music was filled with references to biblical themes, chaos magic and the works of *Aleister Crowley* and *HP Lovecraft* (specifically the *Cthulhu mythos*).

Their image included spaghetti western elements – band members wore cowboy attire including dusters and coated themselves in flour before gigs and photoshoots, giving them a *High Plains Drifter* / weatherbeaten look. It looked good for photos and gigs, with these dusty figures looming through the expected dry ice, but did leave them ripe for being victim to a good piss-take.

Melody Maker ran the hilarious 'Nod Corner' for a while, a recurring jokey article where young drummer Nod Wright – a superb and generally underappreciated drummer, by the way – got into trouble at the expense of a more serious, exasperated Carl McCoy (the singer). McCoy often wore yellow contact lenses and, of all the band members, seemed to be the most reluctant to engage with fans and media.

Early recordings like **Laura** and **Back in Gehenna** were stripped back and somewhat terrifying, especially with Gary Wisker's saxophone screaming across the tracks. After the debut album was completed, showcasing their songs but missing the singles they were best known for (a modified US release featured the singles **Preacher Man**, **Power** and **Blue Water**) the band, now becoming more than accomplished musicians, began leaning towards more elegant, complex arrangements and increased production values, resulting in their phenomenal album **The Nephilim**.

They had a connection with film-maker Richard Stanley, who made early singles videos and featured McCoy in his debut film *Hardware*. The early iteration of the band ended in 1991 and later incarnations, with McCoy the only constant, have struggled to recapture that success.

The very thing that made the band stand out – McCoys growling vocals, which perfectly suited their earlier output – was probably the very same thing that limited the band's appeal for a wider audience, as it began to sound more affected and out of place as the musical arrangements outgrew it. This said, when McCoy sings instead of growls (as in **Celebrate**) he's actually got a decent voice and things may have been different if he'd used it more often.

About This Song
Endemoniada begins with a heartbeat, a few simple guitar licks, a rising tribal drum and a snarl. As an opener for second album **The Nephilim** it's a statement of intent – the band aren't afraid to let this slow build go on for over a minute and a half before the main guitar riff kicks in, and even then it's followed by a wide-open space, ticked by a hi-hat until the riff's counterpart rings out. It's immediately obvious that the production values are better than anything they've done before.

A beautiful, guitar-led instrumental follows and builds up to the four-minute mark before the main thrust of the song bursts through. It's a bold statement, possibly an unexpected one from what was perceived as a poor man's Sisters of Mercy, but one that they more than followed through on. **Endemoniada** is an epic tune, a real evolutionary leap for the band and a gateway into a superb album.

Essential Album
The Nephilim is that album. It's not only one of the best gothic rock albums from the 1980's, it's one of the best albums from any genre of that time. I'm not joking. Quite how an obscure goth band with a funny name managed to write and record such a majestic offering is open to question. Perhaps they did a deal with one of those great old gods they sang about.

The album transcends goth and joins a wider metal pool, putting a lot of that genre's best efforts in the shadows as well. Unfortunately, despite charting in the UK at #12, it disappeared from the mainstream shortly thereafter and never received the love it deserved.

For those in the know, though, it's rightfully regarded as a masterpiece. Lone single **Moonchild** is actually one of the weaker tracks, and the strength of the album lies in the band's complete submission to where the music wants to take them. Closing track **Last Exit For The Lost** is a spectacular journey that builds and changes speed two-thirds of the way through and clocks in at just under 10 minutes!

Weirdly, it's a fantastic album to accompany driving long distances. It's also great mood music to have on it you're doing something else. It's perhaps best as a focus when you just want to sit on a sofa and do nothing except concentrate on the music.

Second Choice Song
Trees Come Down reflects my main choice in that it's a song of two parts. A more melodic first section features a repetitive and genuinely creepy bass and guitar riff, later accompanied by tinkly goth guitar so loved by similar bands like the Sisters of

Mercy. The drums are crisp and clear with beautiful tom fills. McCoy growls over the top. It builds to a climax and then heavier toms kick in and McCoy sings about some sort of nightmare calling across the fields and a girl in a green dress with eyes like fire. Nonsense never sounded so good.

It's an earlier effort, the colours are primary and the complexity is only just beginning to show. The Nephilim sound is very distinct here, and very powerful. In some ways, what should be the stronger second half of the song, where things come into a tight focus and the urgency increases, is actually weaker than the opening section, which makes the band's choice to regularly perform an abridged version of the song, featuring only the latter section, really baffling. It's like they had the confidence to lay down this sort of music on vinyl but not to trust the material and let it loose live.

Regardless, what you have here is an essential listen.

CURVE

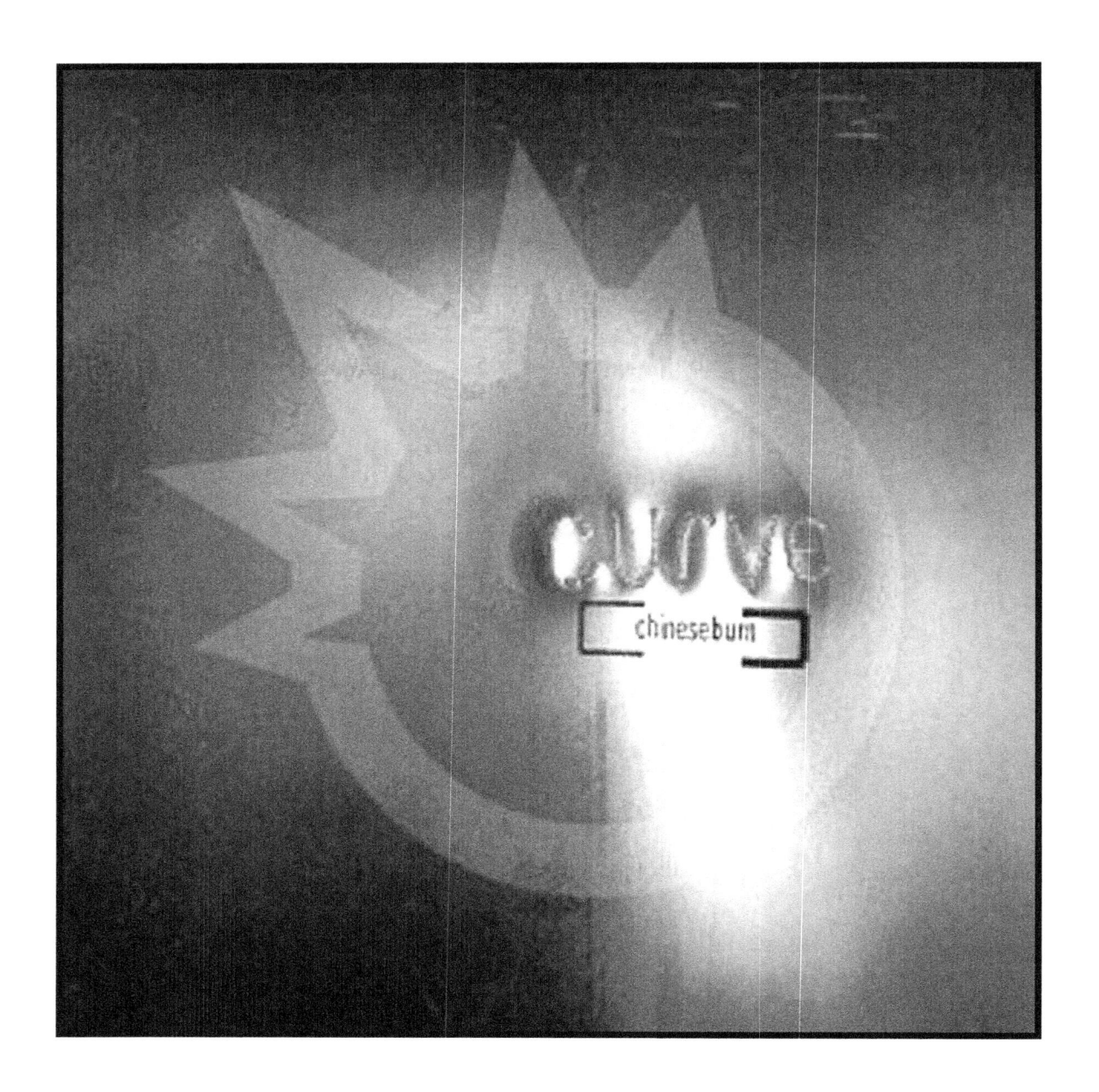

CHINESE BURN

CURVE – CHINESE BURN

About the Band

Curve were an active 2-piece nucleus (with 3 additional members for live shows) that had a 15 year run starting in 1990 (*with a 2 year hiatus between 1994-6*). After 2005, occasional remasters and re-releases have appeared although the band have no plans to record new material.

Dean Garcia was the musical powerhouse behind the duo, writing the songs, playing bass, guitars and dealing with the drum programming. Toni Halliday provided vocals, song writing contributions, lyrics and occasional guitar work. Together they made some of the most underrated electronic rock music of the 90's.

Garcia had form, having been involved with the Eurythmics as part of the live band ('83-'84) and providing guitar work on a couple of albums. Dave Stewart knew Toni Halliday and introduced the pair, who hit it off and formed commercially unsuccessful State of Play before going their own separate ways and reuniting years later to form Curve. This time around, through timing, sheer luck or the fact that they both gained more experience under their belts, things worked out a lot better.

Musically, they opened up new territories, merging Shoegaze, electronica, dance and Industrial elements. When their first release came along, the **Blindfold EP** featuring lead track **Ten Little Girls**, it turned heads and instantly marked the band as one to watch. There was a rap element to the song, which always struck me as a forced concession to anchor this soaring new music to what was popular in the charts. The song really didn't need it and this one element ages it terribly.

The year before their debut album **Doppleganger** dropped in 1992, they put out a couple of outstanding singles in **Coast is Clear** and **Clipped**, both of which clearly laid out what this band were capable of, what they were about. Both are outstanding pieces of work, laying the groundwork for a million bands to follow in their footsteps and steal their thunder. The most obvious pretender to the throne was Garbage, who took copious notes from the Curve rulebook and added a deliberate pop sensibility to blow the charts wide open for themselves.

The video accompanying **Clipped** seemed to have an increased budget from previous videos, and gave us a much clearer, full colour view of the band. At once, ten thousand indie fanboys wet dreams came true. Halliday was a beautiful, if somewhat angry looking frontperson, and subsequent videos only pulled that into a richer focus.

In today's age it might sound slightly misogynistic to single out what a female singer looked like and that's a book-length discussion that I'm going to distil into a single paragraph here. Pop music has always, always been about selling sex. Most of the bands featured in this book did their best to produce music and avoid that path, which is one of the reasons they perhaps didn't chart so well. It's a sad fact that the entire music industry relies on sex appeal to try and sell songs and that the singers fronting the bands, both male and female, are often objectified and the music can seem like an afterthought. Back when Toni Halliday burst onto screens in lush colour, she was competing for attention from the likes of Tracey Tracey (The Primitives), Justine Frischmann (Elastica), Miki Berenyi (Lush), Harriet Wheeler (The Sundays) and so on. Please don't tell me that Curve themselves didn't play up on this aspect of their existence by quickly learning to promote Halliday's good looks in subsequent videos – just check 1992's **Horror Head** to see my point there. I loved the music Curve made, irrespective of what Toni Halliday looked like, but it didn't do her any harm that she was gorgeous. Ok, let's move on.

Unfairly, Curve never received the success they deserved. Although they broadened their scope as their career advanced, a lot of their earlier stuff stuck to a blueprint and could sound a bit samey, and any criticism the band garnered in the press was for this reason. When Garcia was building his sonic temples, walls of sound fizzing with guitars run through all kinds of pedal and studio effects, the architecture for different compositions sometimes only had subtle changes.

They were true pioneers and their music could be released today and still sound totally fresh. They capture a power in their recordings that eludes many bands, and when they choose to relax and loosen up a bit, like in **Coming Up Roses** for example, the results match anything you'd get in the charts (this track peaked at 51 in the UK charts). So many that came after owe them a huge debt, from the recordings they made, from the techniques they used, from their image and attitude. Instead, others stood on the shoulders of this giant and though Curve's influence remained and flourished, their name and back catalogue did not. But there are many that do remember them, and we still play their music and it never gets boring. Join our club.

During and after Curve, Halliday has worked with a diverse range of acts including The Killers, Orbital, Leftfield and Recoil. At the time of writing, Garcia is a member of no less than seven dormant or active bands.

About This Song
Chinese Burn appeared as a backing track to a *Sony MiniDisc* advert in 1997. In it, a young man pushes a MiniDisc into an MD Walkman, pulls an angry face, performs a showtunes jump and runs from his futuristic house across a rocky desert environment, followed by an exact replica of himself running in his footsteps. They both jump off a bridge onto a moving train and the advert ends by saying how the MiniDisc gives you perfect copies every time.

The track was featured in a truncated, instrumental only version. The full song appeared on the **Come Clean** album released in 1998, and has since been used in TV shows *Buffy the Vampire Slayer* and *La Femme Nikita*, and is associated with the *X-Men*, *Torque* and *Stormbreaker* movies. For a track you've probably never heard of, it's been around the block a bit. All this and it still didn't chart.

And what an awesome track it is, dirtier and harder than earlier offerings, a proper noisy bastard of a song that's just perfect in every regard. The lyrics give a portrait of some horrible female that is hopefully fictitious. The guitar loop/riff is killer, the backing instrumentation thunders along and Halliday's voice is that of an Ice Queen, beautifully melded to the music. Only Curve could make a song like this and make it so goddamned awesome. Seek it out.

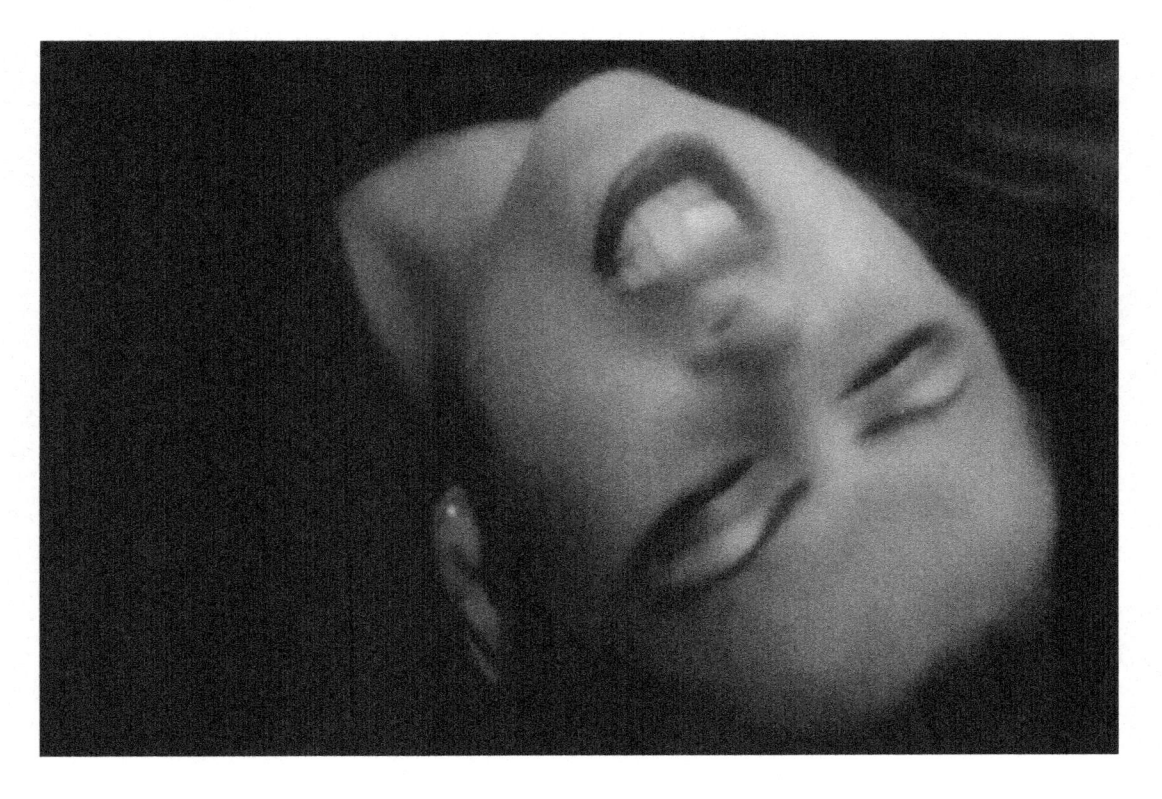

*"She burns friends like a piece of wood,
and she's jealous of me because she never could
hold herself up without a spine
and she'll look me up when she's doing fine."*
Chinese Burn © Curve

Essential Album
The Way of Curve is a compilation album split between two discs. The first features all of their hits and best known songs and the second comprises rare and unreleased recordings. There's no shame in having a greatest hits album chosen as an essential album (a number of acts in this book will have the same treatment) because it offers, in one place, the best possible musical output to familiarise yourself with. The band called it a day after this release so it's effectively an epitaph (or a career retrospective).

Second Choice Song
Slightly gentler fare, but still a mix of heavier beats, guitars and samples, **Coast is Clear** is driven by a thundering bassline, dripping with guitar wash and topped with Halliday's ethereal vocals. Released in 1991 it's one of their first offerings and remained one of their best throughout their career. It's that good. Guitars and vocals shine but for me the star of the song is the drum programming, I just love what Garcia did to make the backbone of the song.

I'm also going to choose **Clipped** as my second choice song. It's another belter, so good that I just can't let Coast is Clear take all the glory. It's not a million miles away in sound, feeling like a sister song to Coast is Clear in some regard, but it's different enough to be held aloft and worshipped in its own right.

Together, both tunes present you with a clear picture of what the band is about and should give you enough info to make a choice about perusing the rest of their catalogue. It's a journey that will be worthwhile, there are many treasures waiting for you. Nobody else sounds like Curve, they were brilliant and unique and they made some exceptional music. Hopefully you will discover that for yourself after reading this.

PRIMAL SCREAM

KILL ALL HIPPIES

PRIMAL SCREAM – KILL ALL HIPPIES

About the Band

Primal Scream are a band that come in many guises and it's probable that you only know one of them - the *indie-dance* version of the band that got bundled in with the *Madchester* scene (even though they are originally from Scotland). Their **Screamadelica** album received vast amounts of critical praise and commercial success and you couldn't escape their era-defining **Loaded** single. (A single that sounded nothing like their original composition **I'm Losing More Than I'll Ever Have** and was basically created by DJ Andy Weatherall in the studio.)

The band also dabble in guitar driven indie rock, having first achieved some level of success in that arena. One of their tracks, **Velocity Girl**, was included on an *NME* cover cassette tape titled **C86**, which became a scene label for a certain type of indie guitar rock around that time. The C86 movement was like a British musical explosion similar to what would happen to Seattle and grunge in the early 90's, but it never caught on in the mainstream - it was far too wilfully amateurish for that - and was soon eclipsed by acid house, then baggy, and shoegaze, then grunge, then Britpop etc. Music scenes seemed to change a lot faster back in the late 80's and early 90's.

I was never a fan of either incarnation of the band, and when they changed direction to a harder, more bluesy rock guitar sound it felt (to me at least) like they borrowed way too heavily from the **Rolling Stones**.

No, the version of the band I'm interested in sharing with you is possibly the least known incarnation but the one that produced by far the best tunes. This version of the band made heavy rock / electronica hybrids with a dusting of Industrial influences.

Primal Scream formed in Glasgow in 1982, and their progress was initially hampered by singer Bobby Gillespie also being the drummer in The Jesus and Mary Chain. JAMC's Reid brothers gave Gillespie an ultimatum - to choose one band to continue with - and he chose Primal Scream, getting the last laugh when they beat JAMC to win a Mercury Prize with 1991's **Screamadelica** album.

After a few years of mis-starts and recordings that were generally poorly received, Primal Scream hit the big time with Screamadelica. The change in musical direction that leant towards acid house / rave had worked really well and the momentum carried on with subsequent albums and new markets like Japan opening up for them.

The band fully embraced the acid house scene and had always fully indulged the rock n roll lifestyle. The following sober but surprisingly hilarious sentence is taken from their Wikipedia page: *Throughout the (Screamadelica) tour the band and their increasingly large entourage gained notoriety for their large narcotic intake.*

Although Screamadelica was at the forefront of this new musical scene, entering the public consciousness and riding the zeitgeist of those times (winning the inaugural Mercury Prize no less), everything that came after may have achieved better overall sales because they were essentially selling to an expanded fanbase. Not as many people know the magnificent **Kill All Hippies** over **Loaded**, for example, and that is a shame because it's a much better tune.

The change in musical direction back to guitar rock with their follow up album **Give Out But Don't Give Up** led to the NME accusing them of being *'dance traitors'*. I never liked that album but what an incredibly stupid thing for a music paper to say. All bands that stay the same grow stagnant and make music papers boring when they cover the same old stuff, so any experimentation on behalf of a band should be applauded. Experimentation and a change in musical direction – plus lots of drugs – turned The Beatles from a pop sensation playing to hordes of screaming girls to a genuinely revolutionary and world-changing band that's often regarded as perhaps the best to ever ply their trade.

Another change in direction followed with **Vanishing Point**, and a notable line up change with the addition of bassist Mani (from the recently split Stone Roses) and drummer Paul Mulraney. The tunes, led by single **Kowalski**, were a darker manifestation of the path begun with Screamadelica, and could be considered a stepping-stone towards the genius pair of albums released between 1999-2005, being **XTRMNTR** and **Evil Heat** respectively. In my view, these albums are just as important to the band's legacy as Screamadelica.

Mani left the band in 2011 to rejoin a reforming Stone Roses, briefly replaced by Debbie Goodge of My Bloody Valentine before Simon Butler took the spot on a permanent basis from 2012 onwards. There were some unfortunate early deaths of a couple of long-standing members (and ex-members) in Robert Young (bass & keyboards, died 2014), Denise Johnson (backing vocals, died 2020) and Martin Duffy (keyboards, died 2022).

Their last studio album came in 2016 with **Choasmosis** and the band continue to tour live (their 2023 incarnation has 12 touring members).

About this Song
Kill All Hippies is the opener to 2000's **XTRMNTR** album, and starts with a sample from a 1980 Dennis Hopper film called *Out of the Blue,* itself borrowing a title from a Neil Young song. Speech is backed with various bleeps and a bit of violin before some phased keyboard and a sampled drum loop kick in. The song starts proper with a machine-gun drum fill and new-ish band member Mani's bass brings on a groove that could shake buildings to dust.

Gillespie repeats the words *'you got the money, I got the soul'* which might be considered a mantra of his, in a falsetto voice and the song builds to controlled chaos. It's brash, confident, brilliant song writing and performance and hard to believe that this could even be the same band that recorded pretty much anything that came before it.

Essential Album
XTRMNTR is a hell of a noisy record, occasionally to the point of being almost unbearable. But underneath all of the noise and chaos are some outstanding tunes brought to you by a band at the peak of their creative powers.

Mani's influence is powerful, it's hard to imagine what the album would have sounded like without him. Underpinning most songs are funky, insistent basslines that drive things forward, locked in tightly with the superb drumlines, the rest of the songs hanging from these solid foundations.

Highlights include the opener **Kill All Hippies**, the crazy hard jazz instrumental workout of **Blood Money** (phenomenal drumming on that one) and the throbbing funk groove of **Exterminator** (which could easily have been my main choice of song here). For the band, the album marks the beginning of a more overtly political stance and has aggressive, anti-authoritarian leanings.

I think of this, and 2002's stellar (but not as critically acclaimed) follow-up **Evil Heat** as sibling albums that work really well together (sort of like Simple Minds and their pairing of **Sons and Fascination** and **Sister Feelings Call**. In short, if you give XTRMNTR a go and love it, Evil Heat is a must.

Second Choice Song
This was a tough choice and I was torn between two songs (three, actually, but I will only briefly mention the wonderful **Some Velvet Morning** cover in passing here). They're so completely different from each other that it's hard to pick one to share... so I'll share both. Coincidentally, both tracks come from the aforementioned **Screamadelica** album.

Movin' On Up is probably their most accessible single (although only their fourth highest charting UK entry) and a brilliant, brilliant pop song, even though it once again wears its Rolling Stones influences openly on its sleeve. This time, I forgive them as the result is so phenomenal.

Of all the songs I highlight in this book, this is one of the most well-known, and radio playlists continue to feature this particular track to the present day, but that's not going to stop me from exalting its pleasures here. The song grooves along in an easy fashion, with a strong vocal delivery from (the sometimes wishy-washy) Gillespie, bringing in a gospel choir halfway through and some sublime guitar work. It's a lovely, vibrant song full of positive energy and always a pleasure to listen to.

The other track I want to mention is a direct follow on from that same album. **Slip Inside This House** is the title, but the autofill on Youtube seems to prefer the title Trip Inside This House, which most people probably think it's called, especially as the actual lyrics never once say 'slip inside' but repeat 'trip inside' no less than a dozen times! Regardless, what you have here is a tune very much of its time but such a banger that being a little dated shouldn't matter in the slightest.

It's another cover version, this time of the 1967 release by **13th Floor Elevators**. Primal Scream use it as a starting point and really turn it into something of their own, almost a totally different song. And although **Loaded** often gets the credit for defining the new scene that emerged in the UK, I think that **Slip Inside This House** better embodies the spirit of the times and is a way, way better track.

One thing about listening to it is a must though – unless you've got a decent sound setup on your TV or computer (or your preferred audio device of choice) you're not going to get the full effect. On the surface, this song can sound a little trebly. It's what lies beneath that really powers this song, an enormous, hulking bassline that you don't just need to hear, you need to sit in a chair in a room with a lot of sub-woofers and let the bass crash into you like a runaway train. It's a religious experience.

PJ HARVEY

LONG SNAKE MOAN

PJ HARVEY – LONG SNAKE MOAN

About the Band

PJ Harvey's first gig left the venue cleared after playing a single song and had the organiser rushing up to the band and shouting at them to stop: *"Don't you realise nobody likes you? Stop playing! We'll still pay you!"*

One has to wonder what that organiser would think upon hearing that Polly Jean Harvey has since been awarded an MBE for her services to music (in 2013), has won the *Mercury Music Price* twice (2001 for **Stories from the City, Stories from the Sea** and 2011 for **Let England Shake**), has been nominated for eight *Brit Awards*, seven *Grammys* and a couple more Mercury nominations for good measure. Despite an inauspicious beginning, she has more than delivered on her aim to produce great music.

With a run of 10 glorious albums over three decades, Harvey has cemented her legacy in the Rock world. A talented singer and multi-instrumentalist, she can play guitar, piano/keyboards, violin, cello, harp, harmonica and saxophone amongst other things. She's worked on projects with artists as diverse as **Tricky**, **Sparklehorse**, **Mark Lanegan**, **Josh Homme** and **Nick Cave**, whom she dated for a couple of years and retained links with afterward by having her music featured on *Peaky Blinders* (including a 2019 cover of Cave's **Red Right Hand**) and recording four albums with former **Birthday Party** guitarist Mick Harvey.

Inspiration for her work comes from a few of the artists featured in this book, such as **Pixies** and **Siouxsie Sioux**, as well as people like **Neil Young**, **Bob Dylan**, **Captain Beefheart** and earlier influences from her parents' record collection (artists like **John Lee Hooker** and **Robert Johnson**). That blues aspect bubbles up through a lot of her work, a common thread despite the variations in her approach.

She has a deliberate policy of making every new album sound different from what has come before, and over the years has embraced all styles of music from post punk, gothic rock, indie rock, folk and electronica. This policy also encompasses the way she presents herself, changing her appearance and dress sense for each period. The results are an impressive body of work, valuable peer and critical recognition and a diverse and broad spectrum of sounds.

As well as music, Harvey is a sculptor whose pieces have been exhibited, and spends her spare time painting and writing poetry, having published two books (*The Hollow of the Hand* in 2015 and *Orlam* in 2022).

Way back in 2004, Harvey posed with contemporary female artists **Bjork** and **Tori Amos**, three strong recording artists with distinct identities riding a wave of recognition and enthusiasm for their collective works. *Q* magazine put them on the cover and then headlined the inside feature '*Hips, Tits, Lips, Power*' which is a headline firmly anchored in that period of history and would probably get a magazine shut down today. Whilst the language and attitudes aren't necessarily complimentary, the act of putting these three artists on a pedestal together was a game changer and these women showed it was possible to succeed (and be themselves, and be recognised) in the male dominated world of rock music, (although artists like Siouxsie had been doing it for years already) and ushered in greater exposure for strong feminist *Riot Grrrl* bands like Bikini Kill, Sleater Kinney and Huggy Bear. This road would eventually lead to the Spice Girls but we can't necessarily blame them for that.

About This Song
Long Snake Moan is an album track from 1995's **To Bring You My Love** (*see below*). From her opening 'mmm-mmm' the track bursts into life, a powerhouse of a guitar-led rock song with a fantastic opening verse and drum production to die for. This song sounds HUGE. When the guitar drops away for the second verse cycle, and you're basically left with just Harvey's voice, some bass and those towering drums, it somehow sounds even bigger.

I love this track immensely, it's one of my favourites of all time. Everything about it is ace, from the power in her voice, the lyrics ('*Dunk you under salt water*') and sense of release at each chorus, the driving guitar line and the overall sound and feel of the track. It's a monster, in the best possible sense.

Harvey has never explained the meaning behind the song (at least not that I could find) so it's open to your own interpretation. Some think it's about desire, vulnerability and the complexities of a certain intimate relationship. Some think it represents seduction, temptation and the lure of the forbidden. Despite containing some pretty vibrant imagery, the song is still a mystery to many and open to interpretations from other people that frankly baffles me. I like that but I think I'm way more literal in reading into things. The music has a raw, primal power all of its own and the words give me the imagery to fill my head with - thoughts of late 17th century witch trials and semi-heretical sentiments. Maybe even the Devil addressing one of his faithful witch servants and offering her power through the ordeal of being drowned (as punishment). I don't know. I don't dwell on the details, I just put the song on and always turn it up as loud as my neighbours or car passengers will allow!

Essential Album
To Bring You My Love is Harvey's third long-player and first as a solo artist. Gone are the tight 3-piece basic setup of her debut and sophomore albums **Dry** (1992) and the Steve Albini produced **Rid of Me** (1993), in come new players and a wider sonic palette.

The leap in sound texture and lushness is immediately apparent. Whatever happened in the two years between albums brought about a maturity and complexity to her song writing and performance skills. Whilst Harvey was always capable of writing powerful songs – John Peel had described her music as *'Polly Jean seems crushed by the weight of her own songs and arrangements, as if the air is literally being sucked out of them ... admirable if not always enjoyable.'* this new batch seemed drawn from a deeper, richer well. They were more textured, with a fatter sound and lusher production. These songs featured added depth and gave space for the compositions to breathe. Perhaps as a result of this, and with a more introspective outlook replacing the aggression of earlier works, much of the album is more emotionally complex and less in your face.

It also marked the first of many collaborations with Flood (who has worked with many of the bands in this book, including **Nine Inch Nails**, **Ministry**, **Pop Will Eat Itself**, **Nick Cave and the Bad Seeds** and **Orbital**) and John Parish.

The seeds of the record came from her isolation living in a remote house bought on the proceeds of her first 2 albums. (Modern Spotify artists will probably implode with rage at reading a sentence like that, where 0.003p a play is the norm and a remote country house purchase would require more than one hundred million streams). Until **Stories From the City, Stories From the Sea** received a massive sales boost from the *Mercury Prize* win, **To Bring You My Love** was her bestselling album.

The single **Down by the Water** received a lot of attention and airplay (and remains one of her best selling songs to this day). With another very strong vocal performance, including a whispered section that still manages to evoke a rich power in her voice, a dark and somewhat gothic tinged backing track and a video featuring Harvey glammed up to the nines basically drowning (an image from the video shoot is used as the album cover), it's a unique offering that redefines what a pop song is and it's fantastic.

Highlights include the amazing singles **C'mon Billy**, led by an acoustic strum and slowly building crescendos of violins, and **Send His Love To Me**. Clearly the album is anchored around the strength of the three singles, with the other tunes needing a little more work for your attention, but all must bow to the true highlight of the album, and inexplicably not chosen for a single, **Long Snake Moan**.

Second Choice Song
There's a lot to like in Harvey's back catalogue, and a range of styles to choose from. I think the early songs, perhaps represented best by **Sheela-na-Gig**, **Dress** and **50ft Queenie** are brilliant, fast and raw and urgent. The jangly guitar pop of **Good Fortune** or **A Place Called Home**. The confident blues rock of **This is Love**. The low key introspection of **Shame**. Like I said, lots of great stuff.

For me, something about **The Wind** just makes it for my second choice. With a bit of jangly guitar to open it, along with Harvey's voice used in whisper mode again, it initially sounds like some sort of film score. Then the subdued drums kick in, along with some almost falsetto vocals, and you get taken on a gentle journey through someone called Catherine's life. She liked high places, up in the hills where she built a chapel. She dreams of children's voices and torture on the wheel. Lonely, moaning, listening to the wind. Again, lyrically there are some pretty strong images brought forth (internet interpretations compare St Catherine, Led Zeppelin's **Stairway to Heaven** and Bronte's *Wuthering Heights* amongst other guesses).

Gentle fare it may be but it's song writing in the domain of genius. Uniquely PJ Harvey, one of England's greatest exports. The song's over before it outstays its welcome – over much too soon in my opinion (it clocks in at over four minutes and feels like two) – but leaving that bit of wanting more only means that it's great to put it on again and have another listen.

THE FALL

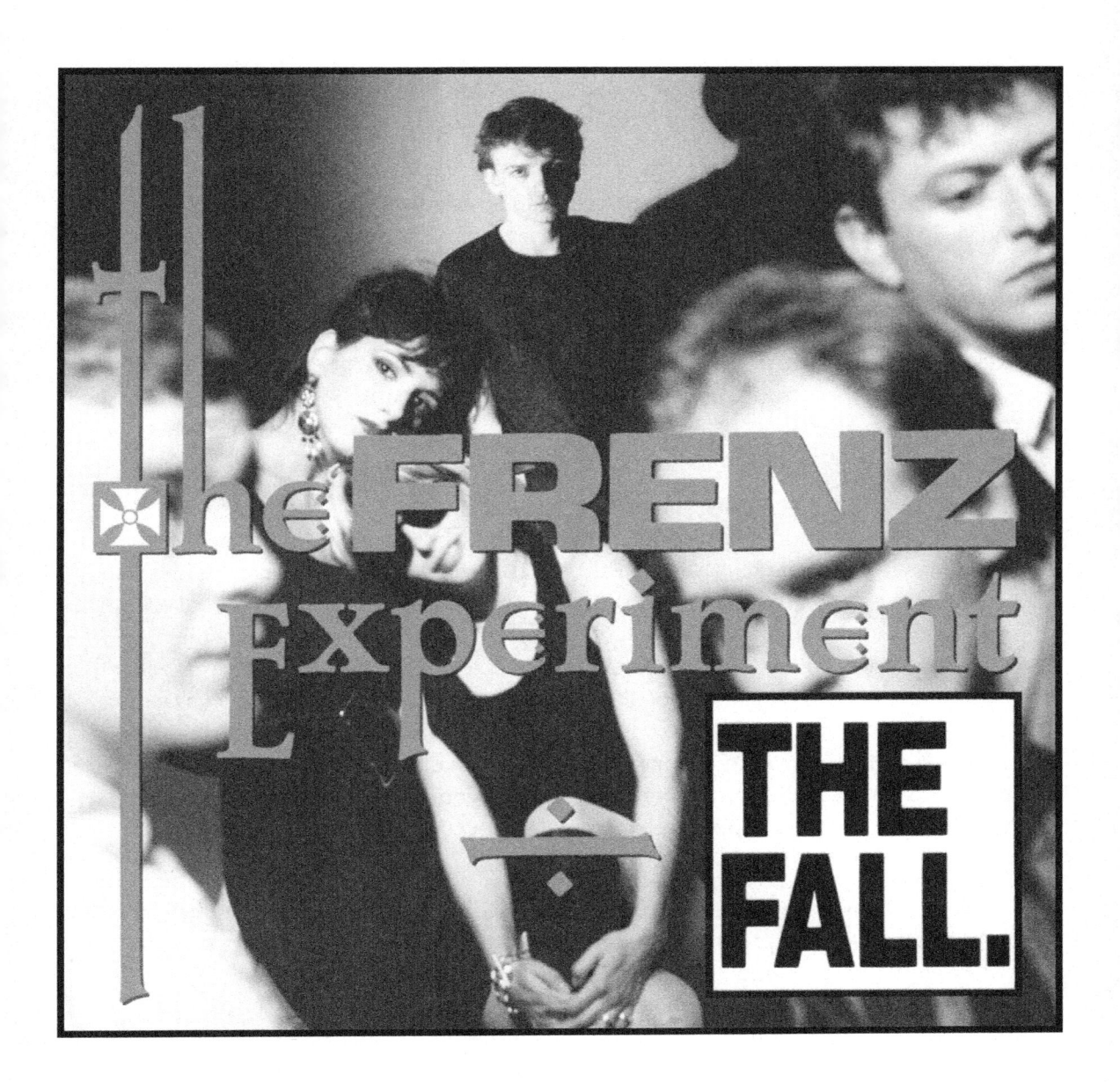

GUEST INFORMANT

THE FALL – GUEST INFORMANT

About the Band

The Fall were essentially one static member – singer and renegade genius Mark E Smith (who sadly passed away in 2018) – and a cast of about sixty bandmates who came and went, sometimes fleetingly, usually on account of Smith behaving in such an upsetting fashion it would cause them to leave. In a truly withering statement about his colleagues, Smith once famously said: *'If it's me and your granny on bongos, it's The Fall.'*

Starting in 1976, the band released 31 studio albums invoking a wide array of sounds and styles. On top of this, there are almost twice that number of live album releases. They were incredibly prolific but whatever they were releasing, the mainstream public generally found their offerings somewhat incomprehensible. They rarely penetrated the charts and were it not for the incessant championing by *Radio 1* DJ John Peel it's likely that their core audience would have been even smaller. I personally like – love, even - some of their music enough to include them in this book, but my window into the world of The Fall is very small and most of their recorded works leave me cold. I've tried, I really have, but I just can't make that leap.

The wild variances in the band's style often came about due to the high churn rate of staff. People with various influences came and went and the overall sound changed accordingly, always sounding like The Fall due to the final layer of whatever Smith came up with for lyrics and vocal lines. Often these would be a worthy icing on the cake, but sometimes they would be like dog shit on pizza, ruining the hard work by the real instrumentalists. Indeed, it seemed that Smith would set out to deliberately make life for his bandmates as difficult as possible, and somehow he managed to get away with it for 42 years, which is astonishing considering they usually did most of the work and he turned up at the last minute and sprinkled some Smith dust on the tracks and generally took all the credit. The fact that they put up with it enough to not murder him is a testament to the man's rogue-ish charm and level of control over the band (and, indeed, the brand).

Despite this constant antagonism, The Fall produced some amazing music. Which part of their ouvre qualifies as 'amazing' is entirely up to the listener, it's a choice that invites nothing but argument. Diehard Fall fans will no doubt be horrified by the works I've chosen here – my favourite 2 albums by the group are often dismissed as a low point in their career but they are how I found my way into the group and I still play tracks from these albums 20 years later. If you ask a Fall fan what the best work is, they'd probably say something like the **Hex Enduction Hour**, and they might be right, but it wasn't for me. When Brix Smith joined the band and infused their music with some pop sensibilities, and when overall production values increased, I pricked up my ears and on the back of their **Kinks** cover **Victoria** I bought **The Frenz Experiment** album and the door opened.

About This Song
Guest Informant is going to sound terrible to the average listener, but with perseverance the hooks and pop qualities eventually emerge and you find yourself reappraising the childish, simplistic dirge and concluding that what you're actually listening to is a rather catchy, spiky piece of pop music with a killer guitar riff. You have to wonder if the sudden rather startling vocal intrusion at 33 seconds into the song is one of the worst ideas ever put to music (I'd imagine Smith came up with the idea and forced it onto the studio engineer at the last minute) or a piece of madness so genius that it not only makes the song but colours the rest of the album to a degree that the offbeat and unexpected should be thoroughly welcomed. I honestly don't know. It always, without fail, evokes a *'What the fuck?!'* reaction whenever I play it to someone new. I love that.

Bonkers lyrics about following a colonel to a hotel and bugging his room degenerate into the shouted ramblings of a madman, accompanied by some excellent backing from the band. Although it can feel totally out there, this track is one of the poppier, most-accessible offerings the group recorded and it only takes a slight shift in your perception to grasp what's going on and love it.

In the burning scorch of another Sunday over
The miserable Scottish hotel,
Resembled a Genesis or Marillion, 1973 LP cover
All the hotel staff had been dismissed,
It was me, the Hoover

Guest Informant ©Mark E Smith

Essential Album
The Frenz Experiment contains a very eclectic bunch of songs, 11 in the original vinyl release but 15 on the CD version I had (the additions including excellent chart-bothering singles **Hit the North Part 1** and **There's a Ghost in my House**, a cover of an R Dean Taylor song).

If you've not heard much of the Fall before listening, it can seem like a strange ordeal.

Opener **Frenz** ambles along doing nothing in particular, an amiable and repetitive curiosity – many Fall tracks could be given that label – before fading out and launching into the superb **Carry Bag Man**. It's a freight train of a rock song, pummelling along with some quirky lyrics and perhaps should have been the opening track, with Frenz left to fade us out at the end. **Get a Hotel** is understated but interesting enough and **Victoria** is a solid cover of the Kinks' tune (a single release with a suitably cheesy accompanying video).

Where the album really takes off though is with its fifth track **Athlete Cured**. I've seen a YouTube reviewer trash this track (and, indeed, the entire album) but have to conclude he doesn't know what he's talking about. This is a slice of mad genius (even if the central riff does borrow heavily from *Spinal Tap*'s **Tonight I'm Gonna Rock You Tonight**). A catchy, repetitive slab of music overlaid with the lyrical investigative story of a German athletic star's illness, ultimately found to be caused by the brother's VW exhaust fumes, for which the brother is punished by being *'sent on a labour beautification course of the countryside north-west of Dresden'*. You just don't get these kinds of songs anywhere else but The Fall.

A couple of indescribably awful they're actually brilliant tracks pepper the latter half of the album, these being the **Steak Place** and **Oswald Defence Lawyer**. I once lent the CD to a colleague who had caught the **Ghost in my House** single somewhere and wanted to hear the album – he returned it to me the following day, ashen-faced. When pressed, it was the **Oswald Defence Lawyer**' track that had tipped him over the edge. It is terrible but repeated listening does bear fruit.

Closing out the record we get the aforementioned **Guest Informant**, the brilliant **Twister** and a couple of bangers in **Ghost** and **Hit The North**. Overall we have an album unlike any other, typical Fall fodder with a slight softening in accessibility and well worth the effort of trying to get to like.

Second Choice Song
Big New Prinz is from the follow-up album to Frenz, the collaborative effort called **I Am Kurious, Oranj**. It borrows some lyrical content from earlier Fall track **Hip Priest**, which to me sounds like some people messing about in a rehearsal studio but it regarded as something of a classic by diehard fans.

Big New Prinz is by far the more polished composition, an exceptionally catchy pop song (or about as close to a pop song as The Fall get), with a throbbing slab of bass repeating all the way through. This kind of bass is something the band does well, most notably in tracks like **Blindness** and **Dr Buck's Letter**, which are well worth listening to if this track makes you like the band even a little bit.

Even if you end up not liking The Fall, you have to give them top marks for determination and perseverance. If music is a rainbow, and you only listen to a couple of colours (those that get in the charts or get played on *Radio 2* or *Heart FM* etc) then you're missing out. When you explore the other colours, you get to experience all of the bands in this book. If only for once in your life, take a closer look at The Fall – it will be an unforgettable experience, one way or the other, and collecting those is surely the point of being alive, right?

JANE'S ADDICTION

BEEN CAUGHT STEALING

JANE'S ADDICTION – BEEN CAUGHT STEALING

About the Band
Jane's Addiction formed in 1985 and quickly gained a cult following on the LA rock scene. Their brand of metal was an adrenaline shot to the heart of an ailing genre comprised of over-the-top hair-metal and glam-metal bands singing about shagging – one way or another, it was always about shagging.

Also rising to prominence around this time were Guns n' Roses, bringing a different sense of freshness and urgency with a brilliant debut album that ended up selling 30 million copies globally. Whereas Guns n' Roses lowered the bar and disappeared up their own arses, with Axl Rose becoming increasingly ripe for derision, Perry Farrell steered Jane's Addiction into art-rock territory and never looked back. They sold nowhere near as many records but they retained their integrity and were lauded for their ground-breaking creativity.

After a live album release in 1987, Jane's Addiction were picked up by Warner Bros and released two studio LP's that would change the alternative metal scene forever. 1988's **Nothing Shocking** and 1990's **Ritual do lo Habitual** are both *bone fide* masterpiece albums that would influence countless bands that came after them. Farrell had the genius idea of setting up the *Lollapalooza* festival, providing a stage for bands like Nine Inch Nails, Siouxsie and the Banshees (and later Ministry and Pearl Jam) to achieve wider recognition, as well as providing the best possible touring experience for his own band.

Like other bands in this book, their upward trajectory was knocked sideways by the emergence of Nirvana's **Nevermind** album in 1991. Were it not for the success of Nevermind, it's likely Jane's Addiction would have become fully global superstars instead of Nirvana... if not for an additional couple of things that would have derailed the band anyway. First, Farrell made excessive demands for the lion's share of royalties, and this created resentment internally within the band that would eventually destroy relationships. Add hard drugs into the mix, with various members trying to rehab back to normality whilst others were going fully rock n' roll, and the fracture deepened enough to cause a split.

Bassist Eric Avery and guitarist Dave Navarro left, with Navarro turning up in the Red Hot Chili Peppers for a stint and majorly contributing toward their unfairly maligned **One Hot Minute** album. When Jane's Addiction finished, they were on the cusp of true greatness, possibly having the credentials and the ability to come up with new music that would see them rise along with Nirvana and ride that wave to immortality. But they split and that was that. Reunions along the line were good – their album **Strays** is a magnificent piece of work – but they never recaptured that initial magic and sales were relatively poor.

Jane's Addiction were so good because they were comprised of four stellar musicians (five if you also include long-time replacement bassist Chris Chaney, unceremoniously dumped in 2022 when Avery returned to the fold again). Drummer Stephen Perkins must surely go down as one of the finest to ever bash the skins, and bassist Avery wrought pure magic with four strings. Eel-smashing bastard Navarro *(yes, some of us remember that, Dave)* was a guitarist that comes along once in a generation and singer/songwriter Perry Farrell was a force of nature with a distinctive voice and a penchant for self-designed album covers of a unique style. Together, they were capable of producing towering compositions like **Three Days** and **Ted, Just Admit It**.

About This Song
Been Caught Stealing is by far the poppiest offering from the band. It's incredibly catchy and upbeat, despite being a song about the joy of thieving. It's JA at their most playful, everyone sounds like they're having immense fun and it includes a dog barking in the intro.

Heavy rotation of the video on MTV paved the way for more ears and more interest for the *Lollapalooza* tour that really broke them to the mainstream rock crowd. It's a gateway song into the band, a very easy listen with just a hint of better, darker things to come.

Essential Album
It would be too obvious to go with either **Nothing's Shocking** or **Ritual do lo Habitual** – either would make an excellent addition to your collection and each are different enough from the other to highlight alternate faces of the same musical diamond – both have been lavished with praise for decades and in retrospect it kind of undermines the work they did on their third studio album, **Strays**.

Maybe it's because I listened to those earlier albums so much that I was slightly worn out with the band by the time Strays came along, ready for something a little less arty. And that's what it brings to the table, a more straightforward take on the genre, a bunch of catchy metal songs played with immaculate precision but still with a seasoning of their former eccentricities.

The record company wouldn't go with Farrell's artwork for the cover, instead opting for a simpler shot of the band in the hope of attracting a more mainstream audience. The music was certainly a little more mainstream than previous albums and some hardcore fans and reviewers were less than kind in their appreciation, which was somewhat unfair. When bands don't evolve, using their old strengths as stepping stones to find new pathways and musical explorations, they stagnate. (A couple of bands in this book would make great examples but I don't want to single them out. So when a band like Jane's makes new music and doesn't try to force the old formulas onto the new material that should be applauded, not criticised.

For my money, the album should be considered another classic. It's full of powerful songs that play really well and occasionally offer flashes of the old Jane's whilst still pointing towards a bright future (which didn't really come for them). **Superhero** was used in the popular *Entourage* show and **Just Because** was nominated for a *Grammy* and appeared in several video games. Overall, a brilliant album and worth an hour of anyone's time.

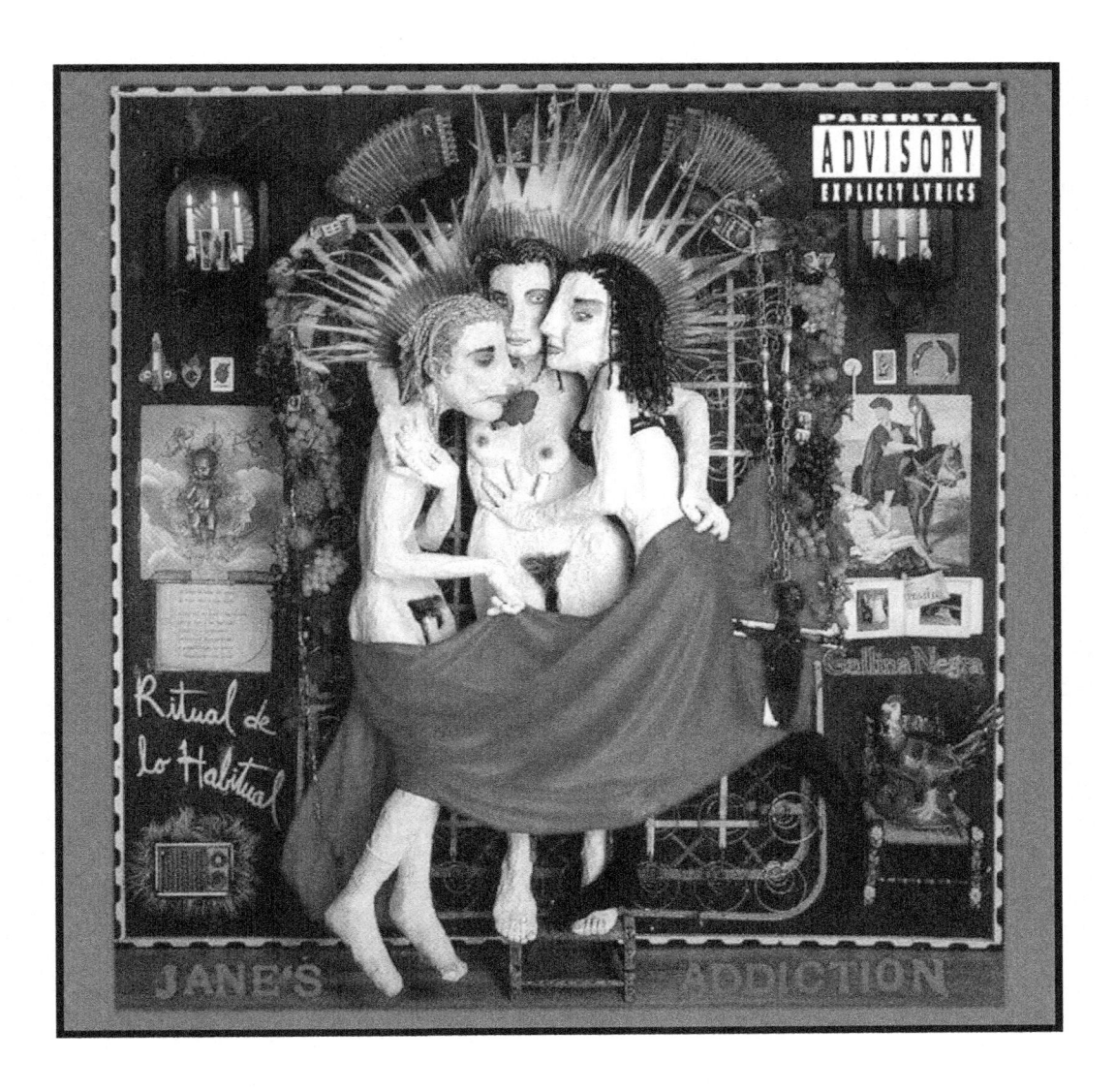

Second Choice Song

Has to be **Three Days**. Just has to be, it's such an epic that it would be criminal of me to ignore it here. Listen to it and see if I'm wrong. If you've never listened to any of the bands or music covered in this book, and all of this is new to you, start with Three Days – you won't have heard anything quite like it. (Well, Radiohead's **Paranoid Android** sort of uses the same blueprint but there's a chance you might not have heard that either. If not, play that straight after!).

If you've only ever been used to hearing what's on the radio, this is what true musicians get up to when they're not hampered by a four minute time limit and a bunch of catchy repetitive choruses. They make songs like this, sprawling epics composed of different movements with space to breathe, take flight and soar. Hearing a song like this for the first time will be genuinely mind expanding for you.

This is music as high art. It might be about Perry Farrell's three days in bed with two women, replicated on the cover of the Ritual album (*left*) by Farrell's physical artwork, but it transcends a mere orgy and becomes something magnificent.

Erotic Jesus, indeed.

INTERLUDE 2

INSTRUMENTALS

INSTRUMENTALS

There are many bands that for the most part produce nothing but instrumentals – some such artists are included in this book. They include Orbital and Jean Michel Jarre. There are also a great many bands that *aren't* featured in this book that focus on instrumentals, such as Mogwai, or Banco de Gaia, or Godspeed You Black Emperor! The reasons that so many musicians devote so much of their time to this branch of music are various - not having to deal with prima donna vocalists is probably the main one.

But another big reason is dead simple to explain – instrumental tracks are ace.

Below are a number of tracks by bands that aren't usually noted for tunes without vocals. They feature singers that have chosen to sit it out on these occasions. I suppose that when being played live, they offer the singer a chance to light up, or nip to the loo, or otherwise stand around like a tit with nothing to do (unless the singer can play an instrument, of course – even a tambourine will do). Sometimes, because the singer has nothing to do, instrumentals just don't get played live.

One common denominator of all these instrumental tracks by 'proper' bands is just how good they are – these aren't just throwaway jams they couldn't be arsed to write words to. Or maybe songs that however many times they tried, the wordsmiths in the bands just couldn't seem to compose lyrics that fitted. Some of them – *all of them here* – are as good as anything else they've recorded. My top pick is a highlight of that particular band's career (in my opinion).

This is by no means a comprehensive list, just a handful of what's available out there to enjoy, and a few of my particular favourites.

THE CURE – ANOTHER JOURNEY BY TRAIN

This was the B-side to **The Cure**'s 1980 mini-masterpiece **A Forest**, itself regarded very highly by fans and the band alike. The classic three-piece line up of the band that would go on to record the landmark **Pornography** album (Smith, Gallup, Tolhurst) were joined by keyboardist Matthieu Hartley, an integral part of both songs and A Forest's parent album **17 Seconds**. His keyboard textures provide much of the atmospheric mood of the songs from this period.

As the band's focus was becoming more downbeat (which caused Hartley to leave The Cure shortly after), **Another Journey By Train** represents an otherwise jolly blip in the increasingly darkening worldview of the band (Smith wouldn't find his sense of fun again until 1982's **Let's Go To Bed**). The track rips through a number of cycles, undercut by Tolhurst's simple but effective drumming, overlaid with perfectly placed keyboard parts whilst Smith's guitar work is beautiful and an early indicator of just how good he was going to become. The real star of the show is Simon Gallup's bassline though, carrying the song and driving it forward. Gallup isn't often critically lauded for his basslines but throughout his career the man has proven his worth time and again with his contributions to the band. This early example is one of his best.

PLACEBO – BULLETPROOF CUPID

Opening **Placebo**'s 4th studio album **Sleeping With Ghosts** with a bang, this short and feisty instrumental showcases head honcho Brian Molko's songwriting ability and aptitude for creating inventive, guitar driven tracks that thunder along without a care in the world for anything else. The word 'brilliant' is admittedly overused in this book but sometimes it's just too good a fit to discard. **Bulletproof Cupid** is a remarkable opening to a remarkable album, fast and urgent and a note to all that the disappointment of previous album **Black Market Music** was not going to be continued.

Placebo are generally adept at writing fantastic pop songs draped in a layer of indie credibility, and their back catalogue showcases some perfect examples of the song writing craft. There were a couple of more experimental tracks on their eponymous debut album that showed a different side to the band, **Lady of the Flowers** and **Swallow** (complete with bonus hidden track after a silent gap of about 10 minutes) which I think the band have never bettered but they continued with this line of musical curiosity with tracks like **Something Rotten** (Sleeping With Ghosts).

BUZZCOCKS – LATE FOR THE TRAIN

There's something about trains and instrumentals (I would have included Banco De Gaia's magnificent **Last Train To Lhasa** in this section if it wasn't for the fact that he is primarily a creator of instrumentals). This one, by punk-pop masters Buzzcocks, is quite simply a work of genius.

Although the band are famous for their single **Ever Fallen In Love (With Someone You Shouldn't Have)?**, which sometimes comes close to eclipsing the rest of their career, fans also know the band for their incredible run of other spiky pop singles and fantastic B-Sides. Delve a little deeper into their discography and you'll see that they were a great deal more than that, with some unbelievable album tracks filling out their inventory.

What they aren't known for is their instrumentals. This particular track brings out the best in all four band members, particularly Steve Diggle and his lead guitar. I'm not sure if the drumming is a mix of drum machine and some extremely tight playing by the incredible John Maher, but it really does evoke the rhythm of the way trains used to sound back in the 1980's (trains were noisier back then, your journeys were often accompanied by a *clackity-clack* as the train wheels traversed the rails – progress has made such wonderful sounds mostly disappear from modern life). One section of the song sonically represents entering a tunnel and suddenly brings all of the instruments down to a dampened, quieter level before a sudden wail of guitar brings the rest of the band whooshing back in as the tunnel is cleared. Utterly brilliant stuff.

BUZZCOCKS – WALKING DISTANCE

Proving it wasn't a fluke, Buzzcocks deliver another great instrumental track with **Walking Distance**. Both tunes are found on their 1978 **Love Bites** album, which is an absolute belter and chock full of great songs. Walking Distance is credited to bassist Steve Garvey, yet once again the track pulls in the best from everyone involved and no-one is idling.

It's a very short piece, clocking in at exactly two minutes, and while not as inventive as **Late For The Train** it's still a perfect example of what a traditional band can do when they leave the vocals out of the mix. There aren't many better ways to fill a spare two minutes.

OASIS – FUCKIN' IN THE BUSHES

Let's get this one out of the way early. I was never a big fan of Oasis. They had some decent tunes, I appreciate that, and I think Noel Gallagher is genuinely talented. Unfortunately, the laddish antics of Liam Gallagher always put me off them. He's just not to my taste, which will probably be upsetting to anybody who gives two fucks about what I actually think (*and I don't believe there are too many of those people around*), but the fact that we all like different things makes the world a very interesting place.

It's possibly because Liam doesn't feature on this track, but more likely because it sounds like very little else the band did. There's a loud and ringing drum beat to kick it off, some **Led Zep** style riffing, fuzzy as hell leads, plus a hint of the awesome **25 Or 6 To 4** by Chicago in the outro. It's Oasis getting their ROCK on.

I think this, the opening track on the fourth studio album (**Standing on the Shoulders of Giants**), is easily the best thing they ever recorded, by a country mile. I can't heap enough praise on this track, it's a 10/10 on every level. It featured in the Guy Ritchie film *Snatch* in one of Brad Pitt's wonderful "One Punch" Mickey's fight scenes, which probably coloured the association in a positive way for me, being a big fan of that film.

Although it is an instrumental, there are a number of samples featured in the song, particularly at the beginning (1970 Isle of Wight MC Rikki Farr giving the crowd some stick with *"We put this festival on, you bastards, with a lot of love! We worked for one year for you pigs! And you wanna break our walls down and you wanna destroy it? Well you go to hell!"*).

The *"Kids are running around naked, fucking in the bushes!"* and the crazy old woman at the end are possibly from the 1970 documentary about the festival but have proven really hard to track down and verify. That's not important for you though, just try the tune out for yourself and see how great it is.

Wal-Mart didn't stock the album due to the title of this track, which possibly affected sales, but the rest of the album is generally considered one of their worst, salvageable mostly by this one effort.

NINE INCH NAILS – THE MARK HAS BEEN MADE

NIN are proponents of noisy Industrial rock, that's the general perception, but they are actually incredibly inventive and diverse in their recordings and have an astounding catalogue of work to their name. I say 'they' but for the most part I'm referring to principal songwriter and multi-instrumentalist Trent Reznor, a classically trained pianist who's currently reaping the rewards of the second phase of his career, producing Oscar winning soundtracks for intelligent movies by the likes of David Fincher, David Lynch and Pixar.

Although NIN have gone onto release fully instrumental albums with the **Ghosts** compilations, the instrumentals produced during the recording sessions for their third studio album, the vastly underrated **The Fragile,** carry far more heft compared to the audio sketches of Ghosts.

The Mark Has Been Made begins in a fairly low-key fashion, a mood piece leading to a violin bridge and bass lead before the drums kick in and the track gains some momentum. The guitars are fuzzy and dirty, the bass jabs at you and when the noise dials back a bit there's a real sense of the song breathing, of being alive. At the end, there's a call-back to **Closer** from the previous album, the mega-successful and career changing (and ultimately career defining) **The Downward Spiral**.

It's a fabulous track, one that would be impossible to improve and it's one of the best tracks on the album, no mean feat as The Fragile is a sprawling double LP with a ton of great songs.

NINE INCH NAILS – JUST LIKE YOU IMAGINED

As good as the previous track is, it's not the best instrumental on **The Fragile**. That spot is reserved for the phenomenal **Just Like You Imagined**, probably the most perfect track the band ever recorded. My God, this is a beast, combining everything that makes NIN so good and topping it out with some piano flourishes that would make Elton John blush with admiration.

I have many, many favourite NIN tracks – between 1989 and 2007 they were the gift that kept on giving for me, they could do no wrong – and this one might just be the top of the heap. Everything about it gives me goosebumps. The opening piano riff surrounded by echoey guitars, the gorgeous bassline and top-notch drums, the noisy guitar and sudden break into a tumbling, tinkling waterfall of piano notes… this is a tune to leave you breathless. There are so many parts to it, it keeps building and throws in a bridge of aligning vocals, numerous stellar guitar riffs, layer upon layer of noise and then a final payoff with a repeating piano riff to fade.

Reznor recruited additional musicians to help bring this piece to life, amongst them Mike Garson (piano), Adrian Belew and Danny Lohner (guitars). As well as the studio version to enjoy, check out the rehearsal of this on *YouTube*, offering another dimension and inside view of the song.

PRODIGY - CLIMBATIZE

Although a lot of early Prodigy tracks were essentially Liam Howlett's music with sampled snippets of vocal over the top, their later work would increasingly feature full vocal performances, whether by band member Keith Flint or guest singers such as Martina Topley-Bird, Jason Williamson (Sleaford Mods) and Juliette Lewis.

Sophomore album, hugely successful **The Fat of the Land** featured 10 tracks, of which eight had a significant vocal presence. It's fair to say the band had made the leap from being an instrumental entity, and this is why I class **Climbatize** (from that album) as an instrumental worthy of inclusion here.

It's by far the least showy, least in-your-face track on the album. Every other track is loud, attention seeking, aiming for maximum impact. Climbatize is a slightly more laidback affair and offers another welcome dimension to a record that is already bursting with brilliance. As a collection of songs, The Fat of the Land has rarely been bettered – I played it to death when it came out, as did everyone I knew, regardless of their musical penchants. This album united everybody.

To paraphrase Danny from *Withnail & I*, this track has '*voodoo qualities*'. The rolling drum machine loop, together with the main keyboard refrain, seem to evoke images of starry Haitian skies, of painted faces and funeral processions. Maybe it's just me. When there's a brief pause in the backing music and that refrain rings out alone (at the 4:34 mark) it sounds like the plaintive, haunting cry of something mournful, unseen in the mists of the river Styx.

I love everything about this song. I love the bassline, the rumbling, looping thread underpinning the song. I love Liam Howlett's choice of instruments, and the arrangement. I think very highly of this band, and I have dozens of tracks by them that I really love, and I can't explain why (considering the excellence of the competition) but if I was backed into a corner at gunpoint and forced to make a choice, this might just be my favourite.

SIMPLE MINDS – THEME FOR GREAT CITIES

I've saved the best 'til last. What's unusual about this track is the fact that apart from a couple of early albums (before the band hit the big time) I generally don't think much of **Simple Minds**' music. Those albums, **Sons and Fascination** and **Sister Feelings Call** are grouped together in the UK and treated as a single offering and are regarded as their fourth studio album.

This was a really interesting phase of the band, before they switched to bombast and huge, stadium-filling pop songs that commercially sent them into the stratosphere. Here, they were more experimental and the songs sounded like little else around, a trait which keeps them sounding razor sharp to this day.

Opening the Sister Feelings Call section is **Theme For Great Cities**. I believe it to be one of the best songs recorded by a band ever – just my opinion, and one that may be laughed at by more serious critics, but it's up there with the best for me. (To qualify that statement, you're currently reading a book full of what I consider to be some of the greatest songs ever recorded, so there's some perspective for you. People may say these tunes won't hold a candle to the Beatles, for example, but I say 'Hold on a minute, let's take another look at this.') Regardless, this tune is awesome. And I mean that not in the trivial sense, but in the sense where the word used to be less common and really did mean something that filled you with awe. It's such a big sounding tune, in hindsight good preparation for the cathedral-sized pieces they'd create in the future.

Speaking of which, the track itself is futuristic and wildly optimistic in that way people used to be about the near future. Unlike the knee jerk reaction you would get today - it's too crowded and polluting and ugly - Simple Minds are saying big cities are 'a good thing'. They are utopian, they symbolise progress and a bright shiny future and we, a lowly Scottish post-punk band, will provide the soundtrack to them. You have to love that attitude.

Singer Jim Kerr sits this one out (he just couldn't come up with vocals that did the song justice and came to the realisation that it really didn't need words – the words of the title were enough) and the rest of the band come together to create this thing of genius, this monument to audio. The bass and drums lock together perfectly, both building on complex rhythms with a simpler keyboard wash backing them up. Charlie Burchill's guitars provide a chugging, fizzing backdrop and occasional stabs, and then gigantic keyboards crash in for the 'chorus' parts. Oh man. I could sit in a room with headphones on and listen to this track for days. I'm not the only one to hold this tune in such high regard. A new book (2022, Graeme Thomson) about the band used this song title as a title for the book, choosing it over hundreds of other possible options and many, many more successful and better-known tracks. Added to this, the song has been sampled 11 times for use in other artists creations, and covered at least 3 times. We know, see. Join our club.

THE CURE

A JAPANESE DREAM

THE CURE – A JAPANESE DREAM

About the Band
The Cure were formed in Crawley in 1978. Early material consisted of spiky pop songs with a smidge of punk before they found their inner gloom and produced three consecutive albums of increasing miserableness – **Seventeen Seconds**, **Faith** and **Pornography**. Each has notable moments of excellence and found an adoring fanbase, who were then subsequently shocked when Robert Smith (the only constant member throughout many line-up changes) went full-on pop and released a run of non-gloomy classics including **The Love Cats** and **The Caterpillar**, from albums **Japanese Whispers** and **The Top** respectively.

The Top was a weird album, flirting with psychedelia and capturing the eternal struggle that would come to define Smith's later career, the yin and yang, the constant battle between producing lighter but well-crafted pop songs and more aggressive, darker pieces. Light-hearted **The Caterpillar** and **The Birdmad Girl** stand opposite darker, heavier tunes **Shake Dog Shake** and **Give Me It**, whilst out-there compositions like **Bananafishbones** look on from the sidelines.

The Head on the Door is a classic pop album with a clutch of ten pretty much perfect songs. Even though it's not quite my favourite, I rate it as probably their best (if that makes any sense). **The Baby Screams** would have made a good single, as would **A Night Like This** (which did get an official video), perfectly complimenting the actual singles **Inbetween Days** and **Close to Me** (see Videos section).

Sprawling double album **Kiss Me Kiss Me Kiss Me** seemed to be critically underappreciated and could also be a contender for their best album, though usually it's the follow up **Disintegration** that gets all the love. It's a great album, no doubt, but I personally enjoyed Kiss Me's greater creative diversity more. Either way, **Disintegration** was arguably the bands high watermark, although 1992's **Wish** performed better commercially, mainly thanks to their high-profile single **Friday I'm In Love**.

After an initial 15 years or so of banging out top quality tunes, they've been in a slow creative and commercial decline ever since, turning up on the festival circuit now and then to headline and blast through their greatest hits, of which they have many, and this seems to satisfy Smith's desire for keeping the band on life support.

About This Song
A Japanese Dream is actually a B-side – the Cure are a band notable for the quality of their B-sides and this is easily an equal to the title track **Why Can't I Be You?,** itself a superb slice of jolliness reminiscent of regular pop tunes like Katrina and the Waves'

Walking on Sunshine. A Japanese Dream is a darker tune, where the band draw out a more powerful sound and the guitars fizz like a swarm of angry hornets. Smith sings about returning to the *'land of the blind'* and worshipping God whilst *'burning like a monkey'* and other such nonsense. Although the lyrics aren't Smith's finest moment they suit the song perfectly and it's altogether a fantastic tune that sounds best when played LOUD. There's a harder to find 12" remix that uses the drumline as a focal point and cleans up some of the general noise, which is a different experience but also great.

Special mention goes to Boris William's drumming. A man whose name doesn't come up as often as it should when discussing rock's greatest drummers, Williams was one of The Cure's finest assets and his work on their albums is often spectacular.

Essential Album
As The Cure are a band with such a diverse range of tunes, it's hard to pin down a specific album because they are so different from each other (although they all still sound like The Cure, which is amazing when you think about it).

You can't go wrong with 1985's **The Head on the Door,** as mentioned earlier. 1989's **Disintegration** is generally regarded as The Cure's best piece of work, and brilliant singles **Lullaby, Love Song, Pictures of You** and **Fascination Street** *(limited release)* – top quality tunes - are all still eclipsed by the title track.

For me though, 1987's **Kiss Me, Kiss Me, Kiss Me** is their masterpiece, a sprawling double album that features a diverse range of songs and showcases the band's ability to attempt anything they fancy and make it sound great. **Hot Hot Hot** is a funky slice of fun, **Icing Sugar** is trippy jazz with a thundering percussion behind it, **Shiver and Shake** is proper angry and about as heavy as the Cure gets. **Just Like Heaven** is one of the best pop singles ever produced by any band but that won't be my second choice song simply because it's so easy to like and I want to give you more of a challenge.

Second Choice Song
There are literally scores of great tunes to choose from. I find 1992's opening track to the **Wish** album, appropriately called **Open**, to be something that still sounds fantastic nearly three decades after release.

Featuring a vocal narrative of a protagonist getting embarrassingly out-of-control via drink and drugs at a social gathering, musically backed by a thick slab of a heavier, rockier sound, the song showcases the band's ability to come up with really decent rock tracks, and I personally wish Smith had focused more attention on this style, especially later in his career. When he turns his hand to things like this, he's one of the best in the world at it, but he seems to prefer to retread older, safer ground.

After all that, **Open** isn't my second choice. The Cure have so many good tunes – albeit from 1992 or earlier, in my opinion – that I could have picked any one of about two dozen. **The Hanging Garden** is a particular favourite of mine, a highlight from their otherwise dour **Pornography** album, and you could throw a dart at **The Head on the Door** and hit any track worthy of being chosen. In the midst of Britpop euphoria, they released the superb **Never Enough**, a standalone non-album track that's up there with their best. It's not all about the singles either with this band – album tracks like **The Kiss** and **Icing Sugar** are phenomenal, as are **Sinking**, **Play for Today** and **Other Voices**.

Smith has come up with so many quality tunes during the course of his career that we can forgive him a dulling of creative sharpness towards the end. The band's induction into the 2019 *Rock and Roll Hall of Fame* (introduced by Nine Inch Nails frontman Trent Reznor) was well deserved.

If I must lock it down, I'm going with the haunting **If Only Tonight We Could Sleep**. When I first heard it as a teenager, I pretty much ignored the track as it was buried amongst a ton of livelier offerings on the Kiss Me album. To me, it sounded like the sort of background music you'd hear in a curry house. And this is why we must all remember that teenagers are idiots. Over the years, as the shininess of the other tracks dulled a little, this quietly unassuming tune grew in power and rose through the ranks of my favourite Cure songs.

I completely underestimated it. It's a beautiful song with some truly gorgeous moments – the drumming, the guitar solo that kicks in just before the two-minute mark and the accompanying – and very brief - layered vocal that rises up ten seconds later. And the lyrics are sublime, some of Smith's best.

Then an angel would come
With burning eyes like stars
And bury us deep
In his velvet arms
If Only Tonight We Could Sleep © Robert Smith / The Cure

Special mention here must go to Deftones, who covered the song at a 2004 MTV Icon Award show in honour of The Cure. They deliver an astounding performance, taking a great song and giving it a harder edge, infusing it with their own sensibility and the result is fantastic, leaving The Cure watching from the sidelines with big smiles of appreciation. Smith liked it so much that he invited the band to his 2018 Meltdown festival and they gave the track another airing.

MUDHONEY

HERE COMES SICKNESS

MUDHONEY – HERE COMES SICKNESS

About the Band

Mudhoney were at the forefront of the Seattle-centric grunge movement, inadvertently spearheading numerous bands into a new era of music and onto the global stage. But somewhere along the way, whilst their contemporaries (and imitators) found fame and fortune, Mudhoney got lost in the mix.

Rarely has a band had such an impact on the entire music industry and remained so ignored.

Singer Mark Arm and guitarist Steve Turner played in what would be, in retrospect, a supergroup called Green River, along with eventual Pearl Jam members Jeff Ament and Stone Gossard. When that band fell apart, Arm and Turner went on to form Mudhoney, embarking upon a career which would see them through 11 albums with some, but nowhere near as much as they deserved, commercial success.

The first EP, **Superfuzz Bigmuff**, was released in 1988. A 1990 reissue as an album-length record added early singles including the glorious **Touch Me I'm Sick**. The band were instrumental in creating the grunge sound and in steering the direction of global music throughout the 1990's.

Nirvana's Kurt Cobain had many influences (perhaps the most overt being Pixies, Buzzcocks and Mudhoney) and he loved – *loved!* – **Superfuzz Bigmuff**. It would heavily influence their own debut album **Bleach** the following year. (Cobain is quoted when asked to define the sound of his own band as saying *'Mudhoney meets the Beatles'*).

Superfuzz was popular in the UK Indie charts too, after the band were invited by Sonic Youth to support them on a UK tour and they started to receive widespread coverage in the UK music press. In 1989, Mudhoney released their eponymous debut LP which beefed up the production values and sounded a little less trebley, and it topped the UK Indie chart.

Unfortunately, Mudhoney will always be in the shadow of Nirvana, despite being true pioneers and showing Nirvana the way. Even though they aren't directly featured in this book, Nirvana's presence can't be avoided, they haunt the pages (and the careers of many bands that were eclipsed by their sudden superstardom) like Du Maurier's *Rebecca* haunts Manderley. Even after Cobain's death, when Mudhoney should have perhaps quietly emerged into global consciousness and recognised for their part in the grunge and alternative rock movement, they were instead ridiculed and attacked by the music press (particularly in the influential English music press, which had once embraced them and given them a platform when no-one else would) for having the temerity to continue. Build 'em up. Knock 'em down, it's a quintessentially British thing we do so well and shames us to the rest of the world.

About This Song
I can't even begin to explain how awesome **Here Comes Sickness** is without feeling the need to personally come around your house and put in onto your stereo at full volume.

It's everything that's great about grunge, about alternative rock, about independent music all distilled down into three and a half minutes of fabulousness. Legendary song from a legendary band, it's criminal that more people don't know it. I'm going to go right ahead and say it's the best grunge record ever made, which is likely to invite some lively discussion but I'll stand by the sentiment.

Opening with a killer guitar lick and pounding drums, the song rumbles along like a filthy juggernaut, Mark Arm's voice adding an extra layer of sleaze with his lyrics:

Here comes sickness
Walking down my street
Shaking her hips
Like she's some kinda treat
All the neighborhood dogs
Licking at her feet
Here Comes Sickness © Mudhoney

Amazingly, this wasn't the lead single off the album, that honour falling to the far more restrained and downbeat **This Gift**. Here Comes Sickness fizzes with energy and would have made a much better choice, capturing the manic sleaziness of grunge in all its glory.

The accompanying video, like many videos from bands just starting out with no money, includes lots of live footage shot on cheap cameras and edited together to make it look like a video for the song in question.

Essential Album
The aforementioned **Superfuzz Bigmuff** is technically an EP, clocking in at just 22.25 minutes, but we'll discuss the extended album-length 1990 version here. It's hard to explain just how influential this EP/album was. To American music, the record provided the same Big Bang energy that the Sex Pistols' debut **Never Mind The Bollocks** did in 1977. It changed *everything*.

There are 6 songs on the EP, 12 on the LP. The longer version brings **Touch Me I'm Sick** and **Burn It Clean** to the party, along with a couple of cover versions (from Dicks and Sonic Youth). It's hard to choose a highlight, particularly with the original 6 songs, but if forced to for your entertainment I'll pick the wonderful **Mudride**, a slowburner that wallows in filthy guitar excellence and gathers speed and momentum as it builds. This said, it's one of those superb albums that can bear different fruit depending upon the day and your mood – sometimes the brutal simplicity of **Touch Me I'm Sick** will win the day, others the complex lunacy of **In 'n' Out of Grace,** which contains the Peter Fonda *Wild Angels* speech sample later used by Primal Scream for their **Loaded** single. The two songs couldn't be further apart in terms of energy and tone.

Second Choice Song

Contrast the early Mudhoney days – tightly packed nightclub venues, everybody hammered, raucous music, hair and sweat flying all over the place – to the band's recent 2023 offering **Little Dogs**, a song I didn't even know existed until writing this book.

With lyrics about how Mr Arm loves his little buddies, and footage of the white-haired elderly statesman talking a little white dog for a walk, this faintly ridiculous song is a ton of fun and really catchy after a couple of listens. The video presents lots of sweet footage of Chihuahuas and the like getting fuss and scampering across the beach. Ah, we all grow mellow and old but not quite so beautifully.

If you'd shown me this video in 1990 I'd have puked six pints of cheap lager in your face but now, as an older man with a number of small dogs, I can't imagine anything better than seeing such a legend put out a song like this.

NINE INCH NAILS

ONLY

NINE INCH NAILS - ONLY

About the Band

Nine Inch Nails are the long-time project of Cleveland, Ohio born Trent Reznor. After a moderately successful stint in a band as a keyboard player, earning an appearance in a Michael J Fox movie no less, the classically trained pianist and fan of Industrial bands like Skinny Puppy and Ministry decided to go it alone.

At the time, he was working in a recording studio as a janitor and the owner let him use the studio equipment in downtime between bookings. On this free studio time and playing all of the instruments himself (except drums), he recorded demos for what would become 1989's industry changing debut album **Pretty Hate Machine**.

Although other bands were working in similar territory – Reznor had even sung on a track by 1000 Homo DJ's *(a fabulous cover of Black Sabbath's **Supernaut**, elsewhere in this book)*, a Ministry side-project headed up by Al Jourgenson – the PHM album somehow captured lightning in a bottle and blew open the Industrial scene to become more mainstream. The work Reznor was doing on this and follow up EP **Broken**, together with the significant chart success of LP **The Downward Spiral**, made Reznor a figurehead for a new generation of musicians and for a brief time he was regarded as one of the top movers and shakers in the industry.

Initially surviving the wrecking ball of Nirvana's **Nevermind**, Reznor succumbed to debilitating drug addiction and took five years to release a follow up record, a sprawling double album called **The Fragile**. During this time, the world had moved onto other things and **The Downward Spiral** is generally regarded as the high-water mark of NIN's output, which does the rest of his catalogue a disservice. **The Fragile** is a spectacular album, brimming with creativity and inventive tracks, though Reznor himself seems almost dismissive of it.

Over time, Reznor cleaned himself up, enjoying outdoor bike rides and lifting weights to bulk himself up a bit – the new Reznor seemed to have the air of a military vet rather than a drug-addled waif of his early days. Free of drugs, he managed to figure out a way to work more efficiently. Over the last 30 years, Reznor (and longtime working partner Atticus Ross) have created numerous albums for Nine Inch Nails, their other band How To Destroy Angels, and have had many collaborations with artists like David Bowie, Queens of the Stone Age, Marilyn Manson, Peter Gabriel and Saul Williams.

As if that wasn't enough, a step into video game soundtracks and also movie soundtracks has proven extremely successful. Working with Ross, who became only the second person to be inducted into NIN as a fully-fledged member in 2016, the pair have won 2 *Oscars* (for *The Social Network* and *Soul*), a *BAFTA*, 2 *Golden Globes*, an *Emmy* and a *Grammy* amongst others. That's quite a haul and that doesn't even count all of the awards and recognition he achieved with NIN.

About This Song
Reznor himself would have to admit that he's a bit of a miserable bastard when it comes to the subject matter of his recorded output. His tunes are generally on the darker side but one that bucks the trend and sounds (dare I say it) almost jolly, is **Only**, a single and track from 2005's **With Teeth** album.

Of course, the lyrics put paid to any notion of jolliness immediately but the vocal delivery style, and the pumping, vibrant music juxtapose against the lyrics nicely and the accompanying video by acclaimed director David Fincher is well worth a watch.

The track reminds me very much of Talking Heads from their **Remain in Light** era (*an album mentioned in this book and a particular favourite of mine*). It's a track that never gets old and the more you listen to it the more secrets it uncovers. Like a lot of NIN music, what may sound simple at first can quickly deepen with complexity once you really listen.

Essential Album
I loved Nine Inch Nails – they were my favourite band for about 15 years or so, losing their place at the top spot with the release of the **Ghosts I-IV** album and their subsequent output thereafter. Their last great album (in my opinion) and one I still play often, is 2007's **Year Zero**.

Although critically well-received at the time of release, as part of the group's historic canon it's often unfairly compared against the earlier work. The album is comprised of 16 really strong tracks. From the opening madness of **Hyperpower!** to the final close-out of **Zero-Sum**, it all flows beautifully. For me, it's their best grouping of songs on any of their records.

It is a concept album though I never really bought into the additional material and am judging the record solely on the music, much of which was conceived using a laptop whilst on tour. For anyone reading that doesn't know this, a lot of music is now produced this way – if you're musically talented (and, ironically, even if you aren't) then such ways of working are quick, cheap and often produce fantastic results.

Whilst promoting the album, Reznor encouraged fans to steal it from the internet rather than buy it from his record label, whom he considered to be pricing the record too high in an attempt to fleece fans (he left the label shortly thereafter).

Second Choice Song
There are so many to choose from that it is impossible to pick just one other song. We're talking about a band here that, even if you discount their singles, you could easily have a better compilation double album than many 'Greatest Hits' packages of most bands out there.

In no particular preference or order of merit, here are a selection of tracks that you should check out and marvel at the fact that they all were birthed into the world by the same person. They aren't all necessarily 'poppy', so I'm bending the aim of this book a little, but all of the following have something about them that should get under your skin and persuade you to listen to the band on a regular basis:

Terrible Lie (1989)
Happiness in Slavery (1992)
Last (1992)
Closer (1994)
Into The Void (1999)
We're in This Together (1999)
The Hand That Feeds (extended version) (2005)
Anything from **Zear Zero** (2007)
Came Back Haunted (2013)

BUZZCOCKS

LIPSTICK

BUZZCOCKS - LIPSTICK

About the Band
A band like the Buzzcocks should never be left to fade into obscurity. For many people, the name is familiar because of the long running BBC quiz show bearing the band's name, and a smaller number of people might be familiar with the anthemic single **Ever Fallen in Love (With Someone You Shouldn't've)?** which gets the occasional *Radio 2* airing. It is a great song, showcasing a blast of spiky pop/punk that they do so well, but there's much more to the band than just that.

Buzzcocks come with a healthy back catalogue of catchy punk-pop songs and a strong collection of B-sides. Formed in Bolton in 1976, originally fronted by Howard Devoto (who left of his own accord to form Magazine and was replaced by guitarist Pete Shelley), they burned fast and bright like their songs, releasing three studio albums before splitting in 1981.

They were a hugely influential band, and together with the likes of The Fall, The Smiths, Joy Division and New Order they consolidated the brilliance of the Manchester music scene, eventually ushering in bands like Stones Roses, Happy Mondays, James and Oasis. Thanks to touring with bands such as Pearl Jam, Maximo Park and Nirvana, their influence crossed oceans and cemented their status as a key player, however minor, in rock history.

Over the years, the band has reformed and split numerous times, releasing another six albums before the sad and untimely death of Shelley in 2018. Despite being mixed in with the punk crowd, his outlook was refreshingly different and worth quoting here:

'I won't be nasty. We're just four nice lads, the kind of people you could take home to your parents.' **Melody Maker interview with Shelley in 1978.**

Upon his death, tributes poured in from bands as diverse as Pearl Jam, Pixies, Duran Duran and representative members of New Order, Red Hot Chili Peppers, REM, The Smiths, The Who, Pink Floyd and Led Zeppelin. Shelley, and his band, were universally loved by those that knew about them. Today, original guitarist Steve Diggle fronts the band and they still tour and release new material.

About This Song
Lipstick is the B-side to the non-album **Promises** single released in 1978. The main chord progression was conceived by Shelley in a noodling session with Devoto and used in Magazine's January 1978 single **Shot by Both Sides**. Devoto said: *"He (Shelley) played the chord sequence and I was really impressed, said so, and he just gave them to me there and then."*

It was such a great little riff that Shelley reused it in this Buzzcocks track later in November '78. It's very rare that non-covers share identical portions and worth listening to both tracks sequentially as a comparison exercise. Not only was Shelley such a nice guy that he would give away a spectacular riff and think nothing of it, he even gave Devoto a writing credit on the Lipstick release.

One of the great strengths of Buzzcocks is their rhythm section, and for me (as an occasional drummer in bands) their original drummer John Maher is one of the best of his era, criminally under-rated and capable of coming up with drumlines of complexity and ingenuity. It's shocking to think that at the time of joining the band he was just 16 years old. **Lipstick** is a relatively straight-forward endeavour but even so, it's a cracking example of his style and skillset.

Whilst we're on the subject of Maher, I can't resist chucking in a couple of interesting titbits. Smiths guitarist Johnny Marr has his stage surname spelled that way because his actual name is also John Maher, and he didn't want people getting the two of them confused (especially as both were knocking about Manchester at the same time). And, in accordance with occasionally noting what ex-musicians get up to after their glory days in a band are over, Maher is an excellent example of a drastic career change, developing an interest in drag racing, building Volkswagen performance engines and eventually relocating the motoring business to the Isle of Harris, where he has also gained a decent reputation as a photographer. Talented guy.

Essential Album
It has to be the best of album, **Singles Going Steady**. It was my introduction to the band and a great starting point for getting into their other records.

Side one of the original vinyl ran through eight of their singles (in order of release) and side two ran through their corresponding B-sides. It says much about the band that both sides were as good as each other.

There's a reason that Nirvana frontman Kurt Cobain chose Buzzcocks as the support act for his own band's final tour and that reason is probably this album. It fizzles, pops and rattles along with a manic energy and often with heartfelt outpourings of angst and unrequited love.

In 2020 it was voted #250 in *Rolling Stone* magazine's list of the Greatest 500 Albums of All Time – not bad for a bunch of songs that most people have never heard of. Buy it, devour it, you will keep playing it for years.

Second Choice Song

Plenty to choose from but **Autonomy** pips it for me. Astoundingly, this was also a B-side, this time to the excellent 1978 single **I Don't Mind** and was written by guitarist Steve Diggle, who also performs lead vocals. Drummer Maher is on fine form yet again (Iron Maiden certainly thought so, borrowing the iconic drum intro to open their own song **Run to the Hills** in 1982, openly acknowledging the influence and paying homage) and the song rips along beautifully.

It was a staple of Buzzcocks live set and continues to be performed by the current iteration of the band to this day. There's an urgency to the song, harnessed masterfully by the excellent musicianship, with simple lyrics (with a deep political undercurrent), a singalong chorus and some beautiful guitar solo work in the middle. This song has everything, it's a masterpiece. If you haven't heard it before, drop everything (including this book) and go and have a listen. You can thank me for the introduction with a glowing book review!

JEAN MICHEL JARRE

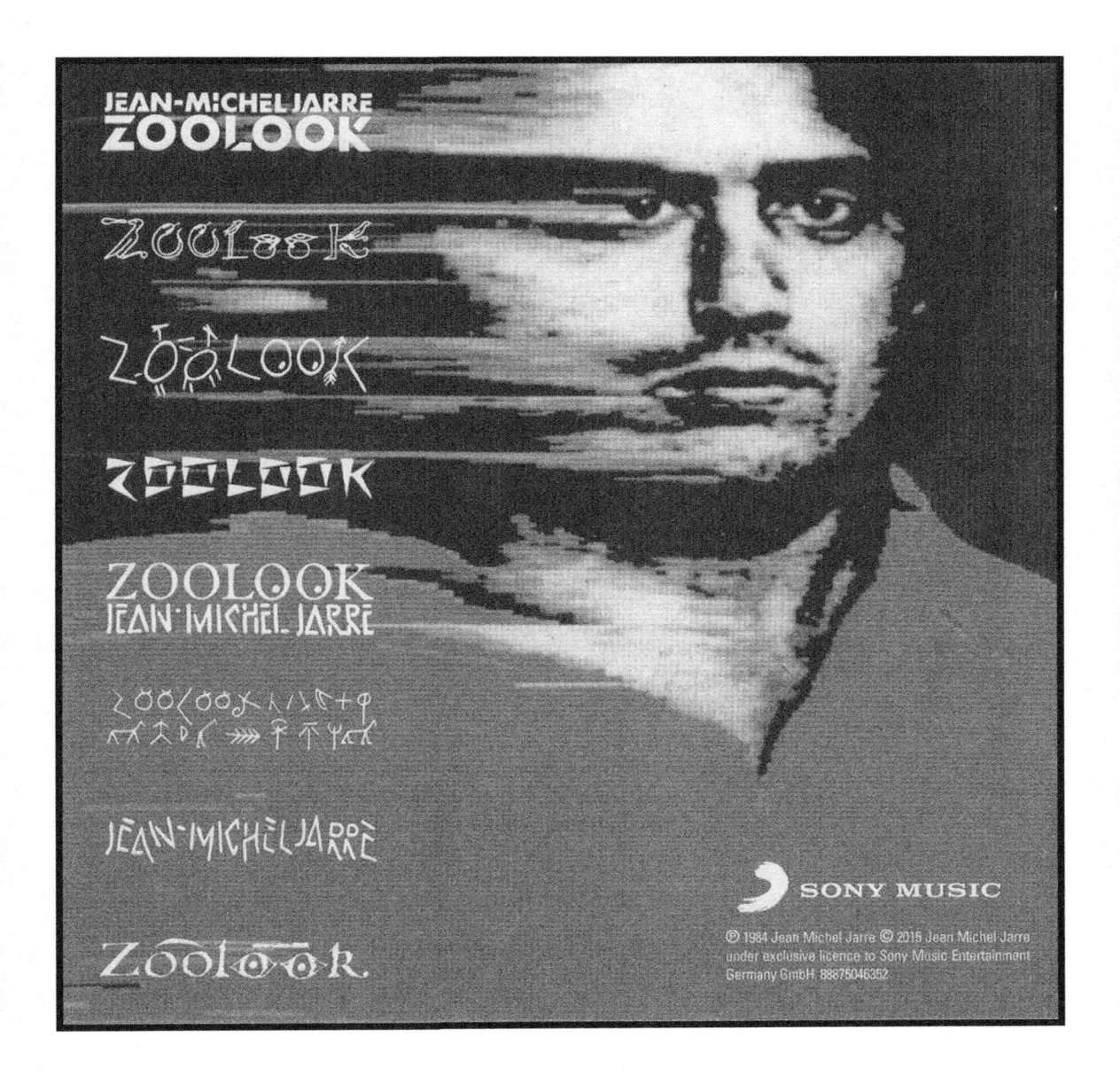

ETHNICOLOR

JEAN MICHEL JARRE - ETHNICOLOR

About the Artist
Frenchman Jean-Michel Jarre is widely known for his record breaking outdoor concerts in places like Houston, Lyon and London Docklands. Attended by up to a million or more people and featuring pyrotechnics, lasers and image projections onto the surrounding cityscapes, his early performances were, along with his early musical output, truly groundbreaking.

He was the first western artist to play in China after the cultural revolution, performing in 1981 and beating Wham! (often incorrectly credited with being the first) by four years. He's also well known for one of his earliest tracks – **Oxygene IV** – which unfortunately, to a large extent, overshadowed the rest of his career to the ears of casual listeners.

Jarre had a phenomenal run of early albums including **Equinoxe**, **Magnetic Fields** and **Zoolook**, all of which were pioneering in the fields of electronic and ambient music and each featuring a palette of sounds unique to their respective album. Nobody was ploughing quite the same furrow as Jarre and his work was totally, uniquely brilliant. In the late '70s and 1980's the man was a giant, a god amongst lesser mortals.

Sadly, as time has progressed, Jarre's work has merged with the multitude of artists also focusing in electronic music, to the point where he now sounds exactly the same as everybody else. Even so, the man will always occupy a higher plane. Had he only ever recorded one album – **Zoolook**, in this instance – the man would still be a legend.

About This Song
Ethnicolor is perhaps a terrible choice for this book as it really wouldn't be considered a chart worthy piece of music in any regard, clocking in at over 11 and a half minutes. It's a lengthy composition that comes in two distinct halves, the first being an atmospheric soundtrack and the latter more traditional rock/pop instrumental. Personally, I love it and it's my favourite piece of music of all time. Even so, I probably won't convince many others to appreciate it as much as I do. But fuck it, I'll have a go anyway.

There is a 2018 official video for a version of the song clocking in at 3.30 mins. *(Quite why this track gets a video 34 years after it was originally released I don't know. Possibly, it was brought out for an airing to promote* The Connection Concert *but he absolutely mauls the track and it's sad to see how much he thinks he needs to portray himself as a geeky figure at mixing desks rather than as the orchestrator of a large band. For a track like* **Ethnicolor** *to work live a real bass is preferable but live drums are essential. Rant over. I wouldn't say it if I didn't care, Mr Jarre.)* Even more bizarrely, it's the first half of the composition that's been chosen for the video, which has surely been made with drug-tripping viewers in mind (and is very similar to the video put out by **Muse** a month later to promote *The Void*).

If you're going to give this track a listen – and that is the point of buying this book, surely? – then take a deep breath, find a comfy seat and listen to the whole thing. Some of you won't last to the end but for those that do I salute you.

My brother gets a couple of mentions in this book, most notably for pissing on Clint Mansell's leg, and he hates this track. He heard it so many times when we were young that it has burned itself onto a deep part of his brain and no amount of therapy or hypnosis will ever remove it. He already knows that if I die before him, I will force him to endure this song one last time, in its full glory, as part of my funeral service. He hates the track so much that he might try to die first, but if he doesn't then he will have this joy to look forward to in our futures. Well, his future anyway. I'll be dead.

Essential Album
Zoolook is my favourite album ever, and without it it's unlikely that I would have found my way to **Orbital**, **Banco de Gaia**, **The Prodigy** and **Nine Inch Nails**. Certainly, these bands (and pretty much any band producing electronic music) would not exist without Jarre first paving the way for more mainstream acceptance. *The album will be covered in more detail shortly, as a separate article in its own right within this book.*

Second Choice Song
Magnetic Fields Part IV was made as dawn was breaking on the emerging electronic music scene. Bands like **Kraftwerk** may have beaten him to the punch but in contrast their music sounds simplistic, and a little too clinical. Jarre brought a warmer palette to electronic music, and the sensibilities of a classical composer along with a complete mastery of the newly emerging synthesizers and the ability to construct larger pieces comprised of various movements.

Considering this track was released in 1981 it holds up surprisingly well. As with his other early albums, Jarre creates (or samples) a unique collection of sounds to build with and they still sound fresh today. It was almost a done deal that **Magnetic Fields Part I** would have taken this spot but it's another longer piece and I thought that was too risky a proposition. Please give it a listen though, especially the first section, it really is an astonishing piece of work.

Part IV is a more subdued, laid-back affair, and a truly gorgeous piece of music. It initially follows a traditional song setup with parts that act out verse, chorus and so on, adding little flourishes as the song progresses through its cycles. Around the halfway point the track changes tone as Jarre takes a musical diversion and somehow manages to completely change the track whilst keeping it the same. The later section brings in additional samples that shouldn't fit but do, culminating in the sound of a train eclipsing the music for a fade out. Bonkers but brilliant.

As a really random side note, Commodore 64 game *Yie Ar Kung Fu* had a main theme cover version of this Jarre track, programmed by Martin Galway on the C64's infamous SID chip*. It's a listen for those with a nerdy side and a quality piece of work.

The following year, Jarre would release **Arpegiator** (on his live **Concerts in China** album), an influence on many bands to follow, including Orbital (f. 1989), Banco de Gaia (f. 1989), The Prodigy (f. 1990) and so on. Jarre was massively influential even if you don't hear the cooler bands referencing his work. He was way ahead of his time and it's just a shame that time caught up with his output.

*

*(The SID chip attracted many talented musicians that might otherwise have found their way into more traditional avenues of making music. I had a ZX Spectrum and suffered through game soundtracks mostly made of single channel beeps, but I loved the rubber-keyed beastie too much to ditch it for the American import C64, even if the 3 channel tunes people were making on that were amazing. I still get goosebumps when listening to Rob Hubbard's **Commando** soundtrack, for example. To this day, people continue to produce tunes on the SID – someone even rebuilt the Nine Inch Nails debut album **Pretty Hate Machine** in SID code in its entirety!)*

INTERLUDE 3

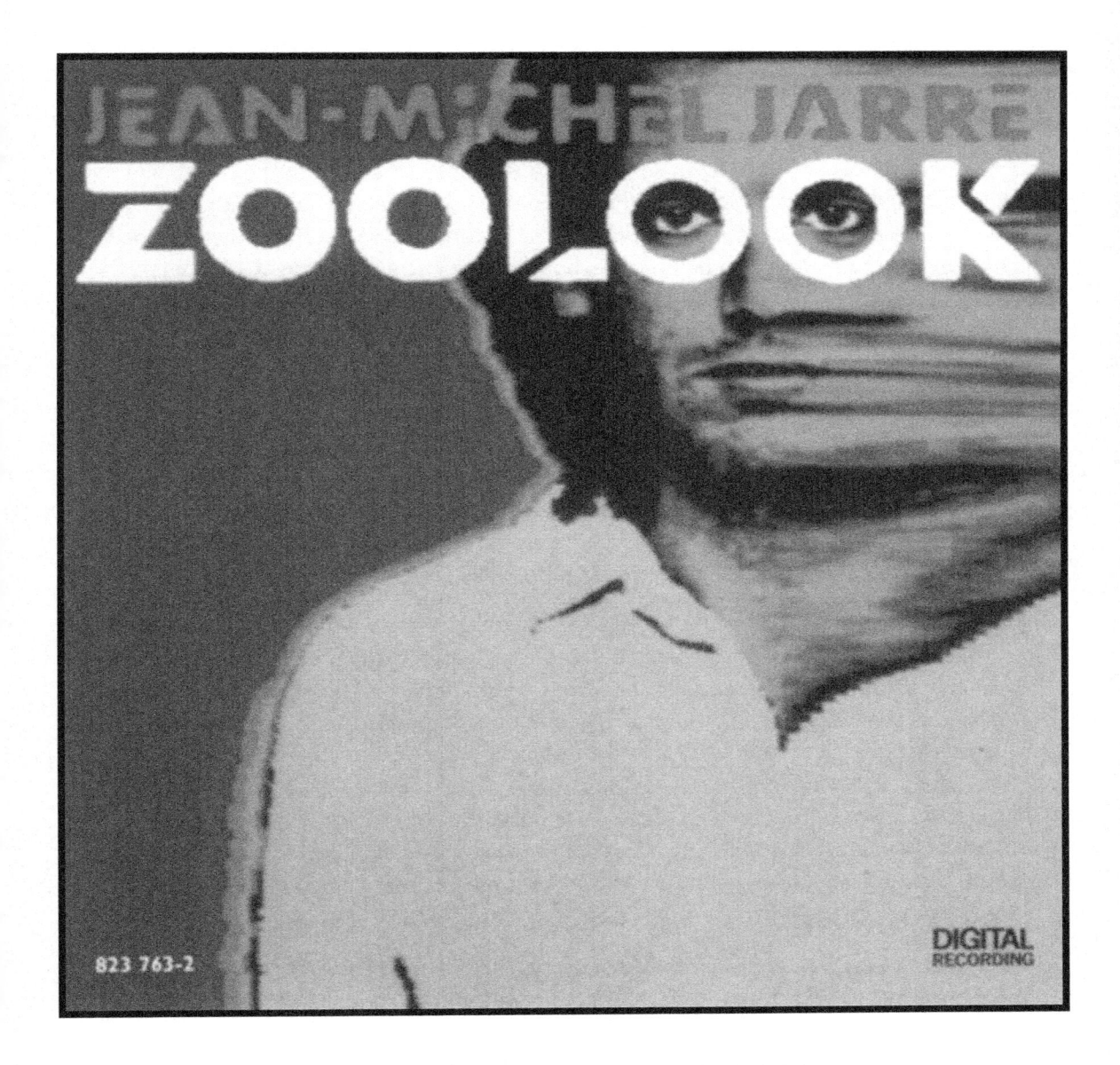

ALBUM SPOTLIGHT: ZOOLOOK

ALBUM SPOTLIGHT: ZOOLOOK

It starts with the sound of an elephant, or maybe even a mastodon. A haunting cry rings out across a sparse soundscape, a lonely desert in some electronic, prehistoric wilderness. Digitised voices lay out a wash of choral ambience. And then somebody starts singing about tits. Welcome to **Ethnicolor**, the opening track of the quintessential 1984 masterpiece **Zoolook** by French keyboard *maestro* Jean-Michel Jarre.

Any serious geeks will already be familiar with Jarre's back catalogue, up to and including **Zoolook**. It's hard to imagine a composer more agreeable to the sensibilities of the average geek, not only for his choice in unique sonic palettes but for the groundbreaking tech used for his compositions. Pictures of Jarre in the early days show him in a room surrounded by banks of keyboards, sequencing equipment, computer screens and wires – he looks like a French proto-Neo from the Matrix.

Before he was a global phenomenon hosting spectacular concerts in Paris, Houston and Moscow (which attracted a record-breaking audience of 3.5 million), Jarre was less known as a performer and more of an electronic *wunderkind*, having had enormous critical and commercial success with his 1976 low budget (home recorded) album **Oxygene**. One track simply titled **Oxygene IV** remains his most well-known composition, a poppy piece of instrumentalism that has provided background ambience to countless television commercials and between-programme links the world over. To date, the album has sold over 12 million copies.

In the UK, Jarre came to prominence at the same time as the emerging punk scene and his early albums were criticised (even derided) by the mainstream music press. The *NME* had written off **Oxygene** as *'just another interminable cosmic cruise'* and *Melody Maker* was even less kind to **Equinoxe**: *'Pseudo-galactically crass and vapid as last year's* **Oxygène**. *The melodies are trite, harmonies predictable, textures almost determindly hackneyed'*. This didn't stop millions of sales but it did mark Jarre as decidedly uncool, a view not helped by his hopeless fashion choices in jackets and hairstyles when he eventually stood in front of millions and unintentionally looked like a overly serious prat playing perhaps the most pretentious instrument ever invented - the laser-harp.

Retrospective reviews of his early work have been kinder and have recognised his pioneering use of electronic music and sampling techniques, and his canon has arguably been hugely influential – it's hard to imagine bands like Orbital, the Prodigy and even Nine Inch Nails existing without Jarre's groundwork. A track like Eat Static's **Survivors** arguably wouldn't exist without like Jarre's **Arpegiator** providing the evolutionary blueprint.

And things come full circle, as they always do. Bands that have sampled Jarre's music for use in their own compositions include Norweigan electronic artists Röyksopp, The Future Sound of London , a plethora of semi-professional musicians self-publishing tracks on websites such as *Soundcloud* and, perhaps bizarrely, Jarre himself (on many occasions).

So why single out **Zoolook** from all his other work to lavish with geeky praise? Arguably his least known and least commercially successful album it sounds like nothing recorded before or since and stands alone even in Jarre's discography. Built around samples of speech from 25 different languages, little of what you hear makes any kind of sense and the mood alternates between upbeat, funky pop and weird soundscapes that could comfortably provide the soundtrack to any number of art-house films.

From the child's creepy laughter in **Diva** and the sample of pouring water in **Blah-Blah Café**, to the exquisite gong that marks the entry into the second half of **Ethnicolor** – a sound buried so deep in the mix it's barely audible – there isn't a wasted note on the entire album. A prevailing sense of sadness hangs over long stretches of the music, evoking an air of melancholy, of loneliness, of creatures on some exotic migration that will ultimately lead to their extinction.

And that's one of the great things about this album, especially when listened to in its entirety – it becomes a soundtrack to your own imagination, where personal meaning is formed from an interpretation of the essentially meaningless lyrical samples, and your mind drifts and melds with the music. Conversely, a handful of tracks could easily sound perfectly at home in a dance-oriented nightclub. Even today, this album is one artefact from the Eighties that hasn't dated – it could be released a decade from now and still sound fresh, and is one of a small number of albums recorded in that particular decade that has stood the test of time so well.

Although Jarre's previous albums had been solo affairs, **Zoolook** marked a real departure in the recording process. He brought in session musicians and instruments more suited for a traditional recording artist. And these session musicians weren't just any old journeymen but internationally renowned recording artists in their own right.

On guitars, Adrian Belew had already worked with Frank Zappa, David Bowie, King Crimson and **Talking Heads** (whose 1982 album *Remain in Light* soars in part thanks to Belew's contributions). It's easy to imagine this particular album having a profound effect on Jarre and the monumental change in attitude and direction that led to **Zoolook**.

Marcus Miller has played bass guitar on more than five hundred tracks by other artists and is a writer/producer who has worked with the likes of Miles Davis, Aretha Franklin,

Jay-Z and Snoop Dog. This is a man so talented (and busy) that he probably doesn't even remember the sublime bass parts laid out on **Zoolook**, but nonetheless these remain integral to the record's identity. Frankly, without Miller's exceptionally funky basslines and Yogi Horton's spectacular drumming driving sections of the album, it's fair to say that **Zoolook** would have been merely a very interesting recording experiment rather than the masterpiece it turned into.

For an album that casual listeners often overlook, Zoolook just keeps coming back. **Blah-Blah Café** and parts of **Diva** originally appeared on the album **Music for Supermarkets** (1983), noted for Jarre's unusual approach to marketing by being broadcast once on radio (for the benefit of anybody wishing to pirate it) and then the only pressing being sold at a charity auction whilst the master tapes were destroyed.

Zoolook debuted a year later and has since been reissued a further 3 times (the last being a 2014 30th anniversary edition). The one to seek out is the second edition released in 1985 featuring slightly beefed up remixes of the title track and **Zoolookologie** (itself rewritten and re-released by Jarre himself on the 2004 compilation album *Aero*).

This album deserves to be remembered. It deserves to be adored. Download it and lose yourself in the tumbling rhythms of **Ethnicolor**, the funk of **Zoolookologie**. Let us keep listening, long into the future, until the world around us resembles the bleak landscapes suggested in **Wooloomooloo** and **Ethnicolor II**. And try to suppress a snigger when someone keeps singing about tits.

PRODIGY

THE DAY IS MY ENEMY

PRODIGY – THE DAY IS MY ENEMY

About the Band

Prodigy emerged from the underground UK rave scene in the early 1990's. An explosion in the availability of ecstasy meant that empty fields in the middle of nowhere suddenly became a most attractive proposition for tens of thousands of wide eyed youngsters who wanted nothing more than to hear a certain type of new music and dance the night away. Previously they would have probably been falling in gutters, fucking in the bushes and fighting in the streets but ecstasy brushed aside all of that muck and filth and made everybody love each other.

And Prodigy loved the scene. Four young men from the Cambridge / Essex / London area of the UK gravitated towards these fields and warehouses and songwriter Liam Howlett drew inspiration to come up with an album's worth of material.

But initial tracks like **Charly** and **Out of Space** gained an unwanted reputation for the band as *'kiddie-rave'* merchants and something to not be taken seriously. This view changed overnight with the release of their second album, the epic, genre crossover masterpiece **Music for the Jilted Generation**. Howlett's song-writing skills had acquired depth and complexity, and the album was nominated for a *Mercury Music Prize*. As their discography grew in the years that followed it became blatantly obvious that Prodigy were anything but novelty record merchants.

Over time, founding member Leeroy Thornhill left and the band coalesced as a three piece. Keith Flint and Maxim Reality took a more active role in the music side of things, particularly with regard to adding vocals. Flint completely reinvented himself with a punk makeover for the 1996 **Firestarter** single and the iconic video catapulted the band into the mainstream. The accompanying album titled **The Fat of the Land** entered the UK and US charts at #1, and gained controversial press coverage for the choice of **Smack My Bitch Up** as a single.

Quality dipped very slightly for the next 2 albums, both featuring some excellent tracks but with weaker compositions padding out the long players. An interim singles collection and a live dvd kept the fans ticking over before 2015's **The Day is My Enemy** delivered the corking title track – see below - along with **Ibiza** (featuring Sleaford Mods) and *Wild Frontier* (with a superb accompanying stop-motion animated video).

Their most recent album **No Tourists** underwhelmed the critics and underperformed commercially, although like every album released by the band since Jilted Generation they had all topped the UK charts, so underperforming in the Prodigy's sense is always going to be a comparison against the crazy success of the Fat of the Land, still the band's high water mark.

In 2019, founding member Keith Flint committed suicide, a truly shocking moment for fans of the band and one that still seems a little unreal to this day.   Prodigy continues with founder members Howlett and Maxim, with additional members for live shows.

About This Song
Choosing two songs from their collected works is difficult – the group have an embarrassing amount of superb tracks in their inventory. Ultimately, I chose **The Day is My Enemy** as the main track, it being representative of everything the group does well. It's dark, heavy, unsettling and is one of their many tracks that sounds even more sensational the louder it gets. It opens with droning bass notes beneath drums that sound like a maniac hammering on your front door at 3am.

The vocals, performed by Martina Topley-Bird and borrowed from a Cole Porter song, add a nice feminine touch to counterbalance the otherwise unrelenting brutality. To clarify, 'unrelenting brutality' here is a compliment.

With many of the best Prodigy songs, Howlett manages to wring a totally unique soundscape, predominantly from computers and samples, and TDIME sounds like something only The Prodigy could produce. It's a powerful, flawless piece of music, a thing of great beauty.

Essential Album
Whilst **The Fat of the Land** is their commercial high point, earlier album **Music For The Jilted Generation** is the work that solidified their reputation as serious artists. Rooted firmly in dance music territory, it contains 12 tracks and is a superb listen from top to bottom.

Essential cuts include **Voodoo People**, **No Good (Start the Dance)**, **Poison** and **Break & Enter**. The track **Their Law** features a collaboration with Pop Will Eat Itself, themselves a band who built songs heavily influenced by the art of sampling.

Jilted Generation was critically well received, getting recognition from major influencers like *Rolling Stone, Mojo, Spin* and *NME*. Although not fully crossing over into the mainstream, it gained the band a solid fan base and paved the way for follow-up album, **The Fat of the Land**, to be a huge success.

Second Choice Song
I'm not being controversial for the sake of it, I'm choosing **Smack My Bitch Up** because it's a terrific composition and never fails to sound 10 out of 10 awesome whenever I play it. Which is often.

To truly appreciate the genius of this song, I recommend watching DJ and producer Jim Pavloff's YouTube video *Making of The Prodigy - Smack My Bitch Up in Ableton*. Pavvloff deconstructs the sound and shows where Howlett procured his samples. In front of your very eyes, over the duration of 10 minutes, Pavloff rebuilds the song from scratch and shows you how it was done.

To some people, this might remove all of the mystery and weaken the track. Once they see how it's done, they might think how easy it all is and their impression of Howlett might be diminished. That would be a mistake. For me, watching the process of how a brilliant track gets made only heightens my respect for the person that made it.

For **Smack My Bitch Up**, Howlett uses samples for bands as diverse as Kool and the Gang, Randy Weston, Coldcut, Rage Against The Machine, and Ultramagnetic MC's (for the controversial vocal line).

To have the ability to rework tiny bits of other people's records, and mould the sounds into something for your own purposes, and then make a song unlike anything that's ever been made before AND have it be as great as SMBU – that takes some serious skill.

Like many other tracks in this book, I am recommending that you watch the accompanying video. The song got a lot of negative press and accusations followed about misogynism and violence against women, which are obviously all virtuous things to get upset about. In the US, chain retailers like *Kmart* and *Walmart* pulled the album from sale. And the controversy grew white hot with the release of the video, a first-person perspective of a night of excessive hedonism involving snorting coke, grabbing at women, puking down a toilet and taking a woman home for sex but watching her gyrating naked first. And then comes the video ending, turning everything you've just seen on its head and somehow making the whole thing even more shocking. But this is cartoon violence, not a statement of intent as such. Interestingly, the song or the video didn't seem to attract much in the way of complaints from the record buying public, only from journalists looking for sensationalist stories to help sell their newspapers. All of which is a long-winded way of saying watch the video – it's ace.

MIKE OLDFIELD

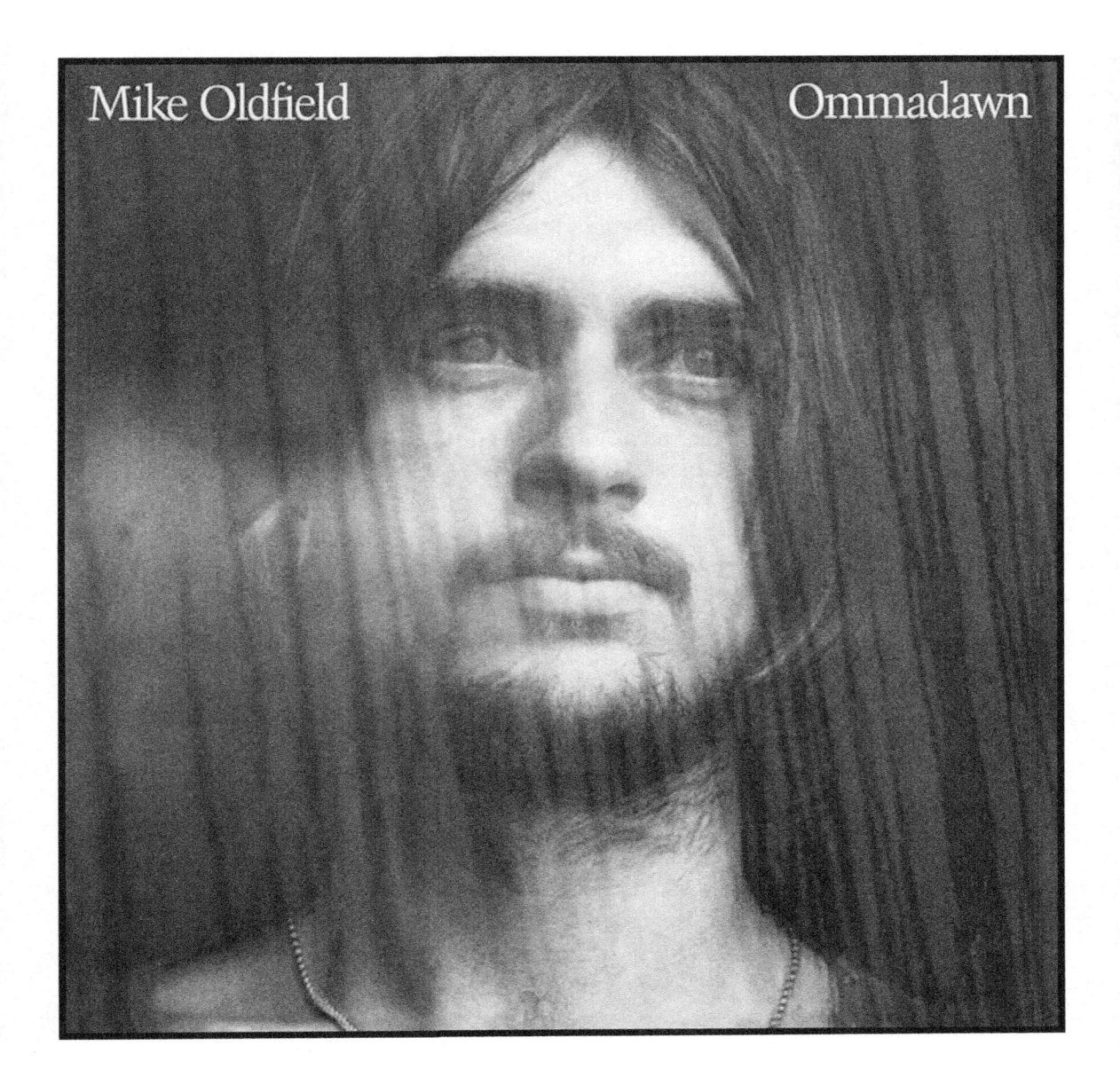

OMMADAWN

MIKE OLDFIELD - OMMADAWN

About the Artist

Mike Oldfield is primarily known for the album **Tubular Bells**, a 1973 vinyl disc consisting of two long instrumental pieces of music, one each side. It was the first release of Richard Branson's new *Virgin* label and basically kept the company afloat for a couple of years whilst Branson learned the ropes. In the UK alone it sold 2.7 million copies (and 18 million worldwide) and is still one of the top 50 albums with most sales to this day.

Oldfield was a determined and willful young man. I use the past tense there not because he's dead but because an Exegesis retreat fundamentally changed the way he interacted with the world. As a schoolchild, he was playing acoustic guitar by the age of 10. When the headmaster of his school told him to cut his long hair short, Oldfield upped and left the school and made the decision to become a full-time musician. He was 15.

A stint in a band with his sister led to a tour of England and Paris and an album release with a major label. A year later, the band split and Oldfield had a nervous breakdown. A shy, sensitive young man, his early family life involved dealing with a younger sibling born with Downs Syndrome that died at the age of seven and a mother addicted to barbiturates and with significant mental health issues. It all caught up with him and added to his sense of isolation and alienation.

The next few years saw him working with various bands, recording other people's music and compiling a demo reel of his own. Early influences include Celtic and classical genres, tribal music and more regular 1970's fare in Led Zeppelin and Free. A couple of engineers at Branson's recording studio *The Manor* heard the demos and took them to their boss, who gave Oldfield a week's worth of studio time to lay down a recording of what would become the first half of **Tubular Bells** part I. The second half was recorded after more studio time was given and Oldfield found himself with another record deal.

Tubular Bells featured Oldfield playing the majority of instruments himself, including acoustic and electric guitars, a mandolin, bass, keyboards and the instrument of the title. The album was a success and received a huge sales boost when the piano section was chosen as the theme for the 1973 horror film *The Exorcist*, ultimately leading to it being a constant in the UK charts for an entire year and a number three spot on the *US Billboard 200*. BBC music show *The Old Grey Whistle Test* (commissioned by David Attenborough!) brought his music to a wider audience by including an excerpt of Tubular Bells with a stock footage backing video of skiers, and the BBC once again delivered a full broadcast of the entirety of side one – played live! - with Oldfield on acoustic guitar and then on bass for the final section. And right there is an incredible feat of endurance all bassists would be proud to achieve, handled superbly by Oldfield.

He went on to record a number of seminal instrumental albums featuring longer compositions on each side. **Hergest Ridge**, **Ommadawn** (*see below*) and **Incantations** cemented his reputation as a world class musician and recording artist but they didn't achieve the same commercial success as his debut.

Around this time, the chronically shy Oldfield attended a life-changing *Exegesis* seminar, a three day self-assertiveness programme that attracted much controversy, parliamentary hostility and a police enquiry. Whatever they were doing, and whether it was a cult or a religion, it worked spectacularly well for Oldfield.

Attendees were invited to workshop through their worst fears, and to quote Oldfield himself: *'It was like opening some huge cathedral doors and facing the monster, and I saw that the monster was myself as a newborn infant, because I'd started life in a panic.'* He was obviously carrying a lot of baggage from his childhood into his adult life, and the three day seminar was a transformative, *'rebirthing experience'*. Oldfield, previously shy and reclusive to hermit-like levels, suddenly blossomed into a confident young man that had no problem going off drinking with music journalists, or giving press interviews, or participating in promotional photo shoots. He even conquered a fear of flying, bought a plane and learned to fly it!

With 1979's **Platinum** (*see Essential Album below*), Oldfield changed his approach to include shorter songs, although they could still be classed as longer pieces broken into sections. Side one includes four parts that incorporate rock, pop and jazz elements, with initial track **Airborne** becoming the theme tune for a UK children's TV quiz show called *First Class*. One of his recordings, a version of Ashworth Hope's **Barnacle Bill**, was also the theme to popular show *Blue Peter* for many years between 1979-1989.

More albums followed, and Oldfield took to having a long piece form the first half of each, with the latter half featuring shorter songs that began to include vocal performances and do well in the singles charts. The album **QE2** was followed by **Five Miles Out**, the gatefold cover of which featured a track sheet for main song **Taurus 2**, and it's a diagram that stayed with me ever since. If any readers use music software such as *Ableton*, you'll recognise a primitive version of a music track blueprint featuring a timeline and separate rows for each instrument. The cover image was very cool too, as was the album's title song.

Crises, released in 1983, featured his bestselling single **Moonlight Shadow** with vocalist Maggie Reilly, which topped the charts in nine countries (not his own though, it peaked at four in the UK), followed by another smash hit (again with Reilly on vocals) in **To France**, taken from the **Discovery** album. Reilly sang on other Oldfield hits including **Family Man** and **Foreign Affair** and worked with other artists including The Sisters Of Mercy on their **Vision Thing** album (see elsewhere in this book).

Oldfield's working relationship with *Virgin* came to a close in 1991. He bore a grudge about the way Branson and his label had treated him when punk came along, choosing to hitch their wagon to this new style of music and more or less ignore the very artist who'd reliably supplied them with numerous hit records and kept them afloat in the early years. Oldfield was totally baffled by Punk, suffering popularity/credibility-wise in its wake and he resented it intensely. He was a musical prodigy, and innately a craftsman, but almost overnight his skill-set and more deliberate approach was deemed redundant and old hat.

Virgin had asked him to use the **Tubular Bells II** title for a new album, to which Oldfield not only refused but then released a somewhat difficult album to listen to (**Amarok**) with a buried morse code message for Branson himself: '*Fuck off RB.*' Oldfield apparently worked hard to ensure that it would be difficult to cut anything like a single from the work and Virgin gave up and underpromoted the album. It was the last one he would record for that label.

He signed to *Warner* and released... **Tubular Bells II**. Yeah, fuck off Branson! Over the years, Oldfield released a number of other records trading in on the popularity of his debut, including a third album, an orchestral version of the first album and a complete re-recording of the original again using modern equipment.

Returning to earlier work is something that he's not afraid to do, culminating in his final release in 2017 with **Return to Ommadawn**. As of writing in 2023, Oldfield is officially retired with no plans to release further music.

To me, Oldfield joins Jean Michel Jarre as a pillar of my musical education, having discovered both of these artists as a child and borrowing their records from my local library. As a youngster with no meaningful musical knowledge, I was primarily motivated in borrowing the records because of the sleeve artwork. My musical tastes could have gone in so many musical directions based on that policy but thankfully it worked out alright for me. Getting older, I eventually moved onto more contemporary alternative music, starting with The Cure and Buzzcocks and many of the bands in this book, but Oldfield and Jarre (particularly Jarre) always stayed with me. I see the things they were doing some forty years ago still being copied by bands to this day. These two artists may stand out a little in this book, surrounded by band such as Revolting Cocks, Sisters of Mercy and Primus, but there are echoes and connections between them and they deserve their space here.

About This Song
For a portrait of the artist as a young man, look no further than the LP cover for **Ommadawn**, where a sad-faced, long-haired Oldfield (photographed by David Bailey) stares through a rain-spotted window at the world outside. Although the album is

great, I'm going to focus on the **Ommadawn Excerpt** section, the latter section of Part One which begins around the 12 minute mark and completes seven minutes later.

Oldfield mixes African tribal drums with Irish folk music and rock guitar. There are lyrics, of a sort, at first coming across like nonsense words but actually English words translated into Irish (sort of). Once you know what the words mean, they kind of lose that layer of mystery, which is why I won't put them down here.

Ab yul ann idyad awt
En yab na log a toc na awd
Taw may on omma dawn ekyowl
Omma dawn ekyowl
Ommadawn © Mike Oldfield

There's an air of melancholy, of sadness hanging over the tune, which builds and builds into something resembling mania, or even madness, and a guitar solo that Oldfield admits nearly gave him another nervous breakdown. It's an incredibly charged piece of music, one that you can put on loud and easily fully immerse yourself into and get lost in.

Undoubtedly contributing to the emotional feel of the album was the death of Oldfield's mother. The final recording seems to bear the weight of this loss. Retreating into the recording process helped him to deal with the bereavement process and provided a level of comfort that might have been hard to find elsewhere.

Many artists process the concept of death through their work, not least because it gives them something to do whilst the world has fallen apart, and the brutal reality of this fact is that creative endeavours laden with the weight of such contemplations become more emotionally complex as a result. As a crass generalisation (that holds an element of truth), happy people do not make great art.

Whilst recording **Ommadawn**, a great deal of early work was ruined as the recording tapes began to disintegrate (possibly due to the many overdubs used as part of the complex recording process) and he had to start over from scratch. Thankfully, in this digital age, those kinds of problems no longer exist for artists.

It is a haunting, beautiful piece of music and one of my all-time favourites. There was no way this book was going to be written without including it.

Essential Album

Of course, I should be saying **Tubular Bells**, the one that started it all. I'll let you discover that one in your own time. Oldfield has released a lot of varied music and covered a lot of styles. A perfect example of an Oldfield album would be **Discovery**, the first where he flips the usual presentation of music so that the pop stuff are the first tracks you hear with longer instrumental piece **The Lake,** now relegated to side two. It's a clear shift in direction and how his music would be marketed to focus on the potential hit singles. It's also a great album.

My personal favourite though, is **Platinum**. Weirdly, I don't think much of the second half of the album, and actually hated the twee **Punkadiddle** track so much that it became a terrorist weapon for me – when burning my brother music cd's, I'd occasionally drop Punkadiddle in as a hidden track in the hope that he'd be playing the disc in public and this would come on and embarrass him. We had a fun youth. (The track was a sort of protest song for Oldfield, a parody of punk rock songs which really didn't resonate in any way with me).

Side one though, made up of four tracks that flow as a larger piece, is amazing. Starting with the heavier rock guitar of **Airborne**, we transition beautifully into a funky pop piece (titular track **Platinum**) with some doo-wop vocals at the end, which turns into a jazz exercise called **Charleston** before the soaring finale of **North Star** (which incorporates elements of a Philip Glass piece of the same name). Together, the lot clocks in at slightly over 19 minutes but what a journey you've been on.

You can pick out individual tracks, or play them in a different order, but a nice sit down and a listen to them in the order they are laid out on the album will be a rewarding and refreshing experience. It's one that's served me well for nearly 40 years and I'm still not bored of it.

Second Choice Song

Covered above - I'm picking 4 songs as 1, which is cheating slightly but I'm going to do it anyway. See **Airborne/Platinum/Charleston/North Star** above.

THE SISTERS OF MERCY

THIS CORROSION

THE SISTERS OF MERCY – THIS CORROSION

About the Band

Led by the dictatorial Dark Lord Andrew Eldritch, the Sisters of Mercy have had a number of incarnations, with acrimonious splits and long-standing grudges with ex-members through the years. Former band members went on to create successful bands in The Mission and Ghost Dance. With a total of three studio albums to their name, each one recorded with a different line-up, the only static members throughout were Eldritch and the drum machine known as Doktor Avalanche (although, like the *Dread Pirate Roberts* ideology, various machines have been used but kept the same name).

The group achieved initial success in the Leeds underground scene, and a number of single releases gave them traction in the Indie charts. Early singles include **Damage Done**, **Body Electric** and a pair of power hitters in **Alice** and **Temple of Love**. Temple of Love was rerecorded in 1992 and featured legendary Israeli vocalist Ofra Haza, who was also the vocalist sampled on The Prodigy's **Smack My Bitch Up** discussed elsewhere in this book. (Haza was a phenomenal singer who sadly died way too young aged 42 in 2000).

In 1985 they released the **First and Last and Always** album, a standout offering that helped to define the era of Goth. Band personnel for this recording is often referred to as the 'classic' line-up, consisting of Eldritch, Craig Adams on bass, Gary Marx and Wayne Hussey on guitar and Avalanche on drum duties. Eldritch, like many of his contemporaries ploughing similar musical furrows, has always refuted the Goth associations but that's always struck me as somewhat biting the hand that feeds him. There's nothing wrong with the Goth label, then or now.

After multiple fallings out, a new and radically different version of the Sisters appeared in 1987. Eldritch emerged from the strobe lights and dry ice to become more of a showman, still dressed in black leather and wearing his customary shades but now accompanied by goth glamour girl Patricia Morrison, who contributed the striking basslines and backing vocals heard on the **Floodland** album. Singles included the excellent **This Corrosion** and **Lucretia (My Reflection),** and Meat Loaf producer Jim Steinman worked on This Corrosion and **Dominion/Mother Russia**, bringing an element of over-the-top pomp-rock to proceedings for a while. If you've ever heard any Sisters music, it's likely to be a track from this period.

In 1990, their third and final studio album emerged with another change of personnel, once again back to a full band line up with new guitarist Andreas Bruhn (whom Eldritch had discovered in a German pub) and bassist Tony James (ex Sigue Sigue Sputnik). They were also joined by Tim Bricheno (ex All About Eve) on guitar. They toured and promoted new album **Vision Thing**, a more straightforward rock effort than anything they had recorded before. Touring ran into difficulties when they partnered up with Public Enemy, with some North American cities banning the shows under the pretext of avoiding any violent clashes between the two different fan bases.

After a long period touring, Eldritch sacked off his management company after discovering that the band were still broke. Shortly after, the band started to disintegrate and by late 1993 Eldritch was at war with his record company and stating publicly that no more Sisters material would be released. And that's exactly what happened. Although technically still a live touring band, still performing as of 2023, no new recorded material is yet forthcoming and the material they play is generally 30 years old (or older).

As a side note, the band were noted for their cover versions, sometimes choosing songs completely at odds with their perceived image – Dolly Parton's **Jolene**, for instance, or **Emma** by Hot Chocolate. They have also played live **Gimme Shelter** (Rolling Stones) and **1969** (The Stooges). Of these, Jolene is arguably the best, and easily found on YouTube.

About This Song
When you talk about this band, it's the elephant in the room. **This Corrosion** casts a long shadow over everything else they've done and any discussion about the band has to reach this song at some point, usually near the beginning. There's no point even considering another song until we've dealt with this one.

It's arguably the best thing they ever recorded. There, I said it. Hardcore fans are probably ripping up this book in disgust to hear me say that but it's true.   The radio edit at four minutes is a great tune but I'm going to choose the extended version that clocks in at just under 11 minutes.

It begins with a clap of thunder and a layered choir singing something that sounds like it could be the soundtrack to a 1970's horror film. Then, in bursts the bassline, sounding synthetic but played by Morrison (who hilariously stated in a 1988 interview that she originally wanted to be a veterinarian but didn't have the money so ended up doing this instead). The drums are loud and crisp, also high in the mix. Together, they form the engine of the song and infuse the Sisters with a little bit of funk. It's worth noting that the singles from the **Floodland** album, which include this song, are the only ones of the band to get positions in the US dance chart, the news of which must have brought a temporary rainbow to the skies of Leeds.

The song throws in an anthemic chorus, long guitar solos, more choral riffs with backing vocals that sound like they're pulled from a pop song, all overlaid with that Steinman production. All of these elements work together beautifully, creating a truly distinctive song, one that easily plays for 11 minutes without getting boring. It's not an overstatement to call this tune 'epic'. I'll leave the last word to a YouTuber and his comment:

@hide904 *I accidentally listened to this song when I was fifteen and it shaped my music taste forever.*

Essential Album
With only 3 to choose from, and each sounding so distinctive from each other, it's a hard choice to make. Debut LP **First and Last and Always** distils the essence of the band at that period of existence into 10 classic tunes. Being honest, their name would have been cemented in goth lore forever if they'd released only this (and the preceding E.P's and singles) and disappeared. It's important to note that all of the early hits weren't included on this album, which retrospectively seems like a mistake. Production costs meant the band made no money on initial sales but eventually did when UK sales reached 100,000 and sales in Germany 250,000.

Floodland has some great singles and an epic feel, but all that bombast can become a bit tiresome before the album plays out. Special mention goes to **Neverland (A Fragment)**, an edit of a much longer (demo) version that didn't surface until the 2006 remaster of the album. If you had to pick a Sisters track that was the most Sisters, this would be it. Sheer genius and very effectively used in an episode of *American Horror Story*'s season *Hotel*.

It's surprising, then, that I'm going to pick what might be their weakest album, **Vision Thing**, but I feel it's the most accessible to a new listener. It rocks out, still retaining some of the edge of First and Last and some of the pomp of Floodland, but is its own beast entirely. The result of a painful recording process, songs were dragged out of the band and some finalised versions were replaced by earlier mixes for the album because they sounded better.

There are some really decent tunes on the album. **More** utilised the talents of Jim Steinman once again and it shows. Built around a violin and piano riff, it brings in some gospel-lite backing singing and might even be the best track. Competition comes from headliner **Vision Thing**, Eldritch's protest song to voice his disgust at the Bush administration. Although not a single, it perhaps should have been. It features the classic opening line *'25 whores in the room next door'* and starts with a high level of energy that it retains right through.

Ribbons is a really good tune as well, but immediately after the quality dips a little with the formulaic **Detonation Boulevard** and doesn't quite recover until **Doctor Jeep** (track six) and follow-on More. Overall the album is a mixed bag but the stronger tracks save the album and if you've not heard the band before it offers a really good starting point.

If you like this, you'll find the other albums worth continuing your journey for.

Second Choice Song
We're going to go all the way back to 1982 for my second choice, for a true classic and an iconic goth anthem. Eldritch, usually a perfectionist that would do many retakes of songs until he was finally happy, who admitted that lyrics could sometimes take six months to coalesce in his mind, apparently knocked out **Alice** on a Leeds sofa, with a *Woolworths* guitar, in 10 minutes flat.

It opens with a simple drum machine loop, instantly recognisable if you're already a fan. Guitar and bass notes mark an extension of the intro before fully kicking in. Compared to later records, the production here feels a little tinny and lightweight, which is an unfortunate consequence of making this recording at the beginning of their career with little studio money. Just turn it up a little bit louder and change the EQ settings on your player of choice to compensate.

The first section of the song, where a verse would normally be sung, is instrumental. The guitars are great, typical Sisters and the style that influenced a thousand other goth bands that followed in their wake, but it's the bass guitar that steals the show with this song, as Craig Adams' playing drives the song forwards in relentless fashion. Eldritch's deep vocals tell of a young girl, Alice, politely yearning for tranquilisers whilst wearing a party dress. More goth nonsense, of course, but sang earnestly enough to sell it, to evoke something Kubrickian, something out of *The Shining* maybe.

When I said earlier that **This Corrosion** might be the best thing the Sisters ever recorded? I was wrong. This is.

CARDIACS

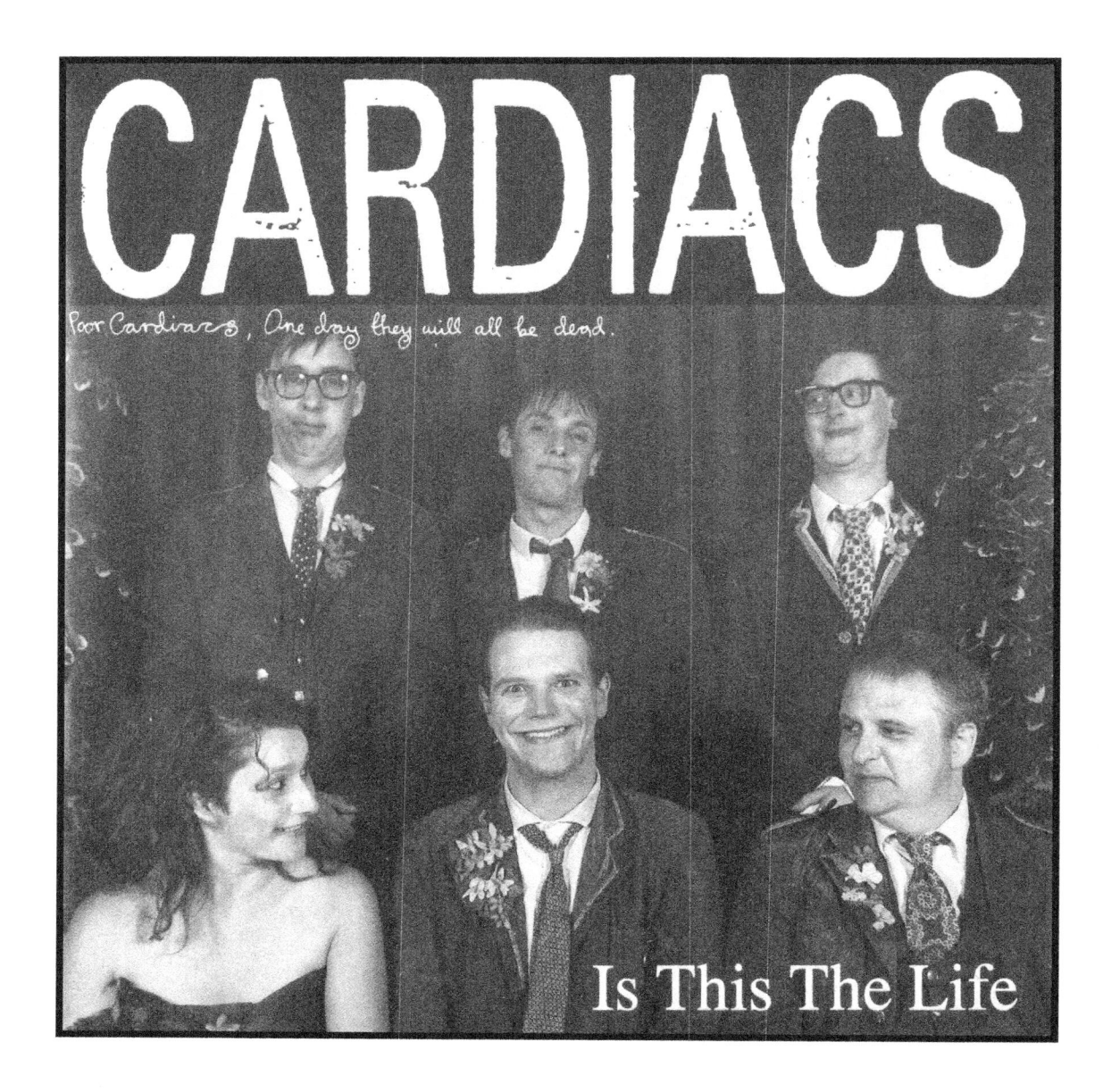

IS THIS THE LIFE

CARDIACS – IS THIS THE LIFE

About the Band

We've seen some pretty strange bands in this book so far. Hopefully you've welcomed a bit of **Primus** into your lives and marvelled at the eccentricities of **Ween**. For all their oddness, such bands can become at least partially palatable to the masses (with a bit of effort and the right tracks). This is, after all, the purpose of this book.

I am highlighting songs that could be shoehorned into the pop category to some degree. I'm not going to try and persuade you to swim in the deep, dark (and frankly unfathomable) waters of, say, Scandinavian Black Metal. Some things are, for the average person, unlistenable – most of us lack the patience, curiosity or willingness to try and understand what some of these extreme fringe bands are all about. Whilst **Cardiacs** aren't unlistenable by any means, they embrace such an oddball approach to creating music that it can all become a little bit too much for most people.

The band employ many different tempos, time signatures and changes of style – often in the same song. At times flirting with punk, heavy rock, prog-rock and psychedelia, they don't limit themselves to any particular genre. A few of their earlier songs sometimes have a whiff of **The Cure**, or even **Madness** about them (*and Blur were certainly listening closely for future reference*) whilst some sound like the soundtrack to a film about toys on a rampage. Or maybe a Joe Pasquale parody, or a nightmare funfair, and bits that sound like *Britpop* played by inmates of an insane asylum… As creators of music, Cardiacs are both exhilarating and exhausting to listen to.

They have a small, very dedicated following who absolutely love them, and a surprising number of artists consider them an influence, but the world at large has mostly ignored their musical offerings.

This wasn't helped by the way the band was treated by the music press in their early days. It's fair to say that the three main music papers back in the 1980's and early 1990's – *NME*, *Melody Maker* and *Sounds* – were populated with quite a few elitist types experimenting with the nature of music journalism. They were constantly trying to make a 'scene' out of bands nobody but punters who favoured the drinking dens of Camden Lock would even be aware of. Front covers would sometimes feature bands who had only been seen by a few journalists, some bar staff and a couple of tramps. I remember reading reviews of albums by my favourite bands at the time and ending up enraged that some dickhead had wasted 800 words on an essay about some abstract concept rather than simply telling me what the record sounded like and why I should rush out and buy it.

However good the music, or however great the live shows, the music press seemed to completely ignore Cardiacs, or even go out of their way to actively censor their existence. They were just the wrong side of the musical tectonic plates shifting and splitting the landscape into punk, post-punk, new wave and so on whilst the unfashionable yesteryear of more layered, experimental progressive music was scathingly condemned to the dumpster of musical history.

Crowds they played to could be hostile, bewildered by their approach to performing. Dressed in odd uniforms and covered in reams of badly applied make-up, often acting out characters from their own *Alphabet Business Concern* soap opera that baffled nearly everyone, audiences found themselves confronted with a level of mania they weren't expecting – pre-Internet with no press coverage, if you weren't one of the tiny minority already in the know, your expectations of a straightforward concert were going to be dashed. If you didn't know it was an act, the sight of singer Tim Smith heaping tons of abuse on the portly bass player (his brother Jim) would have been shocking.

A Cardiff slot supporting Marillion resulted in an increasingly disturbed audience pelting the shit out of them with whatever they could find to throw, and a separate gig on the same tour saw audience members committing arson, setting alight a stage curtain in an attempt to stop the band playing. That's a hell of a reaction, and some bands go out of their way to cultivate such madness, but it just seemed to be a by-product of Cardiacs trying to make a living.

The band was put on permanent hold in 2008 after co-founder and lead vocalist Smith suffered a heart attack and multiple strokes after a My Bloody Valentine concert, resulting in crippling dystonia. It's an incredibly sad turn of events and one that left Smith trapped inside his own frozen body for over a decade, cutting down a vibrant forty-seven year old man and taking away his ability to not only make music but to express himself or even communicate to any significant degree.

The way the world really felt about Smith and his music emerged in the aftermath of this catastrophe. *The Guardian* newspaper offered some rare mainstream praise in an article highlighting a tribute album. Thirty-five artists and bands expressed interest in putting together a record, covering Smith's songs and using the profits to help fund his medical treatment. It was a show of unity that brought tears to Smith's eyes when he heard the results.

He never fully recovered and died in 2020 aged just 59, leaving behind a body of work that is testament to one of Britain's most ignored and misunderstood creative artists.

My including the band in this book is a small attempt at putting a spotlight on them, however dim or fleeting. I only knew them at the time for the single **Is This The Life**, which to me was great but just one more great tune in a sea of intensely brilliant music coming out at the time (like all music is to all adolescents, where musical tastes are forged and songs burn deeper impressions at this time than any other). Back then, I could afford to not try and get into Cardiacs because there were so many other bands taking up bandwidth. The lack of press coverage didn't help to keep any flicker of interest alive. So, I forgot about them until I started working on this book and revisited that single, discovering that time had been very kind and I fell in love with it.

Although they may not be overly popular (maybe this book will change that!) their legacy is huge, having influenced an incredibly diverse number of other bands, including Faith No More, Blur, Napalm Death, Radiohead, Biffy Clyro and Tool just for starters. All hail Cardiacs, we may never see their like again.

About This Song
Is This The Life is one of Cardiacs' most accessible, straightforward songs. It may even be their only one. Released in 1988, peaking at number 80 in the UK charts after decent airplay on *Radio 1* (and a run of four months in the Indie Charts), sales stalled after all available copies of the single sold out – not enough copies were initially pressed after anticipated demand for Kylie's latest took over the pressing equipment.

The song also featured on a VHS compilation of bands (**Indie Top Video – Take One**) and held its place amongst the crowd. No mean feat considering there were songs from Pop Will Eat Itself, Fields of the Nephilim and A Guy Called Gerald on there as well. As a youth, I lost count of how many times I watched that tape.

Is This The Life was filmed at night in an artificially windy and rainswept part of the countryside. The band gurn their way through the song, Smith coming across like an excitable man-child whilst the rest of the band just look demented (and cold).   The vocals are simple, with walls of guitar towering between them. Midway through, an instrumental break layers on a saxophone and the second half of the song builds with some stellar guitar work from Smith. And that's the key to Cardiacs, the fact that rather than stick to a more traditional formula on what would arguably be their best attempt at breaching the pop charts, they opted to ignore the obvious route of returning for another verse or two and instead turn the song into a series of dense and layered guitar solos. Whilst that might sound off-putting to casual listeners, if you stick with it, you'll find something really quite brilliant going on.

Weirdly, the song had been recorded twice before by the band and released on two earlier (cassette only) albums. If you like it enough, it's an interesting diversion to go and listen to them, both can be found on YouTube. The first version appears on the **Toy World** album and is a very low-fi affair that sounds like a Cure demo. The second version, on **The Seaside** album, expands on the early Goth stylings to veer more towards an early Sisters of Mercy sound. Neither are as good as the final, polished version, where production values are increased and Tim Smith utilised guitar-work that would later become synonymous with bands like My Bloody Valentine.

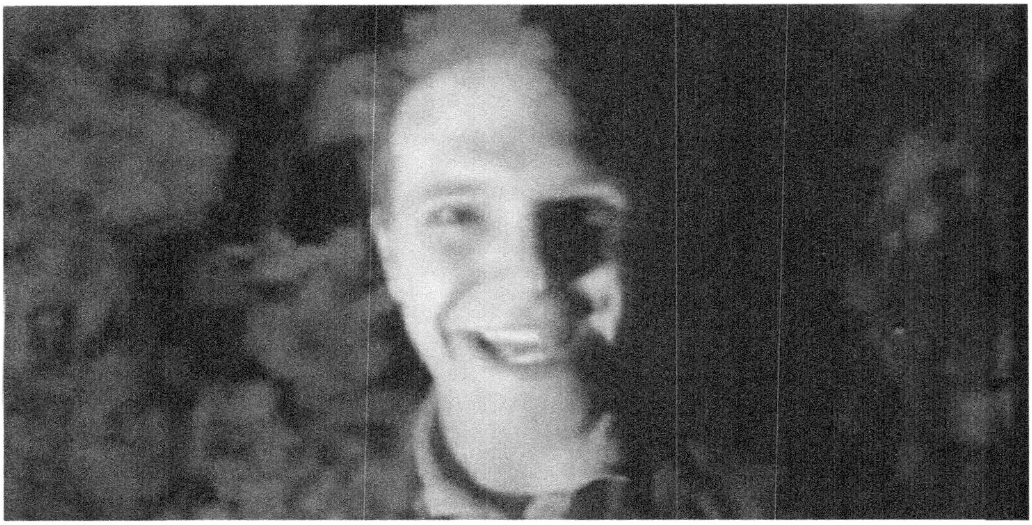

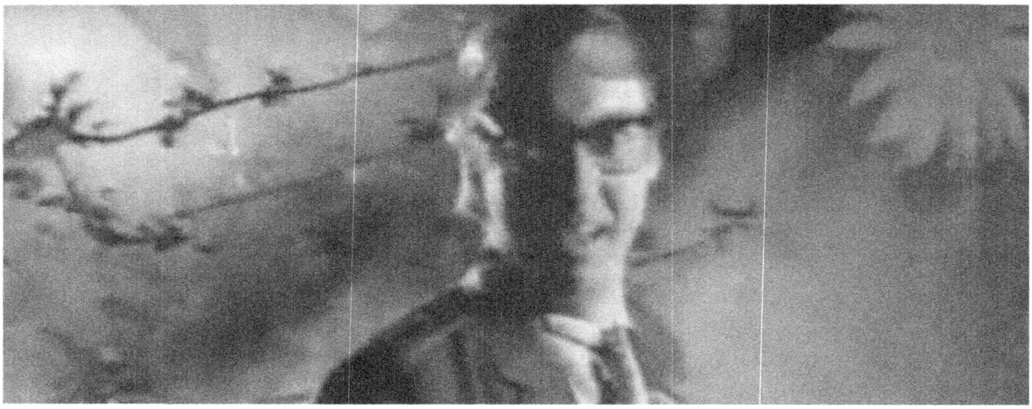

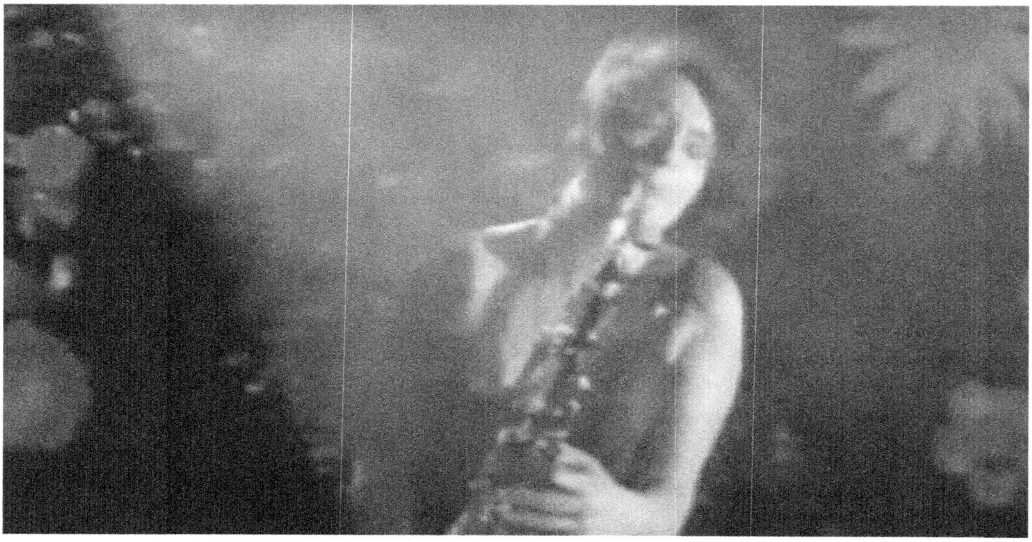

Essential Album
There's a brilliant live concert filmed in Salisbury in 1990 called **All That Glitters is a Mares Nest**, released as a concert film and cd album. It's like a greatest hits of their earlier work and the live setting shaves off a little of the weirdness that casual listeners may find too off-putting. (*This said, there are integrated bits of footage between the songs where the band play caricatures of themselves suffering the wrath of a tyrannical, over-the-top Smith in shouty dictator mode.*)

It's a perfect record of a band caught at the peak of their powers, showcasing their musicianship and song writing abilities. They use **Is This The Life** as an encore, a spectacular end to the concert and cementing itself in their legacy as an essential piece of work. Bizarrely, you won't find any of the tracks highlighted here included in their 2002 **Greatest Hits** album, which largely ignores their own earlier output – for that, go right to Mare's Nest.

As a little note on buying Cardiacs albums, you generally won't find them in shops, including larger chains like HMV. Instead, head to the Cardiacs website (**cardiacs.net**) and find them there.

Second Choice Song
This was a tough choice, mainly because I struggled to find something that wasn't totally shit-house crazy and new listeners wouldn't be scared off by. To clarify that sentence, let's take a look at a couple of their most popular hits on YouTube and see what we're presented with.

Try **Tarred and Feathered** first. I genuinely don't know what to make of it. I must have watched this video twenty times on the day I found it and each time I found myself slightly less appalled to the point of recognising some sort of genius buried within and coming around to totally loving it. The music is quite unlike anything else in my repertoire of favourites and the video itself is utterly mental. I have no idea what they were thinking in making such a video, or why they would choose to present themselves like that. What is certain is that no other bands were doing anything even remotely similar at the time.

Then watch **R.E.S.** It's even more out there. Clearly this is a band unafraid of taking the piss out of a) themselves and b) everything else. They manage to cram an entire album worth of material into a single song. What you'll notice though, after a few listens and acclimatisation, is that the song is insanely catchy.

Something about Cardiacs' music makes me really want to like it but it does take quite a bit of effort. I'm enjoying the challenge. I've also been driving my partner mad with repeated listenings of songs like **There's Too Many Irons In The Fire** (*which she says gives her high blood pressure!*) and the glorious **In A City Lining**.

My choice for a second song, however, is **The Whole World Window**. A slower, gentler sort of ballad that foreshadows the **quietLOUDquiet** *modus operandi* of later bands like Pixies and Nirvana, mixing some disturbing and mildly absurd lyrics with some beautiful string elements. An album track from **A Little Man and a House and the Whole World Window**, the song really soars and begs the question whether a release as a single following a fully-stocked chart assault of **Is This The Life** might have broken them into the mainstream. We'll never know.

And then all life begins to scream
The whole world changes like I've never seen
And then she goes up to the window
And leaps into the sky
So do I
The Whole World Window © Cardiacs, Tim Smith

EMF

LIGHT THAT BURNS TWICE AS BRIGHT

EMF – LIGHT THAT BURNS TWICE AS BRIGHT

About the Band

EMF? Surely there's been a mistake? EMF aren't one of these bands few have heard of, they were in the charts, they were everywhere! They still get loads of radio play to this day - they had *that* single that went to the top of the charts in so many countries!

Well, yes. Everybody knows their song **Unbelieveable**. It was a monster of a hit, gave them their biggest taste of success right at the beginning of their career, and then hung round their necks like a millstone for the rest of it. The proof is in a question for you - what else did they do?

Well, okay then.

And therein lies the sad, savage truth about this band – people think of them as a one hit wonder and don't realise that they kept going, eventually calling it a day after interest diminished to an extent that they didn't want to carry on.

(That's a little unfair of me, as some of you will remember a couple of other great tracks from their first album, namely **Long Summer Days** and **Children** – to see what this band were like live at the time, check out the excellent *Reading Festival 1992* performance of **Children**, and marvel at the energy of all involved, particularly drummer Mark Decloedt.)

The future must have seemed so bright to them, right back at the start. Formed in Cinderford, the band members were knocking about the Forest of Dean music scene for years before coming together in this formation. For any non-UK readers, the Forest of Dean has the same sort of reputation as backwater West Virginia, and residents are noted for 1) their immaculate sense of humour and non-violent tendencies and 2) inbreeding (the reason guitarist Ian Dench was so talented was because he had six fingers on each hand). That is a joke, obviously. People of the Forest of Dean, see number 1) above and please don't hit me for a bit of gentle piss-taking.

After **Unbelieveable**, and the successful album it came from, **Schubert Dip**, the band released a follow up album (**Stigma**, see below) that was more complex, more musically diverse and showed a much better understanding of songwriting and musicianship. It was a superb album, one of the best from that era and it tanked. The oversaturation of their early single meant that even when they put new material out – better material – radio stations would still fill the slot for an EMF song with **Unbelievable**.

Their third album showed how much of a journey they were willing to go on to try and break out from the prison of that one song. After hanging around bands like Jane's Addiction and getting into a harder rock lifestyle, they came back with a totally different sound that seemed to alienate fans that were hoping for more

Unbelievable's. One particularly scathing review by New York based *Trouser Press* said the band were *'groping unsuccessfully for some new musical direction'*. That's harsh. The band were simply trying to escape a hit single that was eclipsing the rest of their career, overshadowing more mature work. They were evolving and progressing as they grew a little older and became exposed to a greater musical *smorgasbord* of influences. What is wrong with that?

There was another brief high point in their career in 1995 with the release of Monkees cover single **I'm a Believer**, in collaboration with UK comedians *Vic Reeves and Bob Mortimer*, but they called it a day shortly after the release of failed non-album single **Afro King** later that year. They would remain mostly inactive but would go on to have a number of intermittent reunions and concerts through to the present day.

Tragedy struck in 2002 when founder member and bassist Zac Foley, just 31 years old at the time, died of a drug overdose. Well known in the UK music press for his antics, once apparently stuffing a whole lime down his foreskin (I have no idea why), it wouldn't have been a total surprise that an accidental overdose may one day have come calling for him. Rock is filled with such casualties, unfortunately, it goes hand-in-hand with that kind of lifestyle. What most of us wouldn't give for 10 minutes of it thought, right? (Just leave the fruit alone).

In 2022, still going strong and with a smaller but dedicated fanbase, EMF released their fourth studio album (their first since 1995's **Cha Cha Cha**, a gap of 27 years) called **Go Go Sapiens**.

Main songwriter and guitarist Ian Dench has reached dizzying heights of critical praise post-EMF with nominations for a *Golden Globe*, two *Grammy* awards and a win for an *Ivor Novello* award in 2008, all for his song writing and production skills. That, more than anything, should serve as a seal of approval on his work in EMF and show that the band was genuinely underrated and underappreciated.

About This Song
Light That Burns Twice as Bright is the tenth and final track of 1992's **Stigma** album. In my opinion it's their most accomplished piece of work, still fundamentally a pop song but bringing in some keyboard/string elements and a fabulous touch of gospel backing vocals. It rocks along, brings in some nice solo work from Dench on the lead up to the choruses, which in themselves are gigantic, effortlessly brimming with power.

I'm not entirely sure what the song is about, like many lyrics from many bands they're kind of vague, but it's something about being lost and needing a sign. The full aphorism that the title borrows from includes the coda *'burns half as long'* and it's hard, in retrospect, to apply that to the early passing of bassist Foley. In a song surging with emotion, does that intensify to either the band or the audience when the remaining band members play it live? It's hard to imagine that wouldn't be the case, turning a pillar of their catalogue into a bittersweet experience every time it gets an airing.

It's a standout track from a standout album, and though it was never chosen as a release for a single it's arguably one of the best tracks they recorded, if not the best. It doesn't have the immediacy of **Unbelievable** or **Children** (for example) but a couple of listens will make it click.

Essential Album
Stigma is superb, a banger of an album in the best possible sense. It's unmistakably EMF, there's a throughline, an undercurrent carried over from **Schubert Dip**, but this feels a little darker and a lot weightier. There are more layers to it, there's a maturity and a complexity to the record that Schubert Dip didn't have.

Opener **They're Here** instantly sets the mood and immediately shows an evolution from their debut album. I'm sure I once read that this song is about the *Cenobites* from Clive Barker's *Hellraiser* but can't seem to find that reference anywhere on the internet now so may have some sort of false belief syndrome in that regard! Whatever it's about, it's a superb opener, followed by another belter in the somewhat slower **Arizona**, further example of song writing maturity filled with a looseness and yet more stellar guitar work from Dench.

The album starts strong and continues that way right through. There are a couple of songs that sound like beefed up ideas carried over from the Schubert Dip sessions – **Blue Highs** and **Dog** – and although they're weaker compositionally they're still a lot of fun and would probably be lead singles for bands with less talent.

The rest of the album maintains a level of quality that elevates the record to classic status, which is why it's so baffling that the public at large turned away from it. You couldn't ask for a better, more accessible pop record stuffed chock-full of fantastic songs. There's absolutely nothing bad you could say about this album and be taken seriously. Why it tanked so hard is one of life's mysteries, and literally the only reason I can think of is because Unbelievable imprinted on the public consciousness to such a degree that they could have released anything that wasn't a shallow derivative, and it would have resulted in failure.

Second Choice Song
I could easily have chosen from half a dozen tunes from the Stigma album but I'm going to spread the love a bit further, go down a more scenic route, and pick one from their third album instead. **Perfect Day**, lead single and opener for the album, sounds like a

different band entirely upon first listen. The lead guitar and bass intro sound like a US funk metal band, with the guitar sounding very slightly out of tune. There's a madness, a mania infusing the music, vocalised neatly by singer James Atkin's childlike la-la-la work in the background.

When the first verse kicks in, you can tell it's EMF again, but distorted and fully committed to this new sound. It's not the catchiest of songs, admittedly, but you haven't heard the chorus yet. It changes everything, bringing in more lunacy and a flute sample and a repeat vocal of '*It's a perfect day*'. Experimentation like this should be applauded and welcomed, it's how bands arrive upon their most interesting material.

I'm not a huge fan of the rest of that album, gotta be honest, but there's some interesting stuff on it, and it's certainly not the (temporary) career killer that it turned out to be. There's no telling what EMF might have come up with had we, the public, bought more of the records and allowed them to keep going. I think we may have missed out on some great albums, particularly as Dench's song writing would earn him some serious music industry recognition – just imagine if that had been focused into EMF, and what wonders we might have enjoyed! Alas, we shall never know. Let's make up for our collective foolishness by giving the above songs a serious listen.

SIOUXSIE AND THE BANSHEES

PEEK-A-BOO

SIOUXSIE AND THE BANSHEES – PEEK-A-BOO

About the Band

Susan Ballion met Steven Bailey at a Roxy Music gig and they began hanging around together, eventually (with a few others) becoming a gang (famously known as the *Bromley Contingent*) that followed the newly formed, and as yet unsigned, Sex Pistols. After a slot opened up at a 1976 concert organised by Malcolm Maclaren, the friends roped in a couple of other musicians and formed their own band two days before playing at that very gig. The additional temporary band members were notable in their own right, being Marco Pirroni (who would later find huge success with Adam and the Ants) and John Ritchie (who would later find infamy as a rebranded Sid Vicious, bassist and then vocalist in a later line-up of the Sex Pistols, before murdering his girlfriend Nancy Spungen and then killing himself in 1979 at just 21 years of age).

Calling the band Siouxsie and the Banshees (and themselves Siouxsie Sioux and Steven Severin), they recruited a new guitarist and new drummer and played a number of gigs. Realistically, I don't think anybody at the time expected much out of them. Their oft-reported debut gig was more a spirit of the times snapshot than a display of musicianship, neatly embodying the punk philosophy of 'just get up and play'.

Both Sioux and Severin were part of the infamous Bill Grundy television interview in December 1976, where the aging presenter with a long history in broadcasting essentially torpedoed his career in the space of three minutes and embroiled himself in one of punk's most defining moments. A dismissive Grundy, possibly inebriated himself (early in the interview declaring *'They're as drunk as I am!'*) and acting in a completely patronising and antagonising manner, goaded his guests – basically punk royalty, including the Sex Pistols and members of the aforementioned *Bromley Contingent* – into swearing live on air. They obliged and it was like a cultural hand grenade going off. Things were never the same again. (In the interview, available on Youtube, Siouxsie and Severin are standing at the back. It is Siouxsie to whom Grundy suggests they meet after the interview, which prompts a barrage of *'dirty bastard'* and *'dirty fucker'* from the Pistols' Steve Jones. What is remarkable now is how polite Johnny Rotten was, and how well-behaved the majority of them actually were in the face of much goading from Grundy. Rotten has to be forced and pushed to swear and when he does he almost mutters under his breath like a naughty schoolboy. Steve Jones was a bit more 'street' and 'yobbish' than all the others combined and needed less goading.)

Nobody would have guessed that with the exception of Johnny Rotten (later rebranded with his real name John Lydon when launching follow-on band Public Image Limited), the person that would ride the wave the longest and have a recording and performing career that would last decades, was Souixsie (and Severin, to a limited extent). It turned out that Siouxsie and the Banshees actually had inherent talent, a previously untapped creative streak and a willingness to work hard which resulted in major label attention, and an eventual signing with *Polydor*. Even at this stage in their career, their decision to sign with *Polydor* was because the label gave them creative freedom to do what they wanted, a sign that whatever came their way the music would always come first.

The band went on to release a number of hugely influential albums. As punk turned into post punk, Siouxsie's image of a spiky haired goth queen grew (she hated any association with the goth scene) and she transcended the music genre to become an alternative 1980's female icon, her face, hair and style a beacon in the alternative scene and distorting the mainstream view of normal as well. If you went to a Siouxsie gig in the 80's and 90's, you'd no doubt see dozens, if not hundreds, of audience members carefully made up to imitate the look of Siouxsie. It was the same with that other iconic moody goth band The Cure, and Robert Smith himself was heavily influenced by Soiuxsie's look and music, even joining her band at one point and debating with himself to ditch The Cure and become a full time Banshee. As their careers panned out, both bands released lighter, poppier fare (especially singles), and though The Cure seemed to have much success in that area, one has to wonder if the Banshees stuff has endured better, and retrospectively provides a more fulfilling platter. I'll leave that up to you to decide.

The Banshees released 30 singles, 11 studio albums and 3 live albums. It's an extremely solid body of work, one that could stand alongside and be comparable to any of the best bands you care to think of.

About This Song
By rights, it should be either **Spellbound** or **Arabian Nights**, both regarded as canon classics. Or it could be **Candyman**, second single from **Tinderbox** album (lead single being the excellent **Cities in Dust**). Or maybe **Happy House**, with that lovely little guitar riff. Some days it would be **Stargazer**. Or the rich, lush pop of **Shadowtime** or **Kiss Them For Me**. You see the problem here, there are just too many great tunes to choose from. I love and recommend all of them.

I am going to pick a song though, and that is **Peek-a-Boo**. I can imagine die-hard fans puking up their intestines in anger at this. Classic thought goes that The Banshees were in their golden period when their guitarist was John McGeogh, and this is when they were at their best. As with many bands – *most, actually* – line-up changes bring out a different side to a band and produces material that contrasts against what came before. The Robert Smith period was an interesting one as well, as was the McCarrick era, or the brief McKay or Carruthers eras. The Banshees are fundamentally divided into periods based on their fluctuating guitarist position, but all of these distinct periods produced great music.

Peek-a-Boo is a weird one, even for their alternative style. It received great reviews, making Single of the Week in *NME* and *Sounds*, and reaching number 16 in the UK charts. It also cracked the US Billboard chart and gave them greater exposure over there, and a video appearance on breakthrough cult tv show *Beavis and Butthead* also helped. Unlike many bands in this book, The Banshees have had some mainstream success at a modest level, and my reason for including them is more to bring their catalogue back out into the open again lest it be forgotten (or ignored by new generations who may not have heard of them).

Built around a brass loop sample, the track reportedly took almost a year to make due to the experimental nature of the recording process. That's a hell of a long time for a song that was originally meant to be an accompaniment to the Iggy Pop cover of **The Passenger** (another great tune, by the way). With the off-kilter beats, the weird funfair accordion and Siouxsie's vocals treating every line separately and using different microphones during the recording, the overall result is one of disjointedness, the kind of music you'd hear if you were tripping in a carnival freakshow. I appreciate that's a hard-sell of an endorsement. Trust me on this, Peek-a-Boo is a work of genius and you'll love it.

Although an original composition, the band had to include a song writing credit to Harry Warren and Johnny Mercer for their 1938 song **Jeepers Creepers**. Fair enough and a legal suit avoided because it does lift the chorus from that song and although some tweaks are made it's definitely worthy of a credit.

Essential Album
Once again I'm going to upset the diehard fans – hopefully they'll forgive me, after all this article shows how much I love the band – and choose one of the various singles compilation albums. This is purely because the singles are so good a collection that, as an album in its own right, it just can't be beaten.

The compilation I choose is a boxed set bringing **Once Upon A Time (singles 1978-81)** and **Twice Upon A Time (singles 1982-1995)** and a third DVD disc of videos. Altogether, this is one of the best collection of songs you'll ever find and the fact that they all come from the same band is just unbelievable. You have all the songs I mentioned earlier, plus fan favourites like **Fireworks, Slowdive** and **Melt!**, and the utterly sublime **Swimming Horses** (built around a hypnotic, looping piano riff) and **Dazzle** (with its sweeping classical intro, the grand, operatic overtones, especially with Siouxsie's voice, which has never sounded better, and Robert Smith's beautiful guitar work).

Just go and separate those two off for a second and take a listen on youtube/spotify – two completely different approaches to making music, both of them resulting in fantastic alternative pop songs with a bit of depth and lots of inventiveness.

Then you have the cover versions, songs which the band make their own. The Beatles' **Dear Prudence**, Bob Dylan's **This Wheel's On Fire** and Ricky Gardiner/Iggy Pop's **The Passenger**. All excellent, perfect covers that pay respects to the originals and bring something new to the table at the same time. All these fabulous songs, and still there's more to come. I haven't even mentioned classics like **Israel** or **Christine** yet!

The singles are a map to the studio albums, and going through them you might find you like some more than others, and this will lead you to the various albums in the Banshees discography. If you've never heard of the band before reading this book, you have a real treasure chest of music to discover and play through, and let's not forget all of the additional material Siouxsie has recorded as part of **The Creatures** and as a solo artist. Enjoy!

Second Choice Song

By 1983 Siouxsie was the post-punk ice queen with hits like **Christine**, **Spellbound** and **Arabian Knights** in the bank. With bassist Severin off with The Cure's Robert Smith making an album under the moniker The Glove, Siouxsie and Budgie stuck a pin in a world map and fetched up in Hawaii to work on their own side-project The Creatures. The result was **Feast**, a vibrant mix of drums, percussion, xylophones and vocals. Not included, but appearing shortly thereafter came their defining track **Right Now**, which will be my second choice song for Siouxsie.

The Creatures recorded four albums during a 20 year period spanning 1983-2003. A couple were slotted in during the years the Banshees weren't recording material and a couple were made after the Banshees had called it a day in 1996. Their overall sound relies heavily on vocals and complex drum arrangements, with plenty of horns and styles skipping between exotica, jazz and blues with a sprinkling of flamenco and later Eastern influences. Recordings are stripped back and often minimalistic, which can occasionally leave them sounding like a cruise ship cabaret act backed up by a Bontempi organ, a Stomp rehearsal, or a town council planning meeting gone badly awry.

Right Now did briefly light up the UK charts, and older readers will probably be aware of it, may recognise it when they give it a listen. So it's for the readers that have never heard it before that I bring this track under a spotlight and wax lyrical about it for a bit. It's short, it's really catchy and it's one of the best things Siouxsie ever did (in my opinion).

It's very rare for a cover of a song to surpass the original in terms of quality – they're often leached of the thing that makes the original so great and resemble paler echoes, however interesting.

Right Now is a cover of **Mel Torme**'s 1962 version (which is itself a cover of **Herbie Mann**'s original instrumental that same year), and takes the blueprint to beef it up to the max.

Previous versions are the sorts of jazz sketches that would end up in the background of an *Austin Powers* film, whereas Siouxsie and Budgie took the material and slammed a syringe full of adrenaline into its heart. The brass sections are punchier than Tyson, the percussion pounds in all the right places, Siouxsie's vocals are sublime and the whole thing oozes with unbridled sass.

The Creatures take on the song changed it forever, with the **Pussycat Dolls** version (2005) using their arrangements and improvements, and **Leon Jackson** using it as a base before layering on the swing and additional jazz (2008). Of all the versions, the Creatures is the best, hands down. They took a fundamentally average tune and turned it into an unforgettable powerhouse of a pop song.

SLEAFORD MODS

JOBSEEKER

SLEAFORD MODS - JOBSEEKER

About the Band
As a thought experiment, if you came up with the idea of a two-piece band, one wearing a baseball cap and dancing on stage whilst 'playing' backing tracks on a laptop, and added the angry bastard son of 90's comedian *Charlie Chuck* to shout (in a broad East Midlands accent) simple and repetitive (although sometimes actually quite elaborate and complicated) verses at the audience, you'd have to admit that such a concept would probably be a bad idea and not much good would come of it.

However, such a band does indeed exist and it turns out they are far better than they have any right to be. Raging about the many things wrong with Britain, the often hilarious and profanity-laden lyrics are the work of a madman/genius, and the simple yet effective musical backing tracks are trim and lean, devoid of any clutter, often as catchy as any pop song you've ever heard.

Together, singer Jason Williamson and cap-wearing music writer Andrew Fearn make a phenomenal team. They describe their work as *'electronic munt minimalist punk-hop rants for the working class'* and, regarding the liberal swearing in their lyrics, Williamson has addressed the issue in a 2014 Ian Harrison Mojo article: *'It's how I speak,'* says Williamson. *'People criticize the swearing. It's not just fucking swearing...'*

Swearwords are just the seasoning to the main themes Williamson is highlighting. Because of his vocal style and delivery, they're also very funny. Even the song titles featuring swearing are funny, with examples like **Jolly Fucker** and **Bunch of Cunts**, and they even called an album **Wank**. To focus on all the bad language would be to miss the point entirely though, and that point is that Williamson is offering up some very sharp insights about the reality of living in Britain as a member of the working class.

They have 12 studio albums in the bank, all recorded since 2007, and a number of collaborations with high profile bands and artists including Orbital (see below), Prodigy, Leftfield and Perry Farrell (Jane's Addiction). They are a prolific entity relishing the chance to work with other artists as their own legend grows.

Williamson also has a number of acting credits to his name, including the final series of *Peaky Blinders*. He may come across as a soapbox preaching lunatic with way too much *Stella Artois* inside him but there's a lot more to him, and the band, than this.

About this Song
Jobseeker was my introduction into the band and makes an excellent track for you to try your luck with as well. Starting with a lo-fi bit of bass and what sounds like a cheap Bontempi organ percussion, Williamson acts out the part of a civil servant asking

himself what he's done recently to find gainful employment, which elicits the response 'FUCK ALL!'. This brings in higher production values, a Bontempi upgrade and some random scores shouted to someone called 'Rob'.

I appreciate that I'm not really selling this to you so far. The magic kicks in when a real bass joins the mix and an insanely catchy chorus fires up. If, by the end of the first chorus, you aren't tapping your foot and roaring with laughter at the classic line *'Fuck off! I'm going home!'* then this might not be for you. This said, I haven't yet met anyone who hears this song that doesn't fall in love with it.

It thunders along to an extended outro, where the word *'Jobseeker!'* is shouted with increasing aggression and, all humour aside, you start to feel that the anger might be a result of Williamson living through this experience, many times.

So Mr. Williamson, what have you done
in order to find gainful employment
Since your last signing on date?
Fuck all! I've been sat around the house wanking.
And I want to know why you don't serve coffee here
Jobseeker © Sleaford Mods / J Williamson

Essential Album
With 12 to choose from, it's a difficult proposition to make a recommendation, particularly because I myself don't know all of their work personally. With that in mind, I'd have to say that the best entry point is going to be one of their compilation albums, although taking a more random approach and dipping in and out of their discography works just as well. For instance, head over to YouTube and look up **Drayton Manored**, with its classic line *'Trip to Spar is like a trip to Mars'*, accompanied by the familiar sound that rings out whenever you cross the threshold of that establishment, which is surely one of the most genius uses of a sample ever.

Or maybe **Moptop**, another repetitive but super catchy tune that opens with the stellar line *'Do you mind? You bit my nose!'* and has a lo-fi video of them performing the song in someone's kitchen. And who doesn't want to listen to a song called **Kebab Spider**, just to see what the hell it's about? Or the collaboration with the aforementioned Perry Farrell called **So Trendy**, a ludicrously catchy (are you seeing a theme emerge?) song that brings Farrell completely into their world, where this gigantic rock star sounds perfectly at home and like he's having more fun than he's had in years (and, I suspect, comfortable in the element as this stuff isn't a million miles away from the stripped-down simplicity of Farrell's project **Porno For Pyros**). I could go on. It's all good. Check it all out!

Second Choice Song

A 2023 collaboration with **Orbital** produced a song that features as a highlight in the catalogues of both parties. **Dirty Rat** is musically less abrasive than the **Ibiza** collaboration Williamson did with **Prodigy** but lyrically just as scathing. There's a certain lilt to the tune, something almost jolly about it, but the intent behind the lyrics is a serious one.

I love the opening line of this song. At once hilarious and dismissive of so many people – entire industries and governments, in fact – that pontificate, sometimes forcefully, about how we should live our lives. So much truth in these words, and although they might look relatively simple I think there's a depth that makes it hard to find an example of any modern lyric that packs such a savage punch whilst critiquing modern society. That's not always a bad thing, for those of you reading this who prefer life to be forcibly positive all the time. Good things can come from anger, dissent and protest.

> "Some people talk about the right way to live.
> Shut up! You don't know what you're on about."
> **Dirty Rat © Sleaford Mods / Orbital / J Williamson**

The accompanying video sees Williamson standing in various spots in what looks like an off-season seaside town, sprinkled with dancing extras that may be locals roped in for the shoot, with a couple of brief cameo appearances from **Orbital**'s Hartnoll brothers, directly shot for a scene each and then lurking in the background at various other locations.

The word 'dancing' in the previous paragraph is a key point – this is a full-on high energy anthem for the club generation but doesn't exclude the casual listener. Orbital bring a beefed-up production to what otherwise sounds like a typical Sleaford Mods song, transforming it for a new audience and opening up SM's world just that little bit more. They complement each other perfectly and it would be an interesting experiment to have both bands collaborate together on a full album. Such an album, should it ever come into existence, would probably be my new favourite thing in the world.

RAGE AGAINST THE MACHINE

BULLET IN THE HEAD

RAGE AGAINST THE MACHINE – BULLET IN THE HEAD

About the Band

In December 2009, long after the band had split up, a *Facebook* campaign brought one of Rage Against The Machine's more famous singles back into the spotlight. In four consecutive years leading up to 2009, the coveted number 1 Christmas slots in the UK Top 40 singles chart were all taken by recording artists that had come from the TV talent show *The X Factor*. And, frankly, a certain section of the Great British public were fed up of it. In particular, a husband and wife called the Morters were so fed up of it, they launched a social media campaign for their fellow countrymen to stick two fingers up to Simon Cowell and buy a particular song in an attempt to make it number one instead that year. That song was Rage Against The Machine's **Killing In The Name**.

It was an act of rebellion, of protest, where the disillusioned and downtrodden came together to show their collective power. It was exactly the kind of thing that the band stood for. And it worked. Backed by celebrity bands and musicians including Paul McCartney, John Lydon, Muse, Prodigy and a host of others – hilariously including a previous winner of the *X Factor*, Steve Brookstein – the song became the festive period's number one song in the UK. RATM's vocalist Zack de la Rocha was so pleased that he gave an interview to the *BBC* thanking everyone involved for their support. Also, in a reciprocal show of generosity, the band played a free concert at London's Finsbury Park in June the following year.

It all began for Rage in 1991, the band forming during the same year that saw the release of **Smells Like Teen Spirit** by Nirvana, **Alive** by Pearl Jam, **Losing My Religion** by REM and, in the UK, Blur's inauspicious start to a great career with **There's No Other Way** (not quite kickstarting the *Britpop* era but making one or two heads look up and take note). The burgeoning Seattle grunge scene was getting noisier by the day and plenty of bands were making records with elements of anger, their attempts at drawing attention to the things the world was doing to upset them.

Nothing really came close to the howl of rage that swept out of Los Angeles in 1992 with the release of RATM's debut album. Never were a band more aptly named. The album cover featured the 1963 photograph of a Buddhist monk immolating himself in protest at the South Vietnamese governments murder of Buddhists (taken by Malcolm Browne, who won the *Pulitzer Prize for International Reporting*). The ten songs on the album took swings at political regimes and social inequality, and (like all their albums) the sleeve notes made a point of saying *'no samples, keyboards or synthesizers used in the making of this record'*, mostly as a validation for the amazing noises guitarist Tom Morello wrought from his instrument.

RATM's sound is heavy but never leaden, furious but always funky. Mixing elements of metal, punk and rap, their songs are like a punch in the face, fronting you up and commanding your attention. Has there ever been written a more powerful protest lyric than the devastatingly simple and direct offering from the single **Killing In The Name**? *Fuck you, I won't do what you tell me.* That's so brutally simple it's genius. Unfortunately, a lot of people focus on the 'Fuck you' bit and not much else, whereas what RATM are trying to get you to understand is the reason *behind* coming out with the statement in the first place. RATM aren't making records to bluster about irrelevant bullshit. They have a point, they're trying to get you to think for yourself and question the lies that you're being fed by those in power. But it wouldn't have any impact if not for those killer songs, riffs and grooves that litter the album. Any protest message always needs that component, that hook and that communal feel to pull you in.

Follow up album **Evil Empire** (1996) saw them land a touring gig with stadium filling U2, a band who sometimes share a (more mischievous) desire to poke a shitty stick at those in power. Coupled with slots on *Lollapalooza* and *Woodstock*, RATM saw some serious commercial success with their music being used on films like *The Matrix* (1999, **Wake Up**) and the sequel *The Matrix Reloaded* (2003, **Calm Like a Bomb**).

Perhaps the culmination of their success, in terms of actual protest, was their brief shutdown of the New York Stock Exchange during filming of their 1999 single **Sleep Now in the Fire**. Directed by Michael Moore, who was detained and taken off the shoot by police (his own fault for not obtaining an advance permit for filming on the pavement area , or having a permit for making loud noise, but no doubt a semi-planned-for happening as it makes such good footage), the band stormed the Exchange and the riot doors were closed, prompting a shutdown of America's capitalist hotspot for just under half an hour.

Unsurprisingly, a band this willing to take on everyone and everything that upset them would also take on each other. Tensions mounted within the band as their career progressed, eventually resulting in numerous fistfights about musical direction and, at a particularly low point, about merchandising. Zack De La Rocha left the band in 2000. The other members – guitarist Morello, bassist Tim Commerford and drummer Brad Wilk (who had apparently once failed an audition for Pearl Jam) stuck together and teamed up with Soundgarden vocalist Chris Cornell to form supergroup Audioslave, which went on to release three commercially successful (non-political) albums between 2002-2006.

Rage have reunited the original line up a number of times, touring globally at periods between 2007-2014. A further 2019 reunion was put on hiatus when COVID came along. Past reunions indicate the band are all now older, wiser and willing to work together again without fisticuffs. Whether they release any new material remains to be seen. With bands like EMF coming together and releasing an album after a 27 year recording lull, anything is possible.

About This Song
Bullet in the Head is from the debut album and was released as the second single. Serving as yet another showcase for the ridiculously talented Morello, the funky bass and drums are overlaid with noises you just wouldn't believe could come from a guitar. He does that live, too. You get a couple of verse/chorus loops before the song changes pace at the midpoint, leading with a tumbling guitar riff that is replaced by the same riff on bass whilst de la Rocha sings the repetitive refrain '*A bullet in your head*'. It rides that out to the end, and it's one of those songs that makes you wish you could play the guitar. Or the bass. Or the drums. Frankly, every band member is fully on-point and they've combined to create an exceptional song, something they did many times during their recording career.

They know how to leave space in the music. It's sometimes sparse but that's why it swings. They never sound too busy even when doing some convoluted stuff. **Led Zeppelin**, who RATM knowingly borrow from on **Wake Up** could also do this - and then some.

Rage Against The Machine were so good that the official video for the song is actually a live performance taken from a *BBC* recording for *The Late Show*. Guitarist Morello's take on the whole thing shows not only how accomplished the band already were at this early stage in their career, but also how seriously they treated the making of a video in the first place: *'The tour bus pulled up in front of the BBC studio, we ran through the song once in front of the cameras, then left to play a club that night.'*

Essential Album
As a full set of ten brilliant songs, with no filler or weaker moments, the debut album has to be classed as essential. Coming out of the blue with such a fully realised sound, with superb musicianship and a singer that somehow manages to rap over metal without sounding like an idiot, plus some very clever, insightful lyrics with many powerful messages embedded in them, it would be a crime not to categorise this album as a masterpiece.

Time has been kind to it as well, mostly because whilst their contemporaries from that era flourished and saturated the world with their product, this album never really took off in quite the same way. A greater commercial success might have diluted the rage somewhat and in retrospect this could have sounded out of touch. The production is near perfect too. Live-sounding, clear and punchy with minimal trickery which helps it in being timeless.

The themes that RATM raised are still prevalent decades later. The overriding theme in **Bullet in the Head**, about media manipulation and control over the public, is even more obvious today, more than 30 years after it was recorded. The album as a whole serves as a snapshot of the time and as a guiding light for today's age as well. Lots of bands get angry about things but none did it quite so well as Rage Against The Machine.

Second Choice Song
Rage weren't noted for their jollity, which is why after three albums of protest tunes, their choice of releasing a record made up entirely of cover songs was something of a surprise. Until one looked a little closer and realised that Rage weren't going soft on us, they were in fact covering a bunch of other people's protest songs!

Taking the Afrika Bambaataa song **Renegades of Funk**, a 1980's piece that has most definitely dated badly, Rage give it a thorough overhaul and turned it into a kickass anthem with some seriously heavy guitar and bass. This song is as funky as a muthafucka. De la Rocha's vocal delivery once again is perfect, with this track particularly welcoming of his style.

As the band had split by the time the single was released, the official video is made up of stock clips featuring the likes of prominent civil rights figures and activists, some of whom are namechecked in the lyrics, including Muhammad Ali, Thomas Paine, Martin Luther King and Malcolm X, along with artistic luminaries like Richard Pryor, Gil Scott Heron and James Brown. So not only do you get a kickass tune – *'Jam Sucka! Groove Sucka!'* – but a concise history lesson in activism and protest mostly affecting black culture.

Would The X Factor give you that kind of experience? Would it bollocks.

ORBITAL

THE BOX

ORBITAL – THE BOX

About the Band

Orbital are two brothers, Phil and Paul Hartnoll. They are an electronic dance act founded in the UK acid house and rave scene – their name is a reference to the M25 Orbital motorway circling greater London, integral to travelling between impromptu raves that were often set up at the last minute to avoid police clampdowns. Back then, the bands and the ravers were pretty much at war with law enforcement, using intel and last minute arrangements to try and thwart the police from stopping them having a good time. Where fields are still used for rave parties to this day – and they do still happen, there are 'survivors' from that era (like 'Tyres' from *Spaced*) still just about functioning in modern society - the same pretty much holds true.

The clearest image of how things were came from the inlay for the Prodigy's **Music For The Jilted Generation**, where a double inner sleeve depicts a chasm connected by a rope bridge, police and industrialised darkness on one side with revellers and clear skies on the other. A lone hippy type stands at the bridge with a large machete, ready to bring it down, looking back at the police and flipping them the bird. It sums up everything about those days, that picture.

Orbital outgrew the constricting parameters of the rave scene (like many of their contemporaries did, including the Prodigy) and started producing music more in-line with electronic music pioneers like Jean Michel Jarre and Kraftwerk. Although a lot of great electronic music works well in a field at 2am when you're out of your mind, bands have to try and sell their wares to people who'd prefer to listen in a club, or at home on their stereo. The bands that achieved this balancing act did so by bringing complexity and subtlety to their compositions, and their music evolved.

Orbital are one of those bands that perform well live, although quite what they're up to during concerts except titting about whilst wearing their trademark torch-glasses is hard for the musical layman to fathom, but rest assured they're doing something clever with keyboards and sequencers and the like, remixing tracks in-situ according to the audience's feedback.

They have contributed music to film scores including *Event Horizon*, *The Saint*, *Spawn* and *Octane*. The band split in 2004 but have reunited on two occasions since, producing further recorded material and playing gigs. At the time of writing, the brothers have recently released a tenth studio album called **Optical Delusion**, which features the single **Dirty Rat** (covered in this book in the Sleaford Mods section).

They've definitely come a long way since beginning their recording career on a four-track tape machine in a tiny under-the-stairs office space at their parents' home. That track, called **Chime** actually gave them an instant hit and won them an appearance on

Top of the Pops, so they began their career with a little boost that really set them in good stead.

About This Song
The Box is taken from the **In Sides** album and comes in two parts. The second part was released (in edited form) as a single and the accompanying video features Tilda Swinton as 'The Traveller' moving slowly through a world sped up with stop-motion photography, taking a look at what we're doing to the planet (all that traffic, all those people, rubbish floating in a river etc) before giving us a sad look and buggering off to a better place.

For the purposes of this book, I will treat parts 1 and 2 as a single piece of music. Their durations are 6:28 and 6:00 respectively, making a total length of over 12 minutes.

The track starts with simple instrumentation and gradually grows in complexity, with movements building and fading, and recurring motifs drifting in and out. It could easily be described as a modern-day piece of classical music performed with electronic instrumentation, although large sections of the piece sound almost medieval with the extensive use of what sounds like a glockenspiel, a harpsichord / zither / dulcimer.

Electronic music is often criticised as being cold/clinical but The Box has a warmth to it, helped by the track bleeding into a more organic structure with the addition of real drums. By the end of part two, all of the elements have come together and the track is really pumping along – in a career dotted with sublime recordings, **The Box** is surely their finest.

Essential Album

The aforementioned **In Sides** is a tremendous piece of work by a band at the peak of their creative powers. Moving away from the more-rave oriented direction of their earlier works, In Sides held crossover appeal and was generally well received across the board.

I rarely listen to the latter half of the album and include it here solely on the strength of the first four tracks – **The Girl With the Sun in her Head**, **P.E.T.R.O.L.** and **The Box (Parts 1 and 2)**. My two choice songs above and below cover most of side one, with the only remaining track being P.E.T.R.O.L., a quick moving soundscape with what sounds like a *Predator* lurking in the background. Another faultless, brilliant piece of music.

Although I don't listen to side two anywhere near as much, there's still some great music to be found. **Dwr Budr** is fantastic, if slightly overlong, and **Adnan's** feels a little like a filler track but even so is still worth a listen. I suppose ordinarily these tracks would come across as excellent in their own right but, for me, they're in a line up with much prettier sisters. That's possibly a terrible analogy but I'm a child of the 70's and it accurately describes my dilemma. Side one is just so good, I doubt anything else would hold up in comparison.

Other albums are worth exploring. Their second album – titled **Orbital** but commonly referred to as the **Brown Album** (mainly because their first album was also, confusingly, self-titled as well!) – begins with a speech loop, duplicated and playing slightly out of synch until both parts align again, for almost two minutes. No music at all, just that repeating speech loop. What a bold start to an album! *(That track is worth a listen just out of curiosity if nothing else, and probably isn't something you'll revisit but it's an interesting experiment, and the rest of the album features a number of their classic tunes.)* Even more out there is the fact that the same speech sample was the very first thing you heard on their debut album (UK release), as a lead in to track **The Moebius**.

This debut album, commonly referred to as the **Green Album** (or Yellow Album, depending upon whether you bought a version with a colour printing error) also features the outstanding, sprawling **Desert Storm**, which has long been a favourite on my playlists and could have easily switched with either of my main choices.

Second Choice Song
The Girl With The Sun In Her Head is unlike anything you'll ever hear in the pop charts. It's a piece clocking in at over 10 minutes and once again features recurring cycles, loops and motifs. It takes nearly two minutes to actually get going and overall I'd probably categorise it as one of the best pieces of music I've ever heard. I don't expect everyone to love it as much as I do but I'm going to recommend it anyway and hope that you all give it a listen.

The track slowly builds, mixing and matching layers until the final cycle where everything comes in at once. This is a common practice amongst electronic bands – amongst all bands, in fact. Simple arrangements of drums, a repetitive bass and a keyboard line over the top drive the song forward. It's not a song you can really dance to, it's not one that would work well in a club or in a field. It's a piece that needs to be enjoyed almost like a work of classical music, sat down and listened to.

When you block out everything and focus on the music, it reveals more layers. The keyboard line – no idea what instrument it sounds like – feels as though it's talking to you, telling a story. A change in direction comes around the six minute mark where a different keyboard bridge takes you into the latter third of the tune, which builds and builds, and the earlier keyboard lead rises up and wreathes around the other sounds, talking to them now as we look on from the sidelines in awe.

One of the reasons I like this track so much is nostalgic and very personal. There used to be an art show on UK tv called Take Hart, where a grey (then white) haired presenter (Tony Hart) used to draw pictures and – well, that's it basically. It sounds crap but was actually a great concept, showcasing all manner of approaches to producing artwork in an endless variety of mediums. I don't know if kids have anything like this nowadays but if they don't they're really missing out!

One show featured a short film clip that I only ever saw once but has somehow resonated with me for decades. It's burned into my brain, I think of it often, still. It was a top-down shot of two hands on an empty desk. I remember the hands were painted blue, and the film was shot in stop-motion. Music played over the top – Glenn Miller's **In The Mood**. And each finger of those hands moved in time to a different instrument. It was a perfectly choreographed, amazing piece of work and I've tried to track it down many times over the years but have never succeeded. That's probably for the best, it's probably nowhere near as good as the version of the film that now lives in my head. But **The Girl With The Sun In Her Head** makes me think of that short film every time I listen to it. I imagine a similar set-up, two hands, each finger moving in time with one of the isolated instruments.

I appreciate no-one else is going to attach a fuzzy, warm and glowing childhood memory to this same piece of music, and that maybe this one is just for me. But even without it, this piece holds up and deserves a listen, especially if you don't normally appreciate music like this. It might just be the piece that opens up a portal into this kind of music and believe me, there are a ton of bands out there working in this genre and there's much to discover and fall in love with.

NICK CAVE AND THE BAD SEEDS

STAGGER LEE

NICK CAVE AND THE BAD SEEDS – STAGGER LEE

About the Band

Here's a fact for you – Nick Cave was a guest at the coronation of King Charles and Camilla. Did any of you that know his music ever expect to read a sentence like that? One has to wonder - did Prince Charles and Camilla get their groove on to the delights of **Red Right Hand** or **Stagger Lee**?

Cave is also an Officer of the Order of Australia, an honorary Doctor of Laws (*Monash University, Melbourne*), an honorary Doctor of Letters (*University of Brighton*), a fellow of the Royal Society of Literature and has won a sack-full of awards including a *Time Out Book of the Year* (for *'And The Ass Saw The Angel'*), *MOJO* awards for Best Album of the Year (twice, 2004 **Abbatoir Blues** and 2008 **Dig, Lazarus Dig!!!**), an *Ivor Novello* award (2014 for song **Push The Sky Away**) and others too many to list.

He is a man of many talents, being an accomplished musician and performer, an author, screenwriter, film scorer and actor. The fact that he penned the screenplay for John Hillcoat's grim and brilliant 2005 film *The Proposition* makes him a hero in my book without even mentioning the music.

And what a catalogue of music this man has produced, either as a leader of The Birthday Party, or The Bad Seeds, or as a solo artist, or as a member of Grinderman. For a man who was a heroin addict for over 20 years, he managed to retain a level of productivity that would embarrass most regular people. So busy, in fact, that his discography covers four separate Wikipedia pages. That much of his work is brilliant is even more remarkable.

It's going to be impossible to neatly summarise Nick Cave in the space I have here. I could easily fill a book just about him alone. Suffice to say he's led a very interesting life, enjoyed some creative highs and experienced some terrible personal tragedies and through it all kept making music and other works of art.

One of his most famous songs (and almost one of the main picks for me) is **Red Right Hand**, a 1994 single taken from the **Let Love In** album and resurrected in 2013 when it was chosen as the theme tune to the popular BBC (now *Netflix*) show *Peaky Blinders*. It's also been used in the *Scream* film franchise, appearing in the first 3 entries. The song is a favourite of Cave's and is one of his most performed.

Whilst never a raging success commercially, he has sold steadily throughout his career, with occasional spikes in sales, but has generally been extremely well received critically. After so long in the field, he's now a musical institution in his own right and long may he continue.

About This Song
I already know that a lot of people are going to hate this choice, and that there are better songs to introduce you to. However, I'm going to take a chance here and really go out on a limb and recommend something that is going to be a really hard sell.

Deep breath, here goes... **Stagger Lee** is one of the downright meanest songs ever laid down, a mad dog of a track with a vision so bleak that any creature within earshot starts weeping in sorrow. It's also the work of a genius and deserves a place in a list of the best songs ever written. This is a fully realised vision of seething violence and madness, a gothic masterpiece tinged with the worst human cruelty and drenched in gore and depravation. If you're having a children's party, leave this one off the playlist.

It also has one of the slinkiest, dirtiest, most sublime basslines you'll ever hear, and a set of lyrics so off the charts mental that you have to take them in the spirit intended and appreciate them for what they are – the work of a macabre storyteller in full flow, so dark they almost become hilarious. Many is the time that my brother and I have sung the odd line or two at each other and dissolved into helpless laughter.

Cave's version comes at the end of a long line of tunes written about American legend 'Stagger Lee' (also known as 'Stagolee' and 'Stack-o-lee'), real name Lee Shelton, who shot and killed Billy Lyons in a Missouri drinking hole on Christmas Day 1895. Shelton was an African-American pimp, known for his snazzy appearance, and he got into an argument with Lyons after the latter nicked his Stetson hat. Shelton shot him dead, casually recovered his hat and calmly left the bar, entering the St Louis night and American folklore forever.

Previous versions have been recorded by the likes of Mississippi John Hurt, Fats Domino, Ike and Tina Turner, James Brown, Bob Dylan, Huey Lewis and the News and the Black Keys amongst many others. It's been an incredibly popular choice for artists wishing to cover it. Cave's version, not strictly a cover but a retelling, is most definitely the darkest take on the tale, having Stagger Lee turn up at a bar called The Bucket of Blood with his Stetson hat and his Colt .45 and a mood so filthy it could curdle milk.

It's a challenging piece of music, containing one of the darkest and most hilarious lines you'll ever hear in a rock song – guaranteed, you'll know it when you hear it – but give it a chance and take it for what it is and you might just be pleasantly surprised at how goddamned excellent this tune is. Cave is on top form, the aforementioned bass glides along like a snake through a muddy swamp, the piano is as heavy as an atom bomb and the guitars worm their way into your brain and refuse to leave. The video sees the band performing on a set more suited to a cruise ship cabaret act, all gold lighting and deep shadows, and Cave himself is dancing like a thin reed in a stiff breeze, dressed in a pink t-shirt and white trousers and presenting as a strangely effete and yet threatening figure at the same time.

I love everything about this song and I want you to love it too. I could easily have recommended something a bit lighter but come on this journey with me, commit to it, and you'll possibly enjoy things you never dreamed you would.

Essential Album
Considering both of the song choices here are from the same album, it would be churlish to not feature it as the essential pick. **Murder Ballads** came out in 1996 and presents 10 songs all thematically linked by the act of murder. It was an unexpected hit for Cave, already nine albums deep into his Bad Seeds career, and drew a lot of attention because of the track **Where the Wild Roses Grow** (*see Second Choice Song*). It received heavy airplay on *MTV* and Cave found himself nominated for Best Male Artist, something which he felt uncomfortable with and asked to be withdrawn from.

The album received much critical praise, some reviews stating that it was Cave's best work. For an album that coalesced around a track he couldn't find a fit for in his usual albums (**O'Malley's Bar**), and which was essentially created to make a home for said track, the project brought in a number of guest vocalists (Anita Lane, Shane McGowan and PJ Harvey) and yielded some amazing results.

Henry Lee, featuring PJ Harvey, is a piano-led piece where she takes turns with Cave to deliver the verses, joining forces on the brief choruses. It was a single and the accompanying video is astonishing, pretty much capturing the moment where the two performers fall in love for real. Similarly dressed, almost a mirror image of each other, it seemed inevitable. The way they look at each other in the video almost makes it feel as though you are a voyeur and shouldn't be watching. After this collaboration, they were an item for a couple of years and their breakup influenced much of his 1997 album **The Boatman's Call**.

Other album highlights include **The Curse of Millhaven** and **Death is Not the End** (a cover of a Bob Dylan song and the only track not to feature any sort of murder). If you have the patience for it, the aforementioned **O'Malley's Bar** clocks in at over 14 minutes, by far the longest track and possibly the least interesting. On the whole though, this is a fantastic album, and the collective grouping of the songs by common subject, and the nature of Cave's extensive lyrics and sublime vocal delivery make it a fascinating one.

Second Choice Song
Brace yourself, here comes the biggest shock in the book. After the madness of **Stagger Lee**, and the dark rainbow of Cave's back catalogue, my second-choice song features a guest performer who you really, really, REALLY wouldn't expect.

Hello, Kylie Minogue.

I bet you never thought you'd see that name in this book. Although much of her work isn't to my taste, I can't deny her a spot at the table. On the basis of this vocal performance and this one creative choice, Kylie changed my view of her forever (and no doubt had the same effect on anyone who heard this song or saw the video). The little princess had finally grown up, and this adult version of Kylie smouldered, far more than the hotpants version parading around on her chart hits, and delivered a vocal worthy of a more serious recording artist. Partnered up with fellow antipodean Cave, they produced a piece of music that transcends rock itself. I'm referring, of course, to **Where the Wild Roses Grow**.

This truly is a beautiful piece of music, opening with violins and alive with the gentle tinkle of piano and acoustic picking and strumming. It's a superbly composed ballad, wonderfully arranged and orchestrated, topped with singing that could make you weep. The fact that Kylie portrays a murder victim who gets her head smashed in by a rock-wielding maniac is almost incidental.

It isn't, of course. I just put that sentence in to highlight the juxtaposition presented by the song, where a single line changes everything that came before. Cave's softly persuasive voice can almost convince you that killing Eliza Day (Kylie) is a sad but rational choice in his world. There is the power of music. Until the murder, it's a wonderful story about two people falling in love and the man showing the woman one of his favourite spots down by the river, where the red roses grow *'all bloody and wild'*.

It's a fantastic duet, a highlight of both performer's careers, and one that the majority of Kylie's fanbase would no doubt have missed. If one song represents the gateway into the world that I'm trying to open up with this book, this is surely it.

TALKING HEADS

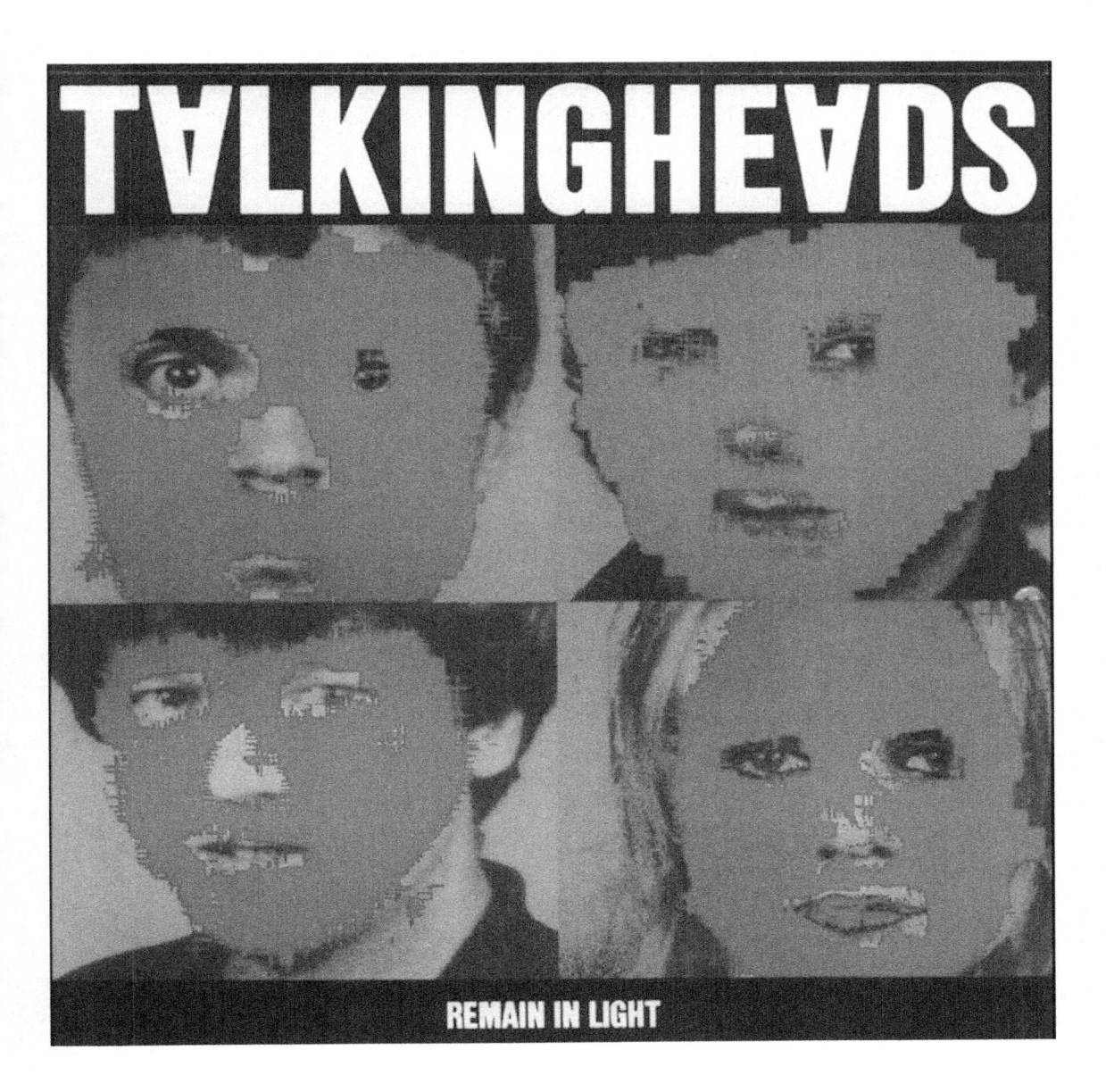

THE LISTENING WIND

TALKING HEADS – THE LISTENING WIND

About the Band

Talking Heads were formed in 1975 and released just eight studio albums. Incredibly, the number of best of albums released, all since the band's demise in 1991, is more with nine (including a remix album). Think about that for a moment. No, I'm not quite sure what it means either but it's a sign that their music endures when record companies keep releasing best of albums and people keep buying them (and with head Head David Byrne reluctant to reform the band, it's the only way the record company has of milking this cash cow).

A selection of their records are hugely influential and are rightly regarded as classics, particularly their most commercially successful album **Little Creatures** (featuring the great singles **And She Was** and the landmark **Road To Nowhere**) and their greatest artistic accomplishment **Remain In Light** (more of which shortly).

Band Members consisted of singer and guitarist David Byrne, Guitarist Jerry Harrison and the husband and wife pairing of drummer Chris Frantz and bassist Tia Weymouth. Frantz and Weymouth also recorded and performed as the Tom Tom Club (that band releasing six albums in their own right).

Weymouth, in particular, deserves an extra bit of love here for paving the way for so many other female band members in groups otherwise consisting of men, and by that I mean Kim Deal (Pixies), Sarah Smith (Cardiacs), Kim Gordon (Sonic Youth), Gillian Gilbert (New Order) and so on. Tina Weymouth did it first and she held her own, her musical accomplishments and musicianship proving any doubters wrong (and in the 1970's, where a lone woman featured in an otherwise male dominated band, playing a typically male gendered instrument such as the bass guitar, there were quite a few doubters to win over! Happily, times have moved on a little bit since then).

Talking Heads style was mostly pop rock with a little bit of punk, a lot of art-rock leanings, a seasoning of World Music and a willingness to radically experiment with the format. Their earlier, weedier sounding recordings with their scratchy guitars and odd vocals stuck out a little in the rapidly changing music scene of the late 70's and early 80's, and it took a couple of albums for some realistic commercial success. That came with the release of single **Once in a Lifetime,** and the accompanying video received heavy airplay when *MTV* launched later the same year. The video for that, incidentally, was co-directed and choreographed by none other than Toni Basil. Utter that name in the presence of a bunch of people over 45 years of age and you'll instantly get a joyous shout of the words *'Hey, Mickey!'*

Towards the end (the band split in 1991) relations in the band were fractious. Drummer Frantz only learned that the band had broken up by reading about it in an article in the *LA Times*. Tellingly, the rest of the band continued touring as a group – calling themselves Shrunken Heads – without Byrne, releasing an album in 1996. The full line up did reunite specifically to play a few songs in 2002 for their Induction into the *Rock and Roll Hall of Fame* but Byrne instantly dismissed thoughts of any further collaborations with a simple explanation of continuing 'bad blood' and a musical divergence that felt unbridgeable.

Their legacy is undeniable. They were part of the New Wave movement in the US along with bands like Blondie, Television and The Ramones. Tellingly, they are all New York bands, they really could only have come from there. That knowing and arty sensibility these bands share (yes, even the Ramones, who were never as dumb as they portrayed themselves) is very NYC.

Accolades include having four of their albums appear in *Rolling Stone* magazine's 2003 list of the *Greatest 500 Albums of All Time*. Influences can be found in bands as diverse as Franz Ferdinand, Radiohead, Phish, The Specials, Nine Inch Nails, Pearl Jam, Foals, Primus and The Weeknd.

About This Song
The Listening Wind is taken from the album **Remain in Light**. Buried on the latter part of side two, almost as an afterthought, and a quieter and more introspective piece of music than the showboat offerings that garnered all of the critical acclaim, The Listening Wind is probably the most powerful piece on the album.

Using Arabic influences scattered about the background patchwork of samples, real instruments and tape loops, Byrne sings about Mojique, young resident of an unnamed village that has been colonised and taken over by Americans and their fancy houses. The wind of the title is a force that talks to him and his people, guiding them, lifting them up and showing them the way. Also, a bomb helps – Mojique has built one and he plants it where these new oppressors will be blown up, destroying their Free Trade Zones.

It's an incredible song for an American to write. Byrne (and Brian Eno) were pulling in influences from World Music years before the likes of Paul Simon (**Graceland**, 1986) and Peter Gabriel (**So**, 1986) made such things popular. But, also, to narrate a story of a terrorist act from the 'other' side, to sympathise with indigenous people and empathise with their wish to remove the interloping Americans, to 'drive them away' – that's a brave, bold point of view to present to the record buying public. Released just five short years after the end of the Vietnam War, a complete and unnecessary disaster from a US point of view, the anti-war sentiment permeated deep and undoubtedly seeps into this song even though it's focussed on a different continent.

A number of other artists have covered this track and it's always interesting to hear what other people do to a song you love. Phish not only cover the song, they performed a concert where they ran through the entire Talking Heads parent album! If you think that's crazy, Angelique Kidja also recorded her version of the entire album in 2018! There are two artists who like the album so much they learned and recorded the whole thing! Showing more restraint, other artists limited themselves to just covering the song, including Girls Under Glass, Geoffrey Oreyama and Peter Gabriel. Legendary English band The Specials released a really interesting version in 2021 with guest vocalist Hannah Hu. If you like the original song, all are worth checking out.

Essential Album
Undoubtedly **Remain in Light**, no question, but I'm going to switch focus and celebrate another of their landmark albums instead. Perhaps a little controversially, I'm not going with a studio album but rather their 1984 live concert offering **Stop Making Sense**.

Even more controversially, I'm going to suggest that this performance, captured on film by legendary *Silence of the Lambs* director Jonathan Demme, is one of the greatest live concert films by any band, ever. Taking a heap of their best songs, delivering them in a really inventive theatrical format, and making them sound ten times better than the originals? That's just amazing. I mentioned earlier that some of the band's songs, particularly the earlier recordings, sound quite weedy and suffer from thin production values. That issue is addressed in this concert, where the sound is beefed up and these great but rather flimsy compositions come out and parade themselves on stage like juiced-up, wildly energetic versions of themselves and they sound so goddamned good. And the 40th Anniversary remaster has just been released – you lucky people!

The core quartet of the band are joined by Bernie Worrell (keyboards), Alex Weir (guitar), Steve Scales (percussion, backing vocals) and the slinky, funky duo of backing singers Lynn Mabry and Ednah Holt. Together, they take a serviceable catalogue of a reasonably successful alt-rock band and blast out one of the best sets you'll ever hear. And all of the magic is captured, from the energy of the performers, the sheer joy they broadcast from their bodies, to the shots of the audience dancing in the aisles.

The best bit is that the whole thing is choreographed so that the band members come out bit by bit for each song. Opener **Psycho Killer** features a boombox on an empty stage, to which Byrne comes out with an acoustic guitar. He kills it, in the best possible sense – the sound sounds incredible. As the concert progresses, the drumkit is wheeled on, then the keyboards and so on, until there's a full compliment of musicians and they're tearing the roof off. Every single song sounds better than its studio counterpart. There are so many standout songs but **Burning Down the House** and **Life During Wartime** seal the deal for me.

Second Choice Song

I could choose maybe a dozen here – most of them from the band's two colossus offerings mentioned earlier (**Stop Making Sense** and **Remain In Light** if you weren't paying attention!) but there's no escaping the fact that this, their second signature tune (after **Once in a Lifetime**), their second most beloved gift to the world (and one that I personally prefer), just has to be **Road To Nowhere**.

Upbeat, jolly, a little bit silly and with a fabulous video, the song is burned into the brains of everybody who was alive at the time of release due to extended airplay from radio stations and just the sheer magnificence of the song and its earworm catchiness.

There aren't many (non-French) songs that can get away with an accordion but this pulls it off magnificently. Opening with a gospel choir singing a verse acapella, the song then fires up with a jolly, quirky bass and drum pairing and Byrne's unique vocals and lyrics. Once you know the words I'd say it's impossible not to sing along, especially when they get to this bit:

There's a city in my mind
Come along and take that ride
And it's all right, baby it's all right
And it's very far away
But it's growing day by day
And it's all right, baby it's all right
Road to Nowhere © Byrne / Talking Heads

Even when the vocals devolve into various screams and shouts, as Talking Heads' songs are sometimes prone to do, the fun only gets better. The accompanying video is suitably madcap, featuring plenty of imagery relating to aging and lots of stop motion segments, including the iconic bit of Byrne's head as he sings whilst a cube rotates around him. Impossible to dislike and although I may not be bringing this song as a new discovery to many people reading this, it's still my pick as it's just such a great tune.

MADNESS

GREY DAY

MADNESS – GREY DAY

About the Band

Madness are probably the most famous band in this book, at least to UK readers who are over 45. The reason they are included is simple – they are one of the best bands the UK has ever produced and they deserve to be remembered and their music kept alive.

Having recently turned the half century mark, I can look back on my childhood and say that certain things had a large presence in my life during that time. The Atari 2600 console. Playing football in the street. BMX bikes. Delicious chocolate (before the Americans bought out Cadbury and started changing the recipes – booo!). Cassette tapes - so many cassette tapes. 7" singles. Arcade games and the early home computer the ZX Spectrum. And Madness.

Now, Madness weren't my favourite band, I'm not entirely sure I had one back then (I seem to have lots now). But they were always there, always providing some sort of soundtrack to my life. Between 1979-1986, when I was 8-15 years old, Madness had the most amazing run of singles and they always seemed to be on the TV. Considering those years felt like forever at the time, and that at any given moment there seemed to be a Madness single in the charts, or one of their wacky videos on the gogglebox, they were a more or less permanent presence and I, along with a great number of my fellow countrymen, developed a real fondness for the band.

The fact that they still tour to this day, and perform sell out concerts to audiences who want to hear them play those singles (*along with some new material, but it's always the old singles that get the most love*), proves that people of my age have not forgotten them.

But do younger generations know about them? Certainly, if your parents were fans back in the day, you'd more than be aware of their music. You'd probably even like a lot of it. To those unfamiliar with his musical past, lead singer Suggs is perhaps better known as a TV presenter these days. If you didn't grow up in a household that played their music, I'm not sure how much modern cultural presence they have, and how visible they are to casual listeners. Possibly, their overall appeal was hamstrung a little by their cartoony image – it just so happened that I was a key demographic target, and maybe older listeners were slightly put off by that, but I'm not overly sure – everybody loved them, surely? Even the Queen, as evidenced by their gig on the roof of Buckingham Palace for the 2012 Diamond Jubilee celebrations.

The band went through several distinct early phases. Formed in 1976 and hailing from Camden Town, they were part of the two-tone movement along with The Specials, The Selecter, Bad Manners and The Beat, influenced by ska and reggae and mixing it with elements of punk and new wave. These bands blended a mix of white, black and multiracial members, something that must have been confusing for some of their skinhead followers with National Front leanings.

The first run of Madness singles showcased their musical influences very obviously, and included **The Prince** (a tribute to Jamaican ska singer Prince Buster), **One Step Beyond** (a cover of a tune actually written by Prince Buster and featuring the iconic opening vocal by Chas Smash), **My Girl** (a UK number three hit and their highest position until **House of Fun** reached number one in 1982) and **Night Boat to Cairo**. During this period the band had six members, with Chas Smash not yet a fully-fledged permanent fixture, reaching that status in 1979 when he officially became a backing vocalist and dancer and eventually proving himself to be a great singer (see **Michael Caine** song) and songwriter in his own right (he co-wrote **Our House**, **Cardiac Arrest** and **Wings of a Dove** for instance).

Their next phase brought a lasting pop sensibility to the music (although My Girl did foreshadow this move) and with the help of an iconic video, classic track **Baggy Trousers** once again propelled the band to number three in the UK. Listing the following singles here will give older readers a warm, fuzzy glow as the memories come flooding back: **Embarrassment**, **Grey Day**, **Shut Up**, **It Must Be Love**, **Cardiac Arrest**. All great tunes that any band would be proud to have written.

Madness then brought out some songs that eased their way into the nation's consciousness and became permanently embedded in the fabric of UK culture. These tunes were everywhere, universally loved by all. Despite not collectively getting the best chart positions, I'd argue that their next run of three songs were creatively the high watermark in terms of popularity: **House of Fun**. **Driving In My Car**. **Our House**. Perfect pop records in every sense, and I doubt there's a person over 45 in the UK who doesn't know the words to all of them.

The next phase of their career – in my mind, possibly not anyone else's, it's just how I think of them – gave the world some slightly more complex, more melancholic fare in singles **Tomorrow's Just Another Day**, **Wings of a Dove**, **The Sun and the Rain**, the phenomenal **Michael Caine** and the bittersweet masterpiece **One Better Day**. During this period, their sales figures were ever so slightly declining and the writing was on the wall. As much as we loved them, at the time it seemed we just wanted them to keep banging out variations of Our House or Baggy Trousers. With age and experience came less poppy but no less rich musical offerings, and I'm not sure why but the mass audience wasn't all committing to that journey with them.

In retrospect, of course, with a distance of a few decades, it's hard to separate out these songs from each other, they all blend into a superb back catalogue of one of our finest bands, all of them equally as inventive and brilliant to listen to. The band split in

1986 after the release of the underrated **(Waiting For The) Ghost Train**, but this was not the end of Madness. Not by a long shot. They would reform a number of times, headline festivals, go onto release critically acclaimed albums and enjoy a longevity to their career that many bands can only dream of.

About This Song
Grey Day has a darker tone than many of the songs the band released up to that point. Written by keyboardist Mike Barson, and first performed in 1978 (although only released as a single in April 1981), in isolation the song could have easily sat alongside the likes of emergent goth band pop-tinged offerings like **A Forest** (The Cure), **Arabian Knights** (Siouxsie and the Banshees) and **Bela Lugosi's Dead** (Bauhaus) and predating other pop-styled downbeat classics such as **Killing Moon** (Echo and the Bunnymen) and **She Sells Sanctuary** (The Cult) by a couple of years. This said, a more obvious influence would have to be The Kinks, and their catalogue of quintessentially English pop songs. I doubt any of these bands would cite Madness as an influence but make no mistake, Madness were experimenting with that style of music and they did it extremely well.

Based on their previous releases to that point, it was a bold move to go in this direction and the results were incredible. It's a very distinctive sounding piece of work, very morose but also clearly a pop song. The verses and choruses feel very downbeat and the lyrics are extremely miserable – we are no longer in the same realm as Baggy Trousers or My Girl, that's for sure – but there's nothing wrong with enjoying music that has a focus on unhappy emotions (**Happy When It Rains** by The Jesus and Mary Chain springs to mind here), life can't always be bunnies and rainbows. One of their follow-up singles the following year, **Cardiac Arrest**, was another hugely downbeat song about a man having a heart attack on a bus, and again it's also one of their best.

I love **Grey Day**, I love the instrumentation, the sounds that they make and all of the additional effects like the bells tolling in the background, the scratchy guitars, the sudden whoosh of a keyboard. As ever, Barson's piano work is beautiful, regardless of context. It's just an all round blinder of a song, one of their best and unlike some of their more obvious hits this track has aged without the period dating and still holds up today.

Essential Album
You'll note that my write up of the band focused solely on their singles – that's mainly because of the way I myself perceive the band. Even though a couple of the album covers are burned into my mind forever – again, the word 'iconic' really does apply here, particularly to the first three LP covers (two of which, **Absolutely** and **7**, pretty much feature the band in poses that would have made great logos) – I never actually

owned a Madness album until 2009's **The Liberty of Norton Folgate** (which, and this is a really interesting development, was widely acclaimed and critically praised, with some reviewers confidently stating that it was the best album of their entire career. **We Are London** got a lot of airplay and I really do like that tune.)

I primarily enjoyed this band through their singles, so for the purposes of recommending an album, it has to be one of their many singles compilations. The best choice, to include all of the songs discussed so far, would be **Divine Madness.** Released in 1992, it reached the top spot in the UK, even after six previous best of compilations were already in the record shops. With a mind-boggling 14 compilation releases overall, they are starting to take the piss a little (or we just really do love them!).

Second Choice Song
Something about the way they handle melancholy adds to my enjoyment of Madness tracks, and my second choice feels initially like another downbeat offering but turns out to be an uplifting love story in the end.

One Better Day came late in their career (the first stage of it, anyway) and was a single off their fifth album **Keep Moving**.

Previous single **Michael Caine** had featured Chas Smash on lead vocal (as did the slightly earlier **Wings of a Dove**) and to the uninformed – which was all of us back then – it got people wondering if Suggs was leaving the band. So when the next choice of single – **Victoria Gardens** – also featured Smash on lead vocals, it was deemed to be reinforcing the wrong message and plans were quickly changed. That became an album track and **One Better Day**, clearly led by Suggs, became the next single.

At the time of release, the band were finishing their record deal with Stiff and the label wouldn't stump up the cash to make a video, so the band funded it themselves. Shot mostly in black and white, presumably to save costs, with some additional colour footage in the latter half, it's a functional offering and unlikely to stay in your memory for long. The music, however, is right up there with the best material this band managed to lay down.

It's a restrained single, not flashy in any way, and has a gentle lilt to it, with lots of warm undercurrents. It's a wonderful pop song, again anchored around Mike Barson's great piano lines and another sax solo where most bands would have a guitar solo. Great tune from a great band. Madness are regarded as a national treasure, which can be a double-edged sword, but if we took the time to listen to them again - to really listen - then we might find ourselves treasuring them a little bit more.

RICHARD HAWLEY

DON'T STARE AT THE SUN

RICHARD HAWLEY – DON'T STARE AT THE SUN

About the Artist

Before researching this book I had no idea that Richard Hawley was the guitarist in 90's indie band Longpigs. They're an unlikely band to have heard of, admittedly, but I do remember owning their rather shouty single **She Said**, which was pretty good but not quite good enough to make me buy anything else by them. After their split, guitarist Hawley went on tour with Pulp and was encouraged by frontman Jarvis Cocker to record some of his own material. He did just that and is consequently eight albums deep into a solo career at the time of writing.

By his third album, Hawley was getting enough attention to be nominated for the 2006 *Mercury Prize*, and when fellow Sheffield musicians Arctic Monkeys won instead, their vocalist Alex Turner graciously cried *'Someone call 999, Richard Hawley's been robbed!'* Hawley went on to work with Arctic Monkeys in 2007, and throughout his career has worked as a co-writer, session musician or guest with many famous names, including Jarvis Cocker (and also Pulp), Elbow, Robbie Williams, Finlay Quaye, Nancy Sinatra, Gwen Stafani, Jools Holland, Texas and Manic Street Preachers. An exhaustive list and not even a complete one.

Speaking of Sheffield, Hawley has a great fondness for the place. His first seven album titles all reference the city in some way and he is a lifelong Sheffield Wednesday football supporter. He went to school with Pulp bass player Steve Mackey and Hawley's father played in a number of local bands, being called a 'Sheffield Music Legend' upon his passing. Before settling for a career in music, Hawley worked at his local HMV store.

Being honest, I should admit at this point that I don't really like a good deal of Hawley's music. That might seem shocking considering I'm writing about him in a book about my favourite tunes. Before his seventh album, **Standing at the Sky's Edge**, much of his music was of the quiet variety with Rockabilly leanings. Nice enough if you like that sort of thing but not my cup of tea. He would have passed me by completely were I not out for a meal with the family one day and I heard something wonderful over the pub's speaker system.

It felt familiar somehow, despite never having heard it before. I knew a bit of Pulp stuff (who didn't after their masterful 1995 performance at Glastonbury?) and wondered if this was a great lost album I'd never heard from them. Even though it was on quiet, in the background, I heard enough to really want to know what the track was and went over to the bar to ask. When the answer came back, I was like *'Who?'* and waited until I got home to *Google* Richard Hawley.

The track I'd heard was **Don't Stare at the Sun.** It blew me away. I bought the album it was from. It blew me away. I investigated his earlier work and that's where this particular journey ended. But I played that one album to death. I loved it. So, whilst I don't rate Hawley as one of my favourite artists, I actually do rate one of his albums as one of my favourites. The music examined in these pages more than earns its place amongst the other greats I'm profiling.

About This Song
Don't Stare at the Sun starts off quietly, a gentle guitar based indie pop song. It's an amiable enough effort, rather catchy and sounds a lot like Pulp on a spa day. In short, it's a pretty good song. But something magic happens as the second cycle of verse and chorus nears completion – this quiet song gently picks up the volume and power and turns into a bit of a beast. It doesn't get any faster, or more aggressive, just keeps surging towards you like a tidal wave until it engulfs you. An electric guitar solo takes the lead and brings a third section of the song into being, one where Hawley is bordering on psychedelia and on the verge of letting go with unrestrained power. But he keeps a tight lid on it, and reigns it back in, and you're left wondering where things might have gone.

The answer is in the rest of the album, and **Don't Stare at the Sun** is your entrance into it. The accompanying video (this was a single from the album, one of four) is unremarkable so the music alone is going to have to win you over.

Essential Album
Standing at the Sky's Edge is a masterpiece. It's a bit of a joke that you may have noticed I use that word a lot in this book – almost as much as 'brilliant' – but it really is. I'm not going to soften it just to avoid being a little repetitive.

A signifier of what's to come lies with the cover. Compared to his more muted album artwork of previous releases, he's gone full-on psychedelic. You can tell he's embraced this aesthetic within a couple of minutes of opener **She Brings the Sunlight**. These songs are full, brimming with riches, alive with stellar guitar work and sitars dazzling in the background mix. His solo work is spectacular, you can feel the looseness, the enjoyment in the way he plays. Here is a man making music he loves and it shows. The first track is seven and a half minutes long and every second of it is glorious. It's a perfect opener, preparing you for what's about to come.

The next song clocks in at over seven minutes as well, clearly showing you that he's going to do whatever the hell he wants and you're going to have to ride along with it. And it's a ride well worth taking. This title track opens and initially resonates with **Nick Cave**'s **Stagger Lee** – there's a single, dark piano note and the lines *'Joseph was a good man but he killed his wife, His hungry little children, he took their lives',* reminiscent of Cave's murder ballads. There's a slight Country and Western edge to the song, until it leaps into a higher gear around the 2:30 mark where louder electric guitars pile in and a minute after that the percussion changes and we go on a bit of an instrumental wig out before the final cycle.

Single **Down in the Woods** is the album's most straightforward rock track, powered by a repetitive guitar riff and bringing the loudness and wall of sound that we're beginning to get used to. He dials it back for the second verse before coming back strong and rocking out for the last third. Follow on track **Seek It** is the most laid back, a call-back to his earlier music. Although I'm not a huge fan of that, it sits well here and I find it an enjoyable track in isolation. If the whole album was like this I wouldn't feel the same way about it.

We already know **Don't Stare at the Sun,** and the next two tracks will be covered as my Second Choice Song below, which leaves us with the closing track **Before**. A familiar template is applied, whereby the opening half of the song feels like a gentle sort of ballad before a sudden change in approach ramps up the volume and the power, and Hawley lets his guitars sing. And roar. It feels like he's going to close out and sign off with an escalating surge of psychedelic rock but there's one last twist as he dials it back again and finishes on a gentler note.

Overall, a great album and one of those that's worth playing in its entirety, in order, to fully appreciate.

Second Choice Song
The Wood Collier's Grave and **Leave Your Body Behind You** come as a package, in my opinion. Like the Afghan Whigs' **Omerta** and **The Vampire Lanois**, they just work as a pair. Feeling like another of Cave's Murder Ballads – maybe this is why I like this album so much – The Wood Collier's Grave is a sad, atmospheric piece. Despite being over three minutes, it feels over in a few heartbeats, and then the opening notes of the guitars ring out from **Leave Your Body Behind You**. The first song really does feel like a build up to this point, an extended intro.

What follows is a track where it feels like Hawley finally opens up the throttle and lets the music take over completely. For the rest of the album there's always been an element of restraint, even on the bits where he's rocking out, but here the song runs the show, sweeping us along with it. There is indeed another lull two thirds in, and then comes the backing choir and the guitar solo work, some buried right down in the mix. It's an epic sound and one that could have easily sustained another few minutes. In my opinion this might have made a better ending to the album but only because there's a deep feeling of satisfaction I feel after playing both of these tracks really loud. And that might be a key to properly enjoying this record – volume. It worked for Hawley, it works for me.

ULTRAVOX

MR X

ULTRAVOX – MR X

About the Band

I've written elsewhere about a band that put out a single that was so popular it eclipsed the rest of their career (EMF was the example I used, there have been may others including The Psychedelic Furs, Talk Talk, Enya, They Might Be Giants and so on). It's much the same story with Ultravox. Their 1981 mega-hit single **Vienna** coloured everything else that came before and after. That single remained at number two in the UK Top 40 for four weeks, three of which had the novelty song **Shaddap You Face** by Joe Dolce edging it out of the top spot. It did reach Number One in several European countries and remains their best known song. It's good but far from their best.

Ultravox share another defining trait with a few other bands (AC/DC, Faith No More and Genesis to name but a few) where the established frontman and vocalist either died or upped sticks and suddenly left the group, only for someone else to then take up the position and steer the band to enormous critical success, whilst at the same time losing some of their unique identity in the process. When original vocalist John Foxx left in 1979, after limited commercial appeal and the ignominy of being dropped by their record label, the band were moving into their trademark sound of incorporating a drum machine for some tracks and pushing synthesisers to the fore.

Arguably they were influenced by Kraftwerk, and some razor-tongued reviewers – my brother, for one! – compared them to a poor man's version of the German synthpop luminaries. This seems a little unfair, as I've listened to Kraftwerk and apart from a couple of singles their music lacks the human touch (possibly deliberately) that bands who followed in their wake and nicked their techniques managed to capture.

Newcomer Midge Ure (formerly of Slick who had a no.1 hit in 1976 with a cover tune - Ure was never a stranger to what works commercially) entered the band like an adrenaline shot to the heart. Their sound moved closer to the mainstream and they started producing a line of chartable singles. To all intents and purposes they were a very successful group and everybody in Europe must have heard some of their music – probably the single **Vienna** – at some point. So why are they in the book? Because they have been forgotten. I never see them referenced, I never hear anything being broadcast unless it's that bloody Vienna.

Much like contemporaries Simple Minds, Ultravox produced some really interesting music in the early part of their career and then success led to less experimental work and a degree of blandness. Unfortunately, chopping off the rougher edges of things equates to better mainstream success, but that just means most people miss all the good stuff. As an example using Simple Minds, their instrumental track **Theme For Great Cities** is a colossus, easily one of the best recordings they ever made (and covered in this book, although the band won't be), but hardly anyone knows that tune and instead the group is remembered for comparably blander offerings like **Sometimes** or – excuse me whilst I vomit for a second – **Belfast Child**, or basically anything after 1987.

Ultravox had a good run of singles, including **The Thin Wall**, **Reap The Wild Wind**, **We Came to Dance**, **Dancing With Tears In My Eyes** and finally **Love's Great Adventure**, which preceded the decline of their success. It's not a gigantic canon of work comparable to peers such as Madness, or Siouxsie for example, but there are enough glittering diamonds to give the band an airing for those that might remember the glory days and an introduction to those that have never heard of them.

About This Song
As a teenager, newly moved back to the West Midlands after schooling in Devon, my musical taste started being influenced by my older brother. Although there was some cross-pollination, his tastes arguably had the larger impact.

He gave me The Sisters of Mercy, Fields of the Nephilim and Pop Will Eat Itself. He loved The Mission as well but I never gelled with them, and now he probably denies ever owning any of their records anyway. In return, I gave him Pixies, Jane's Addiction and Nine Inch Nails. Fair trade. But one day I heard some weird sounds coming out of his bedroom and listened transfixed. Icy keyboards filled the house, a story of a man searching for another man unfolded and by the end of it I had a new favourite song.

That song was **Mr X** by Ultravox. I've played it many, many times over the years. As a writer of short horror stories, I've even nicked the title for a composition of my own. As a haunting piece of music, yet still buzzing with a pop sensibility and all manner of little orchestral effects, it's six and a half minutes of pure escapism. Every time I play it, in my mind I see blurry, shadowy figures crossing mist-covered bridges in some dark corner of Europe. Every single time I listen to it I feel like I've been taken on a journey.

This is perhaps the one song of theirs that is compared, often unfavourably, to Kraftwerk. I say don't listen to the naysayers. Just listen to me. This is a fantastic song – whenever I listen to it, I think it briefly becomes my favourite song in the whole world, and then drops back down to hover in the top fifty or so for the rest of the time. Basically, every song I'm recommending in this book does the same thing, they all become my absolute favourites during those moments I'm listening to them. Even so, this one is special.

Essential Album
Ultravox's fourth studio album **Vienna**, the first with Midge Ure, boldly opens with a seven minute instrumental and contains arguably their best collection of songs. At the time of release reviews were mixed. Some lamented Foxx's departure, some were enthusiastic about the new direction and some were downright scathing.

I appreciate that my trying to turn you onto an album by including the following terrible quotes is a very bad idea but I can't resist sharing them as they're so excruciatingly awful. And wrong, as it happens. Time has been kinder to the group, and this album in particular, but back in 1980 people were saying this:

"the first half of side two reveals the most tedious liabilities" **Melody Maker** (The first half of side two includes my first choice song 'Mr X')

"Vienna is full of conventional electronic rock songs which are beautifully executed but never inspiring" **Record Mirror**

"gaudy, sometimes magnificent, but mostly hollow edifices… wanton plagiarism and less clearly defined ideas" **NME**

If you were in a band and got those kind of reviews you'd probably burn all your instruments! And there are more, some even worse!

But, thankfully, other music press reviews were kinder, in particular *Q Magazine* who stated that **Vienna** was the band's *'best album'* and praised the singles **All Stood Still** and **Sleepwalk** (*see below*). And what a pristine pair of singles they are, both highlighting this new style of synth-based music to perfection and showing contemporary artists such as Duran Duran and the aforementioned Simple Minds how to incorporate these new instruments into a traditional band line up and make something exciting and new.

Although much music from the time has dated, time-stamped at their creation by the instruments and whatever production values were currently in fashion, a lot of this album still sounds fresh. Any accompanying videos, whether official or performances from shows like *Top of the Tops*, are horrendously dated by comparison. And, however genius the music, Midge Ure's ill-advised combo of tiny moustache and tapered sideburns is never going to look like a good idea.

Second Choice Song
Sleepwalk is a more straightforward pop song. It's got a quick tempo and thunders along beautifully, with an extended middle section featuring some great guitar work from Ure (an underappreciated guitarist on the whole and so good, in fact, that Phil Lynott hired him for a brief stint in Thin Lizzy when the late guitar wizard Gary Moore

went AWOL). It's a very enjoyable offering from a band in their creative prime, one that doesn't get old even after decades of playing.

A perfect mix of traditional instruments and the new synths appearing during that period, it melds the two approaches to making music and comes up with something that was arguably ground-breaking at the time. It also means their music sounded less tinny than some of their contemporary artists who only used keyboards. Ure is a confident vocalist – sometimes a brilliant one – and the song features a small but significant drum fill that hinges the entire song at the 2:39 minute mark.

Amazingly, considering the band knew the value of videos – you only have to see the accompanying promotional video for **Love's Great Adventure** to confirm this, it being an expensive looking pastiche of 80's blockbuster fare like *Romancing The Stone* – they neglected to get an official video together for this song. Still, that's one less video in the world with a silly moustache, so maybe it's not a completely bad thing.

MAGAZINE

GOLDFINGER

MAGAZINE – GOLDFINGER
Guest Article by James Griffiths

About the Band

Howard Devoto, Scunthorpe's prodigal son, is hailed by many as an icon of the post-punk movement. But before that, he was a founding member of Buzzcocks, along with Pete Shelley. Not everyone knows that he wrote and sang on their debut EP **Spiral Scratch**. He was widely hailed as bringing punk music to the North of England in 1976, recruiting genre poster boys the Sex Pistols for their legendary first Manchester gig at the Lesser Free Trade Hall. Seen as the beginning of the Manchester music movement, the story is told with questionable accuracy but fully adhering to myth in the movie *24 Hour Party People*. Only four dozen people were there, apparently, but most of them formed bands as a result. Peter Hook, Bernard Sumner and Ian Curtis would form the band that would become Joy Division the very next day; a young Steven Morrissey was there; Mark E Smith, and even Mick Hucknall was in attendance, so you can blame Devoto in some way for the rise to fame of any one of those you don't like.

Devoto eventually became disillusioned with the punk movement, seeing it (correctly, as history tells) as a flash in the pan. He'd leave Buzzcocks to form Magazine a year after the Sex Pistols gig in 1977. Devoto was probably right to do so, as punk as a contemporary movement was beginning to fade. Its legacy is legendary, however, and – as testament to the effect of the Pistols' *'anyone can pick up a guitar'* ethos, a new era of DIY alternative, independent music began, making the act of committing songs to record, or playing shows, accessible to anyone with a dream and a few mates.

Magazine quite deliberately embraced many elements that would be eschewed by any self-respecting, mohawk-sporting, safety pin-supported purist. Out went the stripped-down instrumentation of bands like Buzzcocks, and in came Bob Dickinson and – *Heathen!* – keyboards and synths. Devoto recruited a young, pre-Banshees John McGeoch, at that time an art student, not a musician, and compiled a library of influences as wide-ranging as John Barry (as referenced in my essential track) Captain Beefheart, and the literature of authors like Kafka, Camus and Satre. It was punk's *judas* moment, and then some. Magazine's debut single **Shot by Both Sides** remains an alternative dance floor filler to this day, and their first album **Real Life** followed, bringing a diverse collection of songs. Some capture the punk sensibility, such as **Recoil**, which is less than three minutes of raucous energy; elsewhere, the **Great Beautician in the Sky** channels a freakshow waltz and album closer **Parade** remains the essential twisted post-punk ballad, its opening piano eerie and sentimental in equal measure. The John Barry *James Bond* influence is most prominent on arguably the best track on Real Life, **Motorcade**, with is grinding guitars and highly cinematic atmosphere throughout.

Magazine would go on to release just four contemporary albums. Fan favourite **Secondhand Daylight** followed Real Life in 1979 and further cemented their lack of punk dissonance. At that point, post-punk had fully cemented itself, and Magazine – in my humble opinion – had to try even harder to produce something spectacular and genre-defying. Secondhand Daylight is a moody and atmospheric effort, recalling progressive rock elements that do in places capture a unique edge. Magazine's most commercial album **The Correct Use of Soap** would capture them at their peak both creatively and commercially. Produced by Manchester legend Martin Hannett, this Mangum opus contains its fair share of more poppy moments, producing the single **A Song From Under the Floorboards** (*see second choice song*) which even had a minor effect on the UK charts in 1980. Magazine would extensively tour the album, including playing many shows in the US, generating many American fans who adore their music to this day.

As sometimes happens with an album so perfectly formed, Magazine struggled to follow up on The Correct Use of Soap. 1981's **Magic Murder and the Weather** was again produced by Hannett. However, at this point the mastermind behind the Joy Division sound was in the grip of a heroin addiction and made many questionable decisions on what would become the band's final album, Devoto deciding to disband Magazine before the album was promoted by touring. Whilst the record is not terrible by any means, it's a patchy affair at best. Lead single **About the Weather** plods along but has some redeeming moments; the **Honeymoon Killers** is a nice distraction but other tracks don't really go anywhere and as a result, it was a commercial and critical failure. There is some solace to be found in album closer **Thinking Flame.** What didn't help is that John McGeoch had at this point been poached by Siouxsie, following the near-fatal dissolution of the first iteration of the Banshees. McGeoch's legendary guitar prowess would see the Banshees leap to new heights and is nowadays hailed as their best guitarist, featuring on seminal albums like **Juju** and **A Kiss in the Dreamhouse**.

Magazine served as an epic vehicle for the legendary Howard Devoto, a true but under-appreciated alternative music icon. A solo album followed in 1983 that sadly flopped, leading the man formally known as Howard Trafford to 'grow up and get a real job' in a photographer's archive. However, all was not lost as in the late 90's Devoto returned and created arguably his best work with **Luxuria**, producing two brilliant albums no-one remembers or cares about. Unthinkably, Magazine reformed briefly in 2007, partly as tribute to the late John McGeoch, who sadly died in 2004. Even more unpredictably, a fifth and final album **No Theyself** was unleashed in 2009 to much critical acclaim. Like the greatest stars in the sky, Magazine burned briefly but brightly and their influence is felt today.

About This Song

Yes, it's a cover of the *James Bond* song. However, anyone expecting a faithful rendition of Shirley Bassey's famous orchestral version is in for a shock. Instead of the soaring vocals from Tiger Bay's finest, Devoto drawls and extends each syllable in his almost-speaking style against a backdrop of sawing guitars and weird BBC Radiophonic Workshop synth wizardry. In fact, the cover turns John Barry's essential spy theme into the realms of '60s and '70s science fiction. It could easily become a replacement *Dr Who* theme tune with its unique brand of weirdness. It embodies retro futurism.

It's admittedly not for everyone, but luckily at the time it didn't make the cut on Magazine's debut album, instead appearing as the B-side of non-album single **Touch and Go**. Perhaps Devoto's notion was tongue in cheek, Shirley Bassey of course being about as far away from punk as you can possibly get. Maybe it was an effort to disentangle Magazine from the origins of the short-lived movement, Devoto abandoning ship by unceremoniously abandoning Buzzcocks.

For anyone curious enough to seek out this obscure cover version of a 60s hit, the track features on the 2006 CD reissue of **Real Life**, along with its A-side. Its available on YouTube if the thought of tracking down the long-deleted compact disc is too rich for your blood. A point of interest regarding the original track is that the lyrics were co-written by film musical and amusing pop legend Anthony '*Pop Goes The Weasel*' Newley. Not a lot of people know that.

Essential Album

A much-contested bone of contention - likely because there aren't many to choose from - of the three brilliant albums released by Magazine, I nominate **The Correct Use of Soap**. This opinion would definitely generate a healthy verbal lynching from some fans, who regard their third record as being too commercial. This, of course, is not the point and utter bollocks on the part of anyone who disagrees with me. Ten tracks of perfection, lyrically and musically it's beyond compare within their *oeuvre*.

Highlights include album opener, the anthem **Because You're Frightened**, Devoto screeching out '*Look what fear's done to my body*' as part of a sing-along chorus; it has a few skewed pop moments in tracks like **I'm a Party** and **Sweetheart Contract**, while **I Want to Burn Again** and **Philadelphia** provide a darker edge. Also contained is a weird, deconstructed cover of Sly and the Family Stone's funk epic, **Thank you (Falenttinme Be Mice Elf Agin)**.

Not only is this Magazine's greatest album, but The Correct Use of Soap serves as a good way in, a suitable gateway drug to coerce you into their harder stuff. **Real Life** and **Secondhand Daylight** aren't quite as accessible as this one, but still essential for anyone wishing to seek out their darker side.

Second Choice Song

How many minor hits can you reference containing lyrics as dark as the opening gambit of **A Song From Under the Floorboards** – '*I am angry, I am ill, and I am ugly as sin*' ? Although these dark and prophetic words continue many of the existential, self-loathing lyrical themes featured on **The Correct Use of Soap**, credit is very much due to that staple of Russian literature, Fyodor Dostoevsky. In fact, the lyrics for the entire song are lifted wholesale from Dostoevsky's *Notes from the Underground*. It's doesn't even paraphrase, either; it's key lines from this 1864 novella.

How many minor hits are based on the ideological discourse featured in moody texts written by Russian authors? At the time, in the pre-internet age, if you knew then you knew, I suppose. *(One could easily write an essay about the use of public libraries by post-punk musicians. For instance, J.G. Ballard's books must have rarely been on the shelves in this era.)*

Musically anthemic, the stolen-with-pride poetry contained in the book is backed by whistling synths and memorable guitar work courtesy of McGeoch's axe magic, as well as prominent piano stanza. Weirdly and satisfyingly, the song climaxes with the sort of keyboard pattern not totally unlike that heard on **Sweet Home Alabama**, in a sing-along of the song's chorus – '*My force of habit, I am an insect, and I must confess I'm proud as hell of that fact*' and later, repeat of just the word '*habit*'. Seeing this track performed on the band's 2011 reunion tour was a massive gig-going highlight. Epic stuff.

JULIAN COPE

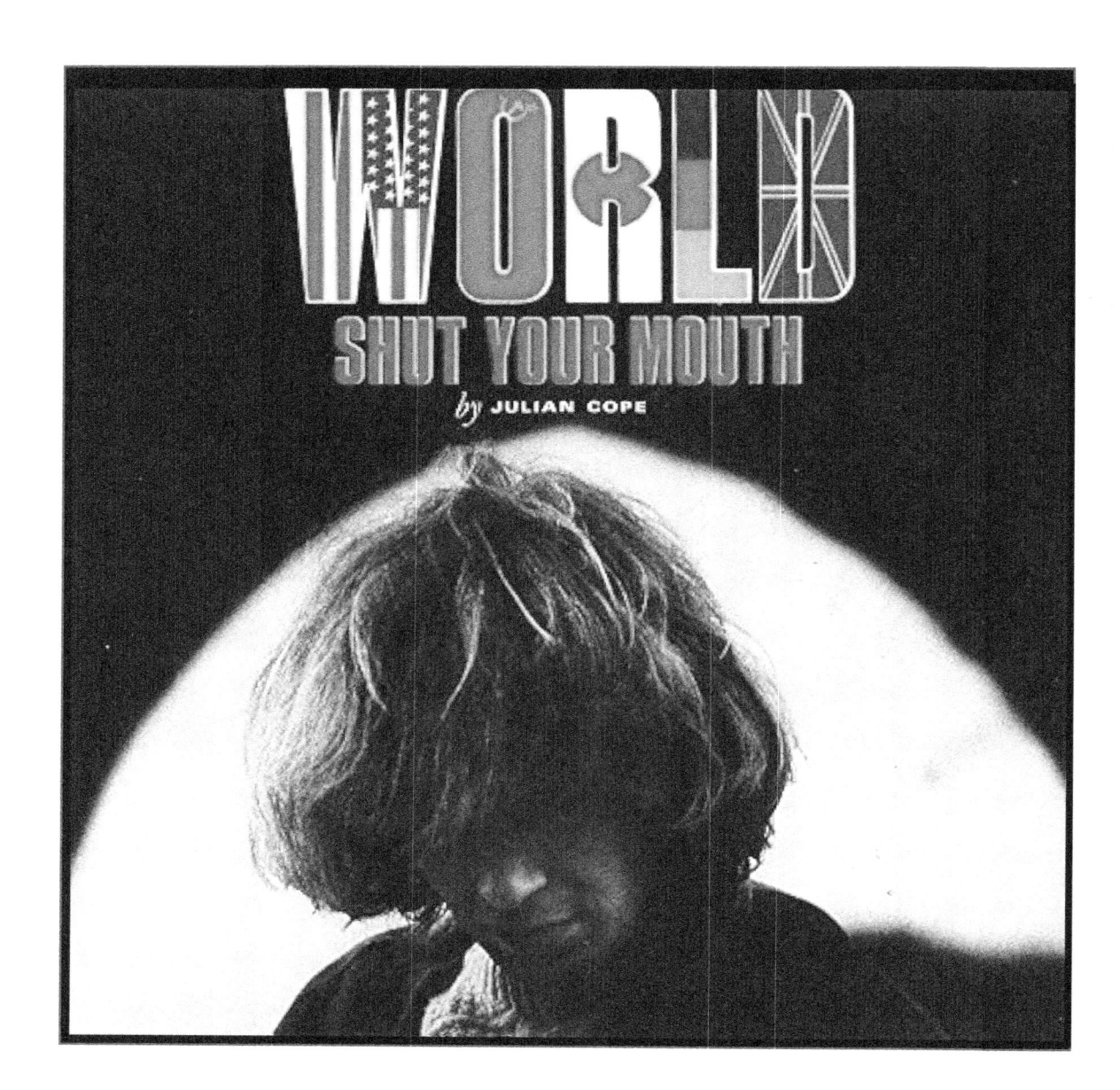

STRASBOURG

JULIAN COPE - STRASBOURG
Guest Article by James Griffiths

About the Artist

To the uninitiated, Julian Cope's discography is a tricky path to tread. Even just trying to count his albums, some of which were recorded under fictitious psuedonyms, is a difficult proposition (much like the legend that surrounds the King's Men stone circle in Oxfordshire, which Cope writes about emphatically in his epic gazeteer *The Modern Antiquarian*).

Nowadays a prolific author as well alternative music legend, Cope is perhaps best known as singer and bassist in The Teardrop Explodes.

He famously left his native Tamworth to attend college in Liverpool, becoming a central part of a thriving post-punk scene (anchored by the famous Zoo club) and forming several bands that went nowhere before the Teardrops were founded in 1978. One these was Crucial Three, the singer of whom was none other than Ian McCulloch, later of Echo and the Bunnymen. Also hanging around looking sullen (*probably*) were the likes of Pete Burns, later of Dead or Alive, Pete Wylie of Wah! and Bill Drummond of '90s weirdos/dancefloor fillers the **KLF** (*who has a producer credit on the Teardrop's debut album*). Even a young Courtney Love was knocking about, allegedly a bit of a 'hanger on' within the scene.

Early Teardrop's single **Sleeping Gas** cemented their post-punk, neo-psychedelia credentials. However, by the time 1980's debut **Kilimanjaro** was released, they were proper major label fodder.

Kilimanjaro is largely all 80's pop brilliance but does offer a smattering of psychedelic moments. They released probably their most well-known single **Reward** as a stop-gap single between their debut and 1981's **Wilder**, an even more sporadic affair which sought (and failed) to prolong their commercial success. Actually, the album works better during its edgier moments, like on the haunting **Tiny Children** or truly epic **The Great Dominions**. No-one remembers the single **Colours Fly Away** and due to commercial failings and general artistic differences the Teardrop's imploded (*ha!*) in 1982.

Cope retreated back to his native Tamworth, bolting the front door and waiting out the inevitable seismic acid comedown. After a couple of years, his first two solo records emerged in 1984. **World Shut Your Mouth** first and **Fried** following later that year. The latter features an iconic sleeve with Cope photographed under an enormous turtle shell and playing with a Dinky toy truck on Alvecote Mound, near Tamworth.

Cope was viewed as pop's greatest weirdo back then, and these two albums failed to set the world on fire. However, they both remain firm favourites of mine.

His next album, **Saint Julian,** was released shortly after and represents his commercial peak. It's a stadium-baiting rock album, and bore single **World Shut Your Mouth**, confusingly *not* on his debut of the same name! Sadly, success wouldn't last and Cope's follow-up record **My Nation Underground** arrived to a lukewarm critical and commercial reception. Quite rightly so, as it's not great.

Things start getting really interesting from here on in though, as Cope discovered a passion for self-recording and self-releasing music outside of the wants and pressures of a major label. **Skellington** (1990) and **Droolian** (1991) are *'slap dash for no cash'*; two-minute songs with titles like **Out of My Mind on Dope and Speed**. Cope termed this style 'acid campfire' and it's easy to understand why.

A trio of albums - hailed by fans as Cope's best - followed in the early '90s, heralding a new era. **Peggy Suicide**, **Jehovahkill** and **Autogeddon** are much darker than their predecessors, the home of songs about more serious issues - the state of the planet, an adverse reaction to the poll tax, the building of the Newbury Bypass and the perils of organised religion are the order of the day here.

Around this time, Cope turned his talented hands to writing and published books on megaliths and German krautrock music. All were well received in the fields of musicology and archaeology alike. Among rave reviews for the music books were some unexpectedly mainstream publications like *Smash Hits* and, bizarrely, girls' comic *Bunty*.

It's worth quoting from the Bunty review for the sheer lunacy of imagining how the average nine-year-old schoolgirl interpreted such praise: *'Brilliantly researched, Krautrocksampler abounds with revelations, and Cope's enthusiasm verges on the lethal ... a sort of lysergic Lester Bangs.'*

Most people aren't aware that Cope's musical career became more prolific despite being under the radar. Nowadays, he continues to self-publish records on his Head Heritage website and has been a central part of several rock and experimental super groups. Outside of the Teardrop Explodes, I think those first two Tamworth albums are Cope's most essential.

About This Song
Strasbourg, from **World Shut Your Mouth** is all kinds of epic. Beginning with a rip-roaring acoustic guitar strum, after a brief intro we get electric guitars and a thumping bassline. In an alternative world, this would be a massive hit. Like a lot of Cope's earlier solo work it presents a slice of pop that isn't afraid to eschew a harder, edgier side.

The lyrics seem to relate to a desire for unity through the metaphor of becoming allied. *If I were France/and you were Germany/What an alliance that would be'*, Cope sings. It's track two on WSYM, sandwiched between **Metranil Vavin** and **An Elegant Chaos**. It's quite straightforward in structure compared to many other tracks on the album and feels like a bit of a belter slap-bang in the middle of two quite strange, slower tracks. The song concludes with the repeated chant *'Look no further'*.

Quite what it all means, no one knows except Cope himself, but we're not in this for lyrical content – this one's all about the music!

Essential Album
Psychedelic Pop. Indie Prog. Call it what you like but **Fried**, Julian's second LP released in 1984, probably doesn't need either of those labels. It's unique but straightforward. Where WSYM is more about being a pop album with little nods to psychedelia, Fried works the opposite way and feels a very alternative record first and foremost.

Opener **Reynard the Fox** is soft and shamanic in equal measure, retelling the medieval literary cycle. The fascination with history continues with the amazing **Bloody Assizes**, an imagining of the trials following the Monmouth rebellion against James II. There's wistful and atmospheric acoustic music on tracks like **Laughing Boy** and genuine joy on **Me Singing** and **Holy Love**.

Fried feels like one of those albums you always want in your pocket. It feels like there are several key themes at play but there is a consistency in its inconsistency. And it's bloody crazy!

Second Choice Song

It would be remiss of me not to acknowledge a song by the band that made Julian Cope famous and who are far more well-known. As a bit of a reaction to this, I'm choosing a b-side. Fuck it, I love b-sides. This is where artists/bands decide to do something a bit different, a bit more edgy.

Use Me is probably one of the best b-sides of the 1980's. Over an aggressive acoustic guitar - *and that's it!* - Cope sings like he's wounded and exhausted. As usual, the lyrics are batshit crazy and probably make no sense to anyone who wasn't on the same trip whilst writing the song. Cope sings about *cats around a marble throne* for some unfathomable reason.

The chords are a thing of beauty, and despite the anger in the song it seems to soar in different directions. I used to play it a lot during the Covid lockdown because it seemed to encapsulate the frustration that I was feeling (that we were *all* feeling).

It's definitely worth checking it out – it's featured on various re-issues of **Kilimanjaro**. What song was it the b-side of? Doesn't matter, it's far superior.

HELMET

IN THE MEANTIME

HELMET – IN THE MEANTIME
Guest Article by Lloyd Hollingworth

About the Band

Helmet are/were a unique group. Heavy but not 'metal', alternative but not in the typical 'indie' sense, they straddled a line between the two genres, with a pinch of hardcore and in their earlier days, a fair dose of noise rock added to the mix. Sometimes this stylistic vagueness was to their detriment because the public – and record companies - tend to like things that are simple to understand and easy to digest.

You have probably read a number of entries in this book that reference the early 1990's as a watershed moment for music previously considered of marginal interest, suddenly and inexplicably 'going mainstream'. I hate to bore you with yet another example of this phenomenon but it is unavoidable if I am to discuss the group Helmet and the story of their unlikely – and sadly quite brief – success.

Formed in New York in 1989 and very much moulded in his own image by guitarist/singer/songwriter, Page Hamilton, the group had quite the alternative/noise rock pedigree but buried deep within the jazz-trained Mr Hamilton was the heart of a teenage metal fan - quite a discerning one too - and this would influence the music of Helmet as much as any atonality or 7th chords.

Their debut album **Strap It On** was released on the archetypal noise rock label Amphetamine Reptile in 1990 and already featured a number of Helmet trademarks such as syncopation, a very stripped back and abrasive approach, and repetition. Just in case it's not clear, one of the standout tracks on the album is simply called **Repetition**.

Nothing about the content of this record offers any hint of marketability or commercial success. It is a fantastic noise rock/alt metal album but sadly, this type of music was always going to be niche and completely invisible to the mainstream. The bands plying that sound did so in small, sweaty clubs, with no airplay, exposure or MTV rotation. Or so it seemed, until just a year, later something unexpected and without precedent happened in 'alternative' music.

In 1991 another noisy and previously very niche band achieved the kind of commercial success and high profile that was previously only the domain of pop bands or heritage rock groups. The unlikely triumph – and tragedy – of Nirvana is an oft-told tale so I'll leave it there except to add that their spectacular success caught EVERYONE off guard, including record companies. What record companies – quite logically – did next was attempt to find 'the next Nirvana' and in attempting to do so they cast their net very wide.

Industry heavy-hitters, Interscope Records, the company to blame for inflicting **Rico Suave** by perma-shirtless, Ecuadorian priapist, Gerardo on the world, got involved in this post-Nirvana major label feeding frenzy. They quickly set their sights firmly on Helmet, offering them a reported 1.2 million dollar advance, which they very gladly accepted.

Fuelled by this cash injection and no doubt brimming with confidence, in 1992 Helmet entered the studio to record their major label debut **Meantime**. Production was handled by noise rock guru and professional divisive character Steve Albini. Famous for his raw 'warts-and-all' recordings, Albini was horrified when hotshot mixer-of-the-moment, Andy Wallace was called in to give the recordings a sprinkle of his audio fairy dust, even going as far as to insist that Wallace wasn't later allowed to remix his work on Nirvana's very flat and lifeless sounding **In Utero**. What a pity.

The album was released to a mostly positive reaction and the band got a genuine major label push in terms of publicity, including regular appearances on MTV and a much-coveted live show support to Faith No More. The album eventually went gold in the US but peaked at just number 68 on the Billboard chart.

Their equally essential follow up album **Betty** from 1994 performed well but sold less. You can guess where this is going by now. Their third Interscope album, 1997's **Aftertaste** was an uninspired affair, sales continued to decline and, near the end of that same year, the band split. There have been Helmet reunions of sorts, starting in 2004 and continuing to the present day, but the magic and inspiration in any new recordings is, to my ears at least, sadly lacking.

About This Song
In The Meantime, almost the title track from **Meantime**, begins with a fusillade of drum rolls, cymbal-crashing crescendos and a suffocating wall of atonal guitar. This is followed by unaccompanied and massive sounding drums, with heavy-handed and heavy-footed John Stanier playing a solid and straightforward beat. What then happens is a lesson in taut riffology and head-snapping musical dynamics that still stays within the structure of a conventional song. Just.

Riff number one makes its welcome *'and you can breathe now'* appearance at the 24 second mark and is an almost prototypical grunge riff, as might be heard on any early Soundgarden or Tad album. This familiarity could lull you into the false belief that what you are going to be hearing is even more of the patented 'Seattle sludge' that was so prevalent at the time.

Instead, what comes next is a little more twisted and a lot more jarring. In a heartbeat, the second riff is introduced. It is incessant, almost illogical, pounding and staccato. It comes out swinging with bad intentions. It's a riff that never delivers the expected turnaround or respite but instead continues to repeatedly poke and jab its hard, calloused fingers into your sternum. It's a thing of malevolent sonic invention and will make you involuntarily clench your teeth. It may even lead your mind to thoughts of violence - or is that just me?

The vocals of Page Hamilton then begin to forcefully berate and castigate the listener in the manner of a US Army drill instructor. The lyrics are deliberately oblique and mostly impenetrable – *'No narratives, I hate singer songwriters'* is a direct Page Hamilton quote – but what you can decipher hints at the menace that is palpable in the music.

Riff number three is a *'parachute deployed'* descending lurch into the chorus, which is simply the phrase *'In the meantime'* repeated three times but in an even angrier and more agitated tone than that used for the verses.

You are then presented with something approaching a traditional breakdown/middle eight, followed by an avalanche of air-drum-worthy fills that segue into the revisited chorus, this time as the outro - and that's your lot.

Did someone at Interscope really think that this band was going to provide them with the next **Smells Like Teen Spirit**?

Unlike Nirvana, there was little to suggest any chart potential in Helmet's body of work. They always had a challenging sound and despite the cleaner production and mix here, to most sane listeners at least, it seemed highly unlikely that they would cross over to the mainstream in the same way as Kurt Cobain & co.

Re-reading the above, I realise that I may not be selling this song as an easy listen but it's actually accessible and extremely memorable. It has multiple hooks and a groove. It is also very concise and in a little over three minutes, it perfectly encapsulates what Helmet are all about. Like all of their songs, it's deliberately lean, sparse and stripped back. Precise but never mechanical and always with a sense of movement, not a second of the composition's short running time is wasted.

Essential Album

I always hoped that the title **Meantime** was a play on words, that as well as its dictionary definition, it might also mean 'Badtime' or 'Hardtime', thus describing a period of particular turmoil, danger and social unrest, as this would suit the sound and aesthetic of the album perfectly. They do flirt very self-consciously with an actual tune on MTV staple, **Unsung** but it's mostly – fantastically - just HUGE riffs with space and a pissed-off sounding Page Hamilton free-associating on top.

It's a front-loaded album and the majority of the stronger and more well-known songs appear early on, with the aforementioned **In The Meantime**, the relentless, choppy chug of **Iron Head** - just check out that anguished cry around the two-minute mark - and the almost bouncy **Give It**, hitting you hard straight out of the gate.

As with all Helmet songs, the almost telepathic rhythmic interplay between guitars and drums is the real highlight. They lock together in grooves that are punishing but that also swing. Light and shade, dynamics and space, all are present in what initially may seem like a barrage of noise.

Occasional forays into melody aside, the vocals primarily serve as another instrumental layer, with the lyrics mostly a cut-and-paste cross section of 90's pop- culture references and soundbites. The phrases that peek out above the parapets and lodge in the memory are a prescient *'die young is far too boring these days'* on **Unsung**, a particularly sarcastic *'self-help, self-help confidence'* during **Give It** and a knowing reference to much-maligned early-days MTV veejay *'Downtown Julie Brown'* also on Give it.

Helmet have always been smarter than the average band, but never smart-alecks, which is a crucial difference, and this album shows them flexing both brain and brawn in equal measure.

Second Choice Song
I could easily have chosen a number of songs from Meantime follow-up **Betty**. It's an overlooked album that has an even bigger, warmer and less 90's sound and is worthy of your immediate attention. Special mention must again be given to the Led-footed (*pun very much intended*) drums of John Stanier. They may well have caused some structural damage to the studio during recording of this album such is the power and kinetic energy they contain. His tight-but-loose grooves power the songs along like a New York John Bonham, whilst guitarist Page Hamilton's riff-well never runs dry.

However, instead of this option, I have decided on more of a wild card choice with 1993's **Just Another Victim**, from the soundtrack to the long-forgotten Emilio Estevez and 'shock comedian' Dennis Leary (remember him?) thriller **Judgement Night**. It shows just how mainstream the underground/alternative music scene was in the 90's when a non-indie film like this had the likes of Biohazard, Onyx, Dinosaur Jr, Cypress Hill, Mudhoney, plus – and I'm not making this up – Ice T and Slayer singing a medley of songs by the UK's glue-sniffing punks The Exploited on its soundtrack.

The song itself, indeed the whole soundtrack album, is dipping a toe in that none-more-90's genre 'rap/metal crossover' - *eugh, I know* - but despite that, it is still a deliberately boneheaded, knuckle-dragging monster of a tune.

That utterly ferocious and feral *'der-ner dun-dun der-ner'* riff is repeated until you advisedly retreat and those trademark drum grooves are immediately locked in. It is so good that even the mid-song arrival – like drunks gatecrashing a party - of faux- Irish lunkheads, House of Pain can't scupper it.

As we are still referencing the 1990's, I'll leave – nearly – the last word to those inimitable zeitgeist-surfers of the period, *Beavis and Butt-Head*, who after approvingly viewing a Helmet video - a sure fire sales booster in those pre-internet days - were a little baffled by the clean-cut look of the group and said: *'If you, like, saw these guys in the street, you wouldn't even know that they're cool.'*

If I have managed to persuade you to listen to Helmet - *'You said Helmet - huh huh'* - and maybe to appreciate their music, then just like the aforementioned pair of sofa-dwelling, MTV-addled idiot savants, you too will realise that they are indeed cool. Very cool.

BONUS CONTENT

ONE-OFFS

BONUS CONTENT

There are a number of bands that have produced just the one song that I like – really like – but I don't much care for the rest of their catalogue. Many of these songs are so good that it would be a crime for me not to mention them in a book specifically written to recommend underrated songs that you might not have heard of.

So, with that in mind, let's take a look at some of those tunes that made it into my favourites list even if the bands didn't. It might be a different story for you, you might discover one or two new favourite bands of your own in this section.

THE BOLSHOI - AWAY

The Bolshoi formed in 1984 in Wiltshire, breeding ground for other such musical luminaries as XTC, Peter Gabriel and Justin Hayward. They migrated to London a year later and earned supporting slots for The Cult and Lords of the New Church. In the early days, the band were pegged as post-punk goths and compared to acts like Bauhaus.

Frontman Trevor Tanner had an eccentric performance style, and in a chicken-and-egg conundrum one has to wonder whether he nicked his moves from Pulp's Jarvis Cocker or, which seems a little more likely when comparing activity timescales, whether Jarvis intensely studied Bolshoi videos and borrowed the stylings from Tanner. To see what I mean watch the video for this song and imagine JC performing and it's pretty much the same person.

I hadn't heard this song for about 30 years when it suddenly came on in the middle of a background YouTube goth compilation as I was working from home. At once, everything about the song came flooding back – after three decades, I remembered the words and the chorus seemed to have been burned into my brain even though the track wasn't a particular favourite back at the time of release.

Since hearing it again, I played it a lot whilst writing this book and have driven my girlfriend mad. When friends come around we sometimes have a YouTube session where we take it in turns to pick a song and I'd battered her down with so many plays of this tune that she picked it as one of her own choices. Result!

The opening drum roll sounds like a bunch of puppies falling down a stairwell and the driving bassline is echoed by the rhythm guitar in the background. An upbeat tempo brings some downbeat lyrics along for the ride and, weirdly, a couple of great lines from the album version are edited out in the YouTube version seemingly for no good reason. It's a very pop-oriented song on the whole, though the opening guitar licks sound reminiscent of those utilised by *goth-meisters* The Mission or early Fields of the Nephilim and Sisters of Mercy.

In their videos, the band present themselves as tidy, manicured goths that girls could take home to meet mom.

DAVID BYRNE & BRIAN ENO – THE JEZEBEL SPIRIT

Buried here in this Bonus Content section is one of the most interesting tracks in the entire book. **The Jezebel Spirit** features the voice of an anonymous priest performing an exorcism, set to a backing track mixing tape loops, African rhythms and David Byrne's scratchy guitar work. And not an exorcism performed for the album – an actual event of a real priest trying to dispel an evil spirit from some poor unfortunate woman that for some reason was recorded. *Rolling Stone* magazine found the act of using a real exorcism rather distasteful, primly and somewhat piously saying that it *'trivialised'* the event.

The track rounds out side one of the classic 1981 album **My Life in the Bush of Ghosts**. At the time, Eno and Byrne were light years ahead of most musicians in their thinking (*Eno still is*), embracing the use of samples and utilising painstaking tape cutting and looping techniques to provide soundscapes for the sampled vocals. The LP was recorded in between Talking Heads 1979 album **Fear of Music** and their groundbreaking 1980 masterpiece **Remain in Light**.

Bush of Ghosts was recorded before Remain in Light – The Jezebel Spirit and other tracks would have comfortably fitted on that album – but it had a delayed release due to clearance on the samples. Its impact on later music is undeniable – people are still using many of the techniques Byrne and Eno helped pioneer to this day (albeit with computers doing the work in seconds that used to take weeks, if not months, of manual labour).

Within a few seconds of the song starting you can tell that it's unique. Imagine hearing it in 1981! Eno has summarised the work on Ghosts as *'a vision of a psychedelic Africa'* – I think that's pretty accurate. It's an incredibly funky track, if linear, but the addition of the priest's voice and the act that he's performing – even if you don't believe in any of that stuff – is genuinely thrilling.

The song's (and album's) legacy is deep. Artists as diverse as Kate Bush, Pink Floyd and Public Enemy producing The Bomb Squad have all acknowledged its influence across popular music culture. Andy Gill of The Guardian critiqued the record as *'groundbreaking in its recontextualisation of sampling in a less overtly avant-garde context'*. Whatever the fuck *that* means!

KILLING JOKE – LOVE LIKE BLOOD

This is cheating a little as I actually like a good handful of Killing Joke tunes. Really, I just wanted them to feature in the book and this was possibly the best place for them. They will get their own featured entry in Volume 2.

Killing Joke formed in 1978 and separated themselves out from the punk scene by dint of their music being a lot heavier, and a lot rockier, so much so that they're regarded as an influence for both the Industrial and Grunge scenes (Nirvana were even sued for nicking one of their basslines!).

Early musical releases were sometimes overshadowed by their proto-Photoshopped (interpret that as manual cut-and-paste) record covers, notably Fred Astaire dancing in a battlefield and a promo poster of a high-ranking German religious figure appearing to salute a bunch of Nazis (reused for their early 1992 career retrospective compilation album **Laugh? I Nearly Bought One!**)

1985's **Nighttime** album brought them critical and commercial success, and provides most of my favourite Killing Joke songs. **Eighties** provides an accompanying video that'll be a sour-tasting trip down memory lane for anybody that remembers that period, as well as providing the influence for Nirvana's **Come As You Are**. **Kings and Queens** and title track **Nighttime** are gigantic slabs of granite awesomeness but it's **Love Like Blood** that steals the show.

Love Like Blood is a brooding track that features their trademark icy keyboards over a huge bass riff, pounding drums and chuggy guitars. Jaz Coleman's vocals are a haunting presence and most band videos make him look like an absolute lunatic – well, he makes himself look like that, to be fair. And he has been fervently predicting imminent armageddon since roughly 1982 - even briefly relocating to Iceland to avoid the Soviet warheads - but let's not hold that against him. In Killing Joke's world the doomsday clock is always set at one minute to midnight (and they are all the better for it).

Coleman is actually one of those fellows with various interests, like we used to get in the Victorian era before we all had to buckle down and specialise in increasingly obscure fields. He is a singer, a conductor (of music), an occultist, a priest, an actor and he also has his own brand of hot sauces. Someone's even painted a huge mural of him on the side of a house in Cheltenham, which I duly took a pilgrimage to during the writing of this book.

FREELAND – WE WANT YOUR SOUL

I'm surprised that this wasn't a huge hit. It's a funny, scathing attack on consumerism and the creeping grip of corporate entities taking over our lives, stealing our data, turning us into consumerist zombies. I assumed that the rest of the world was now in on the joke, but perhaps not. This song should have been number one in every country of release, a stark (and yet danceable) warning to all of us about the road we're being led down.

Adam Freeland is a British DJ and music artist and this was the first of his tunes that he wrote lyrics for. As a first attempt, it's a pretty stellar effort. Instead of getting a singer, he ran the words through a speech synthesizer, which was 100% the right thing to do. He also samples the late, great comedian *Bill Hicks*, who recognised the same issues with society years earlier and used his comedy to try and get the rest of us to wake the fuck up.

Incredibly, the Target Corporation (a huge US retailer) tried to license the song for an advertising campaign, which is either a sign of incredible stupidity on their part or one of the most genius attempts at marketing ever. Freeland rightly told them to do one and the track wasn't used.

The accompanying video – award winning at that – is a fun watch but this shortened version of the song completely omits the Hicks samples, which I would recommend listening to. To offer a comparison with a track that is sort of in the same ballpark – actually it's not but it's the best I can come up with – think of Baz Luhrman's mega-hit **Sunscreen**. Snippets of loosely connected lyrics are read out over a muzak backing track. Freeland's song ramps up the ante and sweeps aside the occasionally sage New Agey / self-help advice in favour of a scathing critique of modern civilisation's obsession with material things and indentured slavery to corporations and their warping of the fabric of reality through advertising.

They try to convince us that we need to buy everything.
They're wrong. The only thing you need is this song.

GRIMES – PLAYER OF GAMES

Grimes might seem like an odd choice to include in this book. She is, after all, really well known. Regrettably, this might not be for her music, more because of her status of being Elon Musk's ex and the fact that she agreed to call her child X Æ A-Xii (surely a winner in *Chat* magazines legendary and hilarious *'You Called Your Child What?'* column.)

Her penchant for exotic names wasn't inherited – Grimes' real moniker is Claire Elise Boucher and she's a Canadian woman who has packed quite a bit into her life so far, not least a trip down the Mississippi in a houseboat she built with a friend, which Wikipedia provides sparse info about: *'several mishaps, including engine trouble and encounters with law enforcement'* before the boat was impounded. I would have loved to have seen a documentary about that but the best we have is an animated short you can find on YouTube under the title 'Grimes in Mississippi (Animated)' which, at the time of writing, had been previously viewed by a sum total of just 12 people. Twelve. (A check 2 weeks later and the figure had gone up to 30).

It's astounding to think that an artist like this is so criminally ignored. In the UK, her music hasn't lit up the charts. The Official Charts website shows that none of her singles have even entered the Top 75 and only one of her albums (**Miss Anthropocene**) breached the Top 10, which may be a consequence of more people checking out her music after being in the news through her association with Musk. More success has come in the US Dance charts, where her releases regularly appear.

I can say that in my social circles, featuring people from all walks of life with diverse tastes in music, I seem to be the only one that is playing any Grimes tracks. I'm not sure why that is and when researching her chart positions, I was left genuinely shocked. For **Player of Games** (and **We Appreciate Power**) to fail commercially to such an extent is mind-boggling. Maybe the world just isn't ready for her yet.

I generally find Grimes a bit wishy-washy overall, with a couple of stellar exceptions, but that may be because I don't know enough of her work. Even a basic check of her videos on YouTube shows that she has a unique creative vision and is unafraid to experiment with musical styles and genres. She has created a lot of sugary, synth-drenched stuff, but we'll ignore that for this book. She seems like a cool person and the world of music is undoubtedly better off with her contributions. Further exploration might make me like more of her work, it might not. Grimes wouldn't care less either way, I suspect.

As a devoted *Rocket League* player, I've also encountered the work of Grimes during Season 5 of the game, where they had a special Grimes event and pushed her music in a big way. Although not particularly liking it at first, **Player of Games** is a grower and I eventually bought it from Amazon and now give it a regular airing. Released late December 2021, the track is generally thought to be about her ex-partner, the super-nerd and multi-billionaire with ambitions to colonise the solar system, Elon Musk.

If the song is based on fiction, it's got some great lyrics that showcase an overtly sad relationship coming to a close, with a heart-breaking outpouring of angst from the narrator. If it is indeed about Musk, and her relationship with him, then it a toe-curling baring of Grimes' soul and she's putting it all out there for her art.

In the song, the narrator laments the fact that what she has to offer cannot compare to the adventure awaiting the subject of her affections, namely a journey deep into the solar system (specifically Europa, one of the moons orbiting Jupiter). She asks why he can't love her the way he loves the idea of sailing away into the *'cold expanse of space'*. You just don't get a depth of lyrics like this in 99% of the shit cluttering up the charts:

I'm also going to mention **We Appreciate Power**. For a song that's so good, it's not easy to get a hold of. I don't mean that you can't just buy it as a digital download if you already know about it, but that it should have been included on her most recent album **Miss Anthropocene** and wasn't (unless you bought the Japanese release by import). That's a genuinely baffling decision as it would have been the best song on the album.

I adore this song. That's probably because it has Industrial leanings and has been favourably compared to the work of Nine Inch Nails. Noisy drums, a terrifying guitar loop, crunchy background guitars with beautiful, almost ethereal vocals and a brilliant chorus. The song repeatedly switches between floaty pop and heavy Industrial breaks and over the top of it all Grimes sings about Artificial Intelligence and our inevitable submission to its coming reign.

It's pop music but yet again there's a depth to the lyrics and an approach to the artistry that puts Grimes leagues above the competition. All she has to do now is wait for the public to catch up with her vision.

MY BLOODY VALENTINE - SOON

There are some bands that I think I should have liked more than I actually did. The idea of them, reading about what they were up to, buying into their experiments and getting on board with their visions of the world. My Bloody Valentine is one of those bands. However, whenever I played their stuff it just didn't seem to gel with me. Except for this one track, which I love.

The band took a long time to get going and find their sound. It's fair to say the existence of the band has never been plain sailing and has always been troubled. When they finally found a label with the resources to fund singer/guitarist Kevin Shields' vision, he nearly bankrupted them. The recording process for the 1991 album **Loveless** (of which **Soon** closes out as the final track) was protracted and expensive. Creation Records, later to regain financial stability by signing the incredibly successful Oasis, nearly went under and dropped MBV shortly after the release.

Soon was released as part of the **Glider EP** in 1990, as the lead track, and a remixed version was used on the **Loveless** album. The sound incorporated Shields' 'glide' technique, wherein he would create a wall of noise, consistently strumming whilst using the tremolo arm of the guitar - a unique technique of his own - to shift pitch and create a warped sound, then adding multiple overlays to further add to the density.

The vocals, provided by Shields and other band guitarist Belinda Butcher, are ethereal and dreamy (and nonsensical) becoming more of an instrument rather than a way of expressing actual words. The drums, after an initial sample, are catchy and almost Britpop-esque, the bass weaving around them in the build-up to the sections where Shields lets loose his guitar, and the dreamy vocals ride the lush yet powerful river of instrumentation beneath. It's a hard song to describe, almost dancey in parts and loud indie shoegaze in others, but all blended perfectly without the dynamic jolts of a Pixies or Nirvana song, for example.

Listen to this song and you'll realise that the critical plaudits Kevin Shields has received for his guitar work are all well deserved. What he's doing with his guitar in this song is amazing, and if trying to bankrupt Creation to get a sound like this down on vinyl was the cost, then I say it was worth it. This is as close to perfection as you can get, it's a really beautiful piece of work and one of my all-time favourite tunes from the last 30 years.

EAT STATIC - SURVIVORS

If I ever win the lottery, top of my list of things to do – well, near the top anyway – is to take six months out of normal life and spend the time pulling together animation videos for two particular tracks.   One is Jean Michel Jarre's **Ethnicolor**. This is the other one.

Whenever I hear it, my head is filled with the most fantastic imagery, of an alien world and creatures communicating with each other in rhythmic bleeps and noises (that rather conveniently sound like they may have originated in an Earth-bound synthesizer from the early 1990's). I see a vast ocean, like Clive Barker's *Quiddity*, and enormous mountains made from frozen methane. I see round creatures with lots of frondy bits noodling around. And I'm imagining all this without even being stoned out of my mind – just imagine what this track can do to committed weed-hounds!

Speaking of which, the band Eat Static were formed from the already existing Ozric Tentacles, a band that would deserve a whole chapter on their own, originally building a career (of sorts) out of playing free festivals and handing out cassette tapes. As that band experimented with a little electronic music but remained steadfastly attached to traditional instruments, the drummer and keyboard player from the Ozrics, Merv Pepler and Joie Hinter respectively, peeled away and formed a side project with the intention of playing around with a bunch of synths and seeing what happened. They were both drawn to the late '80's new world of rave music and acid house and results were so encouraging that they left the safety of the Ozrics in 1994 and continued as Eat Static.

They've released 11 studio albums to date, nine of which I didn't know existed until researching this book. I will give that lot a go, but my focus here is on their track **Survivors**, which appeared on 1995's **Implant** album. Although I've listened to the album and find it decent enough, Survivors does seem to have that additional unknown ingredient that makes it that little bit special. For me, anyway. Hopefully for you, too.

At just under eight minutes in length, you have a fully instrumental track (not included in that section because the band focus on instrumentals) that starts with some weird, echoey noises and then brings in a fizzing keyboard bassline, some light percussion and then something that sounds like someone playing a washboard. It's intentionally strange stuff, but it's ordered and there's a logic to it. Some of the background noises sound like an alien creature talking and trying to communicate, and other 'voices' join in to compliment and enjoy the party. Then, at the 4:06 minute mark, a fantastic new voice enters the mix and steers the song briefly in a different direction. I always, always imitate this new voice whenever I have the track on in the car. I love the sound it makes inside my own mouth. There's no rational way to describe it, you're going to simply have to hear it for yourself.

OZRIC TENTACLES – HALF LIGHT IN THILLAI

Speaking of the Ozrics, now would be the appropriate time to mention their little masterpiece **Half Light in Thillai** taken from the **Jurassic Shift** album in 1993. Masters of their instruments (and no doubt the bong) the Ozrics are a group that have always stayed true to their vision whatever the cost, producing music that they want to make regardless of whether or not other people like it. Luckily, lots of other people do like it and their long career has produced six cassette only albums, 16 studio albums and 10 recorded live offerings. Joined with the catalogue of Eat Static, these are some seriously industrious people!

One of a couple of quieter, more low-key pieces from the Jurassic Shift collection, chock full of echo and reverb, evoking images of Indian temples and mist slowly drifting across rivers, the Ozrics prove that sometimes less is more with this tune. It's funny how I keep describing these instrumental tracks with pictures that I can see in my head, as though I'm suffering from a mild form of synesthesia (good name for a dance band, that) – that might be the case, although in this example, the title of the track pretty much creates the image and I imagine most people would imagine the same sort of thing. Thillai refers to the Thillai Kali Temple, a Hindu religious building dedicated to Shiva and Govindaraja (I suspect Crispin Mills of Kula Shaker also must have visited at some point!).

Beginning with a gong and otherworldly vocal samples, a gentle rolling bongo leads the way for a traditional rock kit, again so loaded with echo that it could have been recorded in a cavern somewhere, a bit of flute and some nice guitar work on the chorus bits, which are a little livelier before fading back down again for the verses. It's a gentle piece with a bit of a kick, never going mad, never overstaying its welcome.

Essentially what you have here is a bunch of extremely talented musicians with the freedom to do whatever they want, and they take a step back from some of the more energetic instrumentals on the rest of the album to breathe and unite with the energy of the cosmos, or something equally trippy. You don't need drugs to appreciate the mastery on display with this tune though, it's way too good for that. The music itself, with some quiet relaxation, can do all the heavy lifting and alter your state of mind on its own.

AMYL AND THE SNIFFERS – GUIDED BY ANGELS

You know when you hear a song and you hate it? And then you hear it again and you still hate it. And you forget all about it and suddenly find yourself humming it, and decide to go back and check it out again to see if you maybe misjudged it the first couple of times? And you find you still hate it? But by this time the song is already in your head, like an audio tapeworm hiding in your brain, popping into your ears unexpectedly at odd moments and gradually it wears you down so much that you put the record on again and find that you now love it.

That's how this song worked for me. It just felt like any one of a thousand bands with an in-your-face vocalist, and in this case a really annoying one - like a deranged toddler whacked out on speed, constantly demanding your attention, jumping up and down with the exuberance of youth - and even watching the video is exhausting because this singer is throwing off so much energy…

In a BBC interview, vocalist Amy Taylor describes the origin of the band's name: *'In Australia we call poppers Amyl. So you sniff it, it lasts for 30 seconds and then you have a headache – and that's what we're like!'*

Amyl and the Sniffers are indeed Australian, something which becomes obvious after hearing just a few bars of singing, though sometimes *shouting* is a more appropriate description. They've only released two albums and a couple of EP's to date, from which no less than nine singles have been harvested. They've won three *ARIA* music awards (recognising Australian music) and been nominated for five more. That's a lot packed into a relatively short career. They do things fast, apparently writing and recording all four songs on their first EP in the ridiculous timeframe of just 12 hours.

What initially appears to be a simple, cartoonish track yanked from the 1970's grows more complex the more you listen to it. The vocals are repetitive in parts, deliberately so, and the band buzz through the song so fast (2:59 in length) that there are more lyrics than you'd expect, and the deeper you get into the song the more you realise that actually, despite all of the obvious punk leanings, Taylor is a pretty decent singer. Not brilliant, which would probably be the last thing even she would want, but perfectly suited to the killer hooks and riffs this tune is stuffed with. Unfortunately, for me, I can only take the band in small doses, but whilst they're on the stereo I'm having a whale of a time (until I get a headache).

THE TEMPER TRAP – SWEET DISPOSITION

Another Australian band, they must be doing something right over there! Formed in 2005, the three-piece relocated to London and released their debut LP in 2009, of which **Sweet Disposition** was the lead single.

This track, arguably one of the most straight 'pop' songs of the entire book, did well in the UK, Irish, Belgian and Australian singles charts, and even made a small impact in the US. Deservedly so, it must be said. The guitar immediately stands out and singer Dougy Mandagi has the voice of an angel. And then in come the drums – mostly toms at this point, until the song kicks into a higher gear at the 1:21 min mark and the snare and hi-hats come crashing in to power the song along beautifully.

They know how good this song is, adding another two minutes onto the length when playing it live with an extended intro.

Bizarrely, the song has three videos, with a different version released in the UK, US and AUS territories, each with a different approach and a different director. Most bands struggle to get the money together for a single video, so not sure why the band (or their management) were so flash with the cash on this one. Having watched two of the three (the original Australian version is particularly difficult to track down) I couldn't pick the best so give them both a go, you really won't get bored of this song by playing it twice over.

They did a headlining tour in the UK, playing at well-known local Birmingham venue *The Hare and Hounds*, a place that most West Midlands musicians are well familiar with (I'm sure I've played there myself in one of the bands I was in, although lots of drink was involved and I couldn't say for certain. Seen a few bands there though.)

They worked their way up to music festivals – big ones like *Roskilde*, *Reading* and *Leeds* – and headline tours in the US and Australia. Their last album release was in 2016 but a new single is slated for 2023, possibly heralding a new full-length work.

JAMES RAY AND THE PERFORMANCE - TEXAS

One of the more obscure artists in the book, for a long time people who knew this man's work thought it might be Andrew Eldritch from the Sisters of Mercy working under a different name. Sometimes, musicians under dispute with their record companies can't control the urge to create and need to find outlets for their talents.

But this is not the case here – despite sounding alarmingly like Eldritch, James Ray is a performer in his own right who just happens to write music that sounds rather a lot like the Sisters as well. And once even worked with the Dark Lord Himself on Sisters side project The Sisterhood (ostensibly set up out of spite to stop band defector Wayne Hussey from nicking the 'Sisters' brand for his new band, which he eventually called The Mission).

James Ray is sort of like a British Al Jourgensen (Ministry, Revolting Cocks etc) with lots of project bands and releases under different band names. A lot of his stuff was on his website, where he gave it away for free, but my most recent check brings back a site that doesn't appear to be fully working. No matter, you can listen and buy in all the usual places.

So, what is **Texas** like? Well, if you already like The Sisters Of Mercy you are in for a right old treat – it sounds like the best record they never made, a danceable powerhouse of a tune with some amazing guitar riffs. For non-Sisters fans, what you have here is a sort of very distant cousin to **You Spin Me Round** by Dead or Alive. Neither artist may have thanked me for the comparison but it's definitely there, and nothing to turn any noses up at – both records are fantastic. Both offer up the same sort of electronic background with a deep-voiced vocal line over the top. James Ray throws in a ton of superb guitar work as a final layer and his association with The Sisters lends it an aura of additional coolness.

Like many of the tracks highlighted in this book, it plays best LOUD.

FISHBONE – BONIN' IN THE BONEYARD

Fishbone provided the blueprint for many of the successful funk-metal bands that proliferated in the early '90s, including the likes of Faith No More, Red Hot Chili Peppers (whom they were great friends with) and Primus (who used to support them). Originally formed in 1979, the band wrote music in whatever style suited them at the moment, including punk, ska, reggae, soul and metal, whilst always making it top level funky, often creating songs that mixed one or more styles to create a hybrid.

Their tunes often offered up some biting social commentary counterbalanced with some oddball humour. The B-side to **Bonin' in the Boneyard**, the madcap **Love and Bullshit**, has to be heard to be believed.

The main track suffers from undercooked production values, in my opinion. Somebody had to say it. For a band so reliant on the funky bass undercurrents, they needed a production approach like Butch Vig gave Nirvana on **Nevermind**, giving their music less treble and more heft, but that's a small gripe when you take in the overall greatness of this composition.

Even with slightly too much treble, the things going on with the bass in this song are incredible. It's a really up-tempo tune, one that will instantly put you in a good mood, layered with plenty of vibrant horn sections (an unfortunate turn of phrase considering the song title). It's been a favourite in the Roach household for decades, although I've never quite made the leap to appreciate their other work anywhere near as much.

Special mention should go to their awesome cover of Alice in Chains' song **Them Bones** at a *MoPOP* 2020 tribute concert after the death of AIC singer Layne Stayley. They take an already phenomenal song and turn it into their own whilst paying the utmost respect to the original. An amazing performance and really worth looking up on YouTube.

MORPHINE – HONEY WHITE

I find the saxophone a hard instrument to love. Normally, when I hear that instrument, it brings a whole load of Kenny G type baggage with it and makes me want to go off and destroy something fragile. But occasionally, the instrument gets through and wins me over. It's all about the context.

When Madness use it, for example, it's an essential piece of their identity and their songs just wouldn't sound the same without it. And then there's **A Night Like This** by The Cure, a fabulous tune from their **Head on the Door** album that features a sax break like a lead guitar solo. And, of course, early Cardiacs managed to do the nigh-on impossible and make me like music with lots of sax in it, but again that's all contextual and mostly down to the musicianship of their pioneering female band member Sarah Smith. Nine Inch Nails put out the sax heavy **God Break Down The Door** in 2018, and very early **Fields of the Nephilim** made the sax sound like a nightmare summoning from Hell itself. That might be it, that might be all the sax I can stand, with one last exception.

Here we have Morphine, a band essentially built around drums, sax and a two stringed bass. Nobody else out there sounded quite like them, they were pretty unique. Bassist and vocalist Mark Sandman freed himself from the tyranny of four strings and soared with just two, having them tuned an octave apart and playing them with a slide technique that has to be heard to be understood.

The band ended with just five albums in the bank after Sandman died of a sudden heart attack on stage in Italy. I remember hearing the news shortly afterwards and not quite believing it. A neighbour had lent me a couple of their albums not long before and I was just getting into them. Whether the abruptness of the singer's death affected me, or whether it was just too much sax at once, I never stuck with the band and only carried a couple of their tunes forward with me.

One was **Honey White** (the other was **Radar**, both from the **Yes** album). The music was distinctive, as was Sandman's voice. Give them both a listen and see what you think. Even for dedicated sax haters like me, there's something about Morphine that transcends the limitations of having to feature the thing in every bloody song, and maybe it's because of the unusual mix of band elements that keeps it fresh sounding, but something about these records just works really, really well.

About the Author

I'm a UK based author with books in a number of genres including horror fiction, micro street art, retro gaming, travelogues and illustrated children's books. I have over 200 four-star and five-star reviews for my books on Amazon. For an independent writer, I feel that's a decent achievement.

My travel books are light-hearted and fun, covering such journeys as a three-month road trip around North America, a grand tour of Europe in a VW Campervan and a month-long cycling trip through France from Cherbourg to Perpignan. They bring the *'get-up-and-go'* attitude to travel and represent the sort of experiences ordinary people have when doing similar things. I have no production company behind me, no personal assistants to organise meetings or events in advance – I just get in a campervan, or get on a pushbike and go, and then tell you what happens.

My fiction is usually quite dark, often with horror elements. My period fiction (such as *'The Whaler'*, or the *'New Orleans Trilogy'* which was set during the days before, during and after the 2005 Hurricane Katrina disaster) usually involve intense bouts of research to bring in authentic background details.

I've also written children's books, working in collaboration with the late artist Simon Schild.

steveroachwriter@gmail.com
facebook.com/writerroach

The author at the legendary Jaz Coleman wall in Cheltenham.

Other Books by Steve Roach

Short Story Collections
Glittering Treats – Selected Stories 2011-2021
The Hunt and Other Stories
Resonance
Tiny Wonders

Novellas
Ruiner
People of the Sun
Conquistadors

Travel
Cycles, Tents and Two Young Gents
Mountains, Lochs and Lonely Spots
Step It Up!

Non-Fiction
Retro Arcade Classics
Small People, Big World

Illustrated Books For Children
Crackly Bones
The Terrorer

facebook/writerroach
Check Out Your New Favourite Author!
Steve Roach
Ruiner
10th Anniversary Edition
Steve Roach
PEOPLE OF THE SUN
10th Anniversary Edition
STEVE ROACH
ARCADE RETRO CLASSICS
STEVE ROACH
A group of young men are invited to appear on a exciting new TV game show.
During filming, they realise they might not have been chosen at random after all.
Their past is about to catch up with them in the most horrific way.
LOOKING INTO A FURNACE
AVAILABLE NOW AS PART OF THE 'GREATEST HITS' COLLECTION
www.steveroach.co.uk
amazon
www.facebook.com/writerroach
Small People, Big World
Micro Street Art
Steve Roach
Deluxe Hardback Versions Available now on Amazon

ARCADE RETRO CLASSICS

The new book by Steve Roach

ARCADE RETRO CLASSICS

STEVE ROACH

'Works brilliantly. Slick design work and lots of lovely images.'

retro GAMER MAGAZINE

PAPERBACK	PAPERBACK	KINDLE
(Colour Interior)	(B/W Interior)	Ebook
£18.99	£7.99	£6.99

available at amazon

Small People, Big World

Micro Street Art

Rules:
No camera trickery
No Photoshopping
No image manipulation or effects
All shots taken with point-and-shoot method

The new book by
Steve Roach
Available now on Amazon

Printed in Great Britain
by Amazon

31524917R00143